The Henry Rolfs Book Series of the Institute of Noetic Sciences

Higher Creativity:
Liberating the Unconscious Mind
for Breakthrough Insights
Willis Harman and
Howard Rheingold

Waking Up:
Overcoming the Obstacles
to Human Potential
Charles T. Tart

Paths to Peace:
An Exploration of the Feasibility
of Sustainable Peace
Richard Smoke
with Willis Harman

The Noetic Sciences Book Series is dedicated to Henry Rolfs, a long-standing member of the Board of Directors, whose leadership, generosity, and personal courage have been instrumental in establishing the Institute of Noetic Sciences.

CONSCIOUSNESS AND SURVIVAL

A Symposium
sponsored by the Institute of Noetic Sciences

Georgetown University
Washington, DC
October 26-27, 1985

Co-conveners:

Carole Angermeir Taylor
John S. Spong
Claiborne Pell

Planned in cooperation with
The Office of Smithsonian Symposia and Seminars

ISBN 0-943951-00-3

CONSCIOUSNESS AND SURVIVAL

An Interdisciplinary Inquiry Into the Possibility
of Life Beyond Biological Death

Edited by
John S. Spong
Bishop, Diocese of Newark

With an introduction by
Claiborne Pell
United States Senator

An Institute of Noetic Sciences Book

Produced for the Institute of Noetic Sciences
by
Carol Guion, Leona Jamison and Samuel Matthews
on a Macintosh and Laserwriter
donated by Henry Dakin.
Special thanks to Karen Murphy at IBM, San Jose.
Cover photo courtesy of Eric Heiner.
Printed by Westview Press.

Dedicated to

CLAIBORNE PELL
Senator from Rhode Island

whose inquisitive mind and probing spirit
made this symposium possible

CONTENTS

PREFACE

THE SURVIVAL OF
CONSCIOUSNESS

It began with a telephone call from Washington to New Jersey in August of 1981. A Senator from Rhode Island contacted a Bishop from Newark. "I would like to talk with you about life after death," the Senator said after identifying himself. "Do you ever come to Washington?" It happened that the Bishop had a daughter in law school at William and Mary. On Thursday of the coming week he would be on the Beltway around the nation's capital returning to New Jersey from Williamsburg. "Could you drop by my suite in the Senate office building that afternoon?" the Senator enquired. The Bishop accepted the invitation and the stage was set for a rather remarkable series of conversations that led to a conference and finally to this book.

I am that Bishop. I have had a number of rich and unusual experiences in my life. Still I was not prepared to find a United States Senator on my home telephone line asking me to come to Washington to discuss life after death. But life has time after time presented me with the miracle of new opening doors. I have always been eager to walk through them.

Before that telephone call I knew Senator Claiborne Pell by name but that was all. Hubert Humphrey had considered him briefly for the second spot on the 1968 Democratic Presidential ticket before opting for Edmund Muskie of Maine. I knew nothing about his interest in life after death, his religious affiliation, if any, or his personal sense of values. I was not even consciously aware of his appearance and had no mental image attached to the name. When I entered his office, the man I met was warm and gracious, tall and thin, greying and in his early sixties. He invited me to sit down. In a moment, others he had asked to gather with us arrived. The Senator opened some splits of champagne and offered them.

Then we began to talk together about the possibility of life beyond the grave. We were not all believers. It was not the typical conversation one might have on that subject. There was a rare degree of honesty. What did we really believe was our focus, not what did we feel we were supposed to believe, or wished we believed. From time to time a bell would ring and the Senator would excuse himself to return to the Senate floor to cast a vote. When he returned from the last vote about 7:30 pm, we adjourned to a restaurant for dinner and the conversation continued uninterrupted until about 11:00 pm. At that point, the four-hour trip to Newark still before me finally overwhelmed me sufficiently to force my departure from one of the memorable evenings of my life.

We made arrangements to meet again. Future meetings took place in Newark, New York and in Washington. Carole Taylor, who had been invited by Claiborne Pell to join us at that first meeting, hosted a dinner party at her home about a year later. Joining us were people engaged in serious study on the issues of survival. The circle was clearly widening.

It is hard to pinpoint the moment that the idea of a conference was born, but it was early. What did I think about the possibility of a Bishop and a Senator sponsoring a national symposium on the subject of the survival of consciousness after biological death, the Senator proposed. We could bring together, he suggested, experts from many fields of knowledge to shed whatever light they could on the subject.

The idea appealed to me on many levels. In 1980 I had published a book entitled *The Easter Moment*. In that volume I had examined, with all the scholarship I could amass, the Christian claim that death had somehow been conquered in the person of Jesus. I had dissected the biblical texts that deal with the first Easter with a surgeon's scalpel, probing them for interpretive clues. That study had whetted my appetite for more and the subject compelled me in a deep and personal way. I had confronted death often both in my personal life and in my professional life. Death had brought me both pain and insecurity as well as some of the most beautiful and profound moments of life. I was not impressed by most of the traditional religious arguments concerning life after death, but I was deeply convinced that life was bigger than the limitations under which it seems to be lived, including the limitation of finitude.

I had also achieved by this time a reputation in religious circles as a critical liberal thinker. No one I knew in the field of theology seemed to me to be addressing this issue. I was intrigued by the possibility that a liberal Christian might be the one to make the case for life after death to the modern mind. It would be so unexpected, so out of the ordinary. I knew that I could not make that case along traditional lines. I am not moved by images of reward and punishment. I am not eager to postpone the human quest for justice to some heavenly place or to use life after death to make fair an unfair world. I was aware that the hope of life after death was a fading hope in the Western world. For an increasing number of dwellers in the secular city, neither heaven nor hell computed. The Church was ambivalent also. In periods of the Church's history the primary prerequisite for entry into the Promised Land was theological, that is, it was right believing in particular creedal formulas. One had to acknowledge Jesus as Lord and Savior for example. As the knowledge explosion and the shrinking globe made the ultimate claims of Christian truth more relative, the prerequisite for entry into heaven increasingly became moral, that is, heaven was the reward for proper behavior rather than proper believing. Whichever prerequisite served the Church's survival and power needs was the one used. Beyond that rhetoric was there reality? I thought so then, and I think so now. But do we have words to convey that reality? That was not nearly so simple a question. I only knew that I wanted to work in this area of our corporate life.

When C. B. Scott Jones was added to the trio of Spong, Pell and Taylor, the conference began to take shape. He was to be the conference coordinator, and the conference's success was due to him in no small measure. The Reverend Timothy Healy, SJ, President of Georgetown University, offered to host the conference on his campus. Wilton Dillon of the Smithsonian Institution agreed to cosponsor it as part of the Smithsonian Symposia. A Bishop, a Senator, Georgetown University, and the Smithsonian began to look like a formidable combination. As a major financial backer, the Institute of Noetic Sciences also came onboard as a major sponsor. The foundation was now complete. The form of the conference came next. We postponed our plans for one year because of Senator Pell's need to run for reelection in 1984, a task he successfully completed with 73% of the vote in a state carried by Ronald Reagan.

We began to line up the speakers. We did it by categories, first of all. We wanted a physicist and a biologist. We wanted a larger sampling of the world's religious perspectives far beyond Western thought. We wanted critics who dismissed this hope as silly or absurd, who believed in absolute nihilism at death. We wanted those who were working with near-death phenomena, parapsychologists who sought to understand mental telepathy, precognition, psychokinesis, and clairvoyance. We wanted doctors and psychologists who worked with the effects of mind-altering drugs and multiple personalities. We wanted the intuitive wisdom of both men and women as well as the voices and insights of representatives of the Third World. We wanted philosophers and theologians—anyone who might open a new angle of vision or chart a new pathway into this subject.

Above all we wanted this conference not to be captured by the interests of religion, or by the occult. We were not eager to propagandize for any group. We wanted an open forum to address in fresh ways this ancient and perplexing human concern, to lift this subject of the survival of consciousness after biological death into human awareness as a worthy subject for discussion, debate, and inquiry. It was our intention to indicate that this subject had implications far beyond the affected individual. There are political, economic, moral, social, and scientific implications that need to be faced, identified, and addressed. The more we planned, the more complex and vast appeared to be our task.

We were thrilled as the acceptances to our invitations to address this conference began to arrive from those who would be our leaders. We had aimed at the top echelons of international scholarship. It was satisfying to realize that they too regarded this subject as worthy of their time and energy. Professor Antony Flew is a world renowned philosopher and an articulate spokesperson for his point of view. Professor Paul Davies of the University of Newcastle-upon-Tyne is a much-published theoretical physicist who is able to make the Quantum Theory comprehensible to the average person. Dr. Candace Pert, chief of brain biochemistry, Clinical Neuroscience Branch, National Institute of Mental Health, was among the first to show that opiate drugs can bind to cells in the brain. Dr. Rupert Sheldrake is a biologist whose experiments with animal behavior moved him to seek a consensus between biology and the work of Carl Jung. Sogyal Rinpoche is a world famous Buddhist teacher and mentor who perceives life from an Eastern perspective and who seeks to bridge the gap of experience and focus that divides East and West. Stanislav Grof, a psychiatrist, has done extensive research on the use of psychedelics in therapy. Kenneth Ring is a psychology professor at the University of Connecticut who has devoted his professional career to a study of what is called the Near-Death Experience. Professor Charles Tart of the University of California at Davis does not eschew the designation of parapsychologist and sees that field as a major new, as yet barely explored, frontier of human knowledge. Dr. John Hick is a philosopher and theologian from Claremont School of Religion who has walked the frontiers of his discipline much to the discomfort of those who exist to guard a narrow orthodoxy. These were the members of our primary faculty. Beyond the formal presentations, we proposed two panel discussions in which panelists could interact with each other and with the audience. Dr. Jacqueline Damgaard, a practicing psychologist in Atlanta, who specializes in treating multiple personality dysfunction, and Dr. Willis Harman, president of the Institute of Noetic Sciences, agreed to chair these panel discussions. We were pleased, satisfied, and filled with great expectations.

The final unknown was whether or not such a conference would have popular appeal. There were two ways available to us by which we could measure that. One was whether or not the conference would attract a large audience. The other was whether or not the conference would attract media attention. On both levels we were destined to be deeply pleased.

More than 700 people crowded into Gaston Hall at Georgetown University, making the conference an absolute sellout. The audience was destined to play a major role both in their enthusiastic responses and in their comments and questions addressed to the panel of speakers. A portion of those are included in the Appendix.

The Washington Post covered the conference with an 18-year veteran reporter. The Voice of America was also present and conducted extensive interviews with the participants. Milton Friedman, the former speech writer for President Gerald Ford, was approached by *The New York Times* magazine about doing a feature article. We believed that we touched a nerve-end of interest in the public arena. We expect to see the subject of the survival of consciousness beyond biological death receive increasing attention across this nation. It is no longer the private domain of the religious establishment. More and more the representatives of organized religion will have to enter the turf of the scientific disciplines if they want to be contributors to this debate.

We present in this volume the content of that conference. It is our hope that the dialogue initiated here will continue and that this volume will prove to be an important element in that dialogue.

Special thanks must be expressed to three people who assisted the editor in the preparation of this manuscript. First there is Barbara

Festa of Berkeley Heights, New Jersey, whose editorial talents helped to shape the material and who placed it on the word processor. She also compiled the panel discussions from rough notes from a tape recording. As the reader might imagine, a tape recording of a panel discussion together with questions from the floor does not lend itself to finished copy. Bobbie Festa brought to her task sensitivity, professional interest, and high levels of competence.

The second person is Susan McConnell of Washington, DC, who was a participant in the conference and who volunteered to work with the editing task. Despite the problem of long distance editing, her efforts were both helpful and appreciated.

Third is Wanda Hollenbeck, the Bishop of Newark's Executive Secretary, who in her usual calm and helpful manner managed the flow of material from inception to completion.

I would like to give special appreciation to my two co-conveners both for the concept of the symposium and for the important energy they gave to this work: Carole Angermeir Taylor and Claiborne Pell, members of the Board of Directors of the Institute of Noetic Sciences.

Additional thanks and appreciation go to the patrons who made the symposium possible, including the following foundations: Astral Foundation/METAscience Foundation, Copernicus Society, est Foundation, John E. Fetzer Foundation, Freed Foundation, Stans Foundation, World Community Foundation and Delphi Research Associates.

John S. Spong
Newark, New Jersey
March 1986

INTRODUCTION
Claiborne Pell

DOES CONSCIOUSNESS SURVIVE PHYSICAL DEATH? IS THE QUESTION IMPORTANT?

Does consciousness survive physical death? Is the question important? These are vital questions. As one grows older and physical death becomes more imminent, the question of survival is of increasing actual importance, rather than theoretical relevance. Thus, it is a question I have asked myself with increasing seriousness.

Death and taxes are traditionally the two immutables of our life. Taxes are specific, predictable, and part of the government process with which I have been concerned as a Senator for the past 25 years. Death, on the other hand, is the ultimate mystery, meaning differing things and providing differing images to a multi-faceted humanity.

What does death mean? What happens? I don't pretend to know. I suspect no living being knows. I feel most humble in my limited knowledge in the presence of so many philosophers, theologians, opinion leaders, and scholars, both among our speakers and among those attending this symposium. Nevertheless, my reading in this area has convinced me that there are four broad possible points of view to this question that we will be examining together.

First, there is the possibility of reincarnation where the soul remains, with or without memory. The soul embarks on a long pilgrimage, perhaps involving many lives, hoping to achieve Nirvana. This view will certainly be discussed by our Tibetan speaker, Sogyal Rinpoche.

Second, there is the idea of the Great One, advanced not long ago in this city by Krishnamurti. Here death means that the soul and its accompanying memory joins the Great One, or Cosmos. And a particular soul's memory simply is an add-on to the sum total of memory, or knowledge.

The third and perhaps the most disagreeable alternative is oblivion. Many doctors and scientists maintain this view. I believe far more people believe this privately than admit it publicly. This, I believe, will be the focus of Antony Flew's presentation.

Finally, there is the idea that the individual soul with its accompanying memory lives on eternally. Some variation of this view has been historically identified with Christianity. It is the view to which many of us incline, and certainly the view we hope is correct.

My wife has proposed another alternative. That is, whenever you die, what will happen is what you believe will happen. I would add, though, that if we survive, it would seem to me that there is a prior fundamental subconscious understanding of this fact. To bring this knowledge to the conscious level might well result in a more integrated personality, promoting mental and physical well-being.

If we survive, knowledge of this fact would have a substantial impact on the present heroic medical procedures used too frequently in the Western world to sustain life, and on the concomitant psychological and financial costs.

I cannot assess the impact of positive knowledge of survival on theology and organized religion, but I suspect that the potential for spiritual unity as the result of this knowledge may not be greater than the potential for spiritual discord. The focus might turn to arguments on how to assure a greater degree of grace at the moment of transition.

What differences would positive knowledge of immortality make in the affairs of individuals in the balance of peacefulness and violence? This is a very complex concept and I am not going to attempt to develop it in detail. I do want to note that there very likely is no direct correlation between peacefulness and the belief in a concept of immortality. Ancient and modern history is replete with examples of great excesses and violence done in the name of God. But we must be careful here about a general judgment. Each case in full historical perspective would have to be assessed. I strongly suspect that an important distinction would be belief based upon faith alone as opposed to belief based upon scientific evidence. How additionally responsible would any of us be if we had full scientific knowledge of immortality and the reasonably assumed karmic consequences that would go with immortality?

Is it an important question? Would knowing the answer make a difference? In my view the answers to both these questions are yes.

These are the views that will be advanced by those who know much more and have studied these matters in much greater depth than I. And I know how much I shall be looking forward to the presentation of papers.

INTRODUCTION
John S. Spong

LIFE AFTER DEATH—
A MODERN INQUIRY

The possibility that there is some survival of consciousness beyond biological death is an intriguing but relatively new idea in the development of human thought. Let me set its newness in context.

Present anthropological views place human life on the planet Earth for 500,000 to 1,000,000 years. Given that span of time, almost all of our ideas are born in the modern age. The great religions of the world which have been well-served by concepts of life after death are themselves recent phenomena. If we propose the call of Abraham as the moment in which the Judeo-Christian faith story was born, then that worship tradition is not yet 4,000 years old. The religious traditions of the East including Hinduism and its developed tributaries are a bit older but their identifiable origins stretch back only perhaps 6,000 years. Islam, which like Judaism and Christianity also traces its life from Abraham, is in its specifically Islamic identity only 1,300 years old, a mere babe in arms on the calendar of the world's history. If we go just 10,000 to 12,000 years into the past, which represents only one to two percent of human history, we find ourselves face to face with that grey area which is illumined only by artifacts discovered on archeological digs.   The human enterprise as we know it with its intellectual concepts, its philosophical speculations, and its theological creeds, is a very recent accomplishment of the species homo sapiens.

The concept of life after death, at least as the Western mind has shaped that concept, was all but impossible for the ancient world to envision.   This concept is built upon a clearly defined individuation in human life which our prehistoric forebears, who thought tribally and corporately, could not have imagined.   Perhaps there was some hint of survival for chiefs, kings, or military heroes, but beyond those larger-than-life figures, individuals mattered little.   The real traumas in the ancient world came not with individual tragedy which was so common as to be expected, but when the life of the tribe was threatened with extinction.   That occurred when captive people were transported to foreign lands following military defeats or when a nation was cut off at its roots in war without a saving remnant through which its life could be restored.

In the Judeo-Christian faith story there was no significant sense of individualism before the sixth century BCE and there was no widespread concept of life after death until the third or fourth centuries BCE.   Both concepts were almost unheard of in the Hebrew scriptures before the time of the exile, yet, by the first century BCE, both individualism and life after death had become dominating themes in Judaism.   Christianity conflated these concepts by merging life after death with an individualistic manifestation making it the central affirmation of the powerful new religion.   So closely identified was Christianity with individualism and individual life after death—complete with individual judgment, individual reward, and individual punishment—that in the minds of many these are identifiable Christian concepts.

There is no doubt that the ability to convince people of the reality of an individualized life after death has been a primary source of power for the Christian church throughout history.   On the promise of the reward of heaven or the punishment of hell, human behavior has been altered and controlled by the church.

The prospect that there was another existence beyond life on this Earth also enabled the church to understand and to accept as inevitable the vast inequities of human life.   A just God and an unfair world were difficult to reconcile unless there was a place where all wrongs and all unfairness were rectified.   When the righteous ones perished and the evil ones prospered, the authority of the church was called into question.   To be able to assert that these apparent discrepancies in the justice of God were redressed beyond the grave had the effect both of providing a divine explanation and of giving the church a powerful line of defense against its critics. In this way the concept of life after death acted to sustain the church's power as the primary agency in the control of human behavior and to provide assurance that the values which the church espoused worked even when it was not apparent to the earth-bound eyes of human beings. An institution that could control eternity, assign individual lives to their place within eternity, and control earthly behavior with the twin whips of fear and guilt was a powerful institution indeed. It is no wonder that the church at the height of its power was allowed to practice the incalculable evils of the Inquisition, to fight the religious wars, and to champion the crusades, all of which today would be impossible on humanitarian grounds alone. Nor is it surprising that the church could require of its most devoted adherents such austere lifestyles as celibacy for the priesthood and the cloistered life of monasteries, convents, and nunneries, complete with practices of self-abasement that today would be highly suspect on psychological grounds alone. There was and is enormous power in the concept of life after death.

As belief in life after death has faded in the last century so the church's power has declined rather dramatically. But the church's lost power has not been the only casualty of that belief shift. No idea empowers an institution for nineteen centuries if that idea does not meet deep and basic needs in the human psyche. If that idea ceases to be credible, then those psychic needs met by that declining idea will demand to be satisfied in some other way. The contemporary quest for meaning and the contemporary passion for justice are surely manifestations of the human attempt to deal with issues that once were satisfied by the conviction that there was life beyond the grave.

If there is no eternal aspect to human life then the meaning of human life is itself in question. Twentieth century men and women exhibit that loss by seeking ultimate meaning in material pleasure, in sex, in drugs, in psychotherapy, in meditation, in a return to the fundamentalistic religious concepts of yesterday (whether in the Ayatollah Khomeini's Islamic Iran or in Jerry Falwell's Christian America), and in many other patterns of modern behavior. The self-evident meaning once found in the unquestioned religious conviction that there was life after death is no longer a possession of the citizens of today's secular city. A new search for meaning is, therefore, a hallmark of modern life.

If life after death is in serious question then the unfairness of human life also becomes overwhelmingly oppressive. For life that is unfair is life that is chaotic. A primary function of all religious systems is to give order to life's chaos, to make fair life's inequities. If life is ruled by blind fate and not by rational deserving, then anxiety rises, for blind fate cannot be controlled, ordered, or anticipated. If life is not fair and if religion cannot give a believable promise of fairness beyond this life, then earthly justice becomes imperative in a way that it was never imperative before.

The decline of belief in life after death is directly responsible, I believe, for the birth and growth of the liberal policies witnessed in the late nineteenth and early twentieth centuries throughout the Western world. When life after death ceased to be a working concept the passion to make fair an unfair world grew. Human oppression becomes intolerable if there is no life beyond this life where grievances are redressed. If there is no Beulah Land to which I might go, nor a sweet chariot that will come to carry me home from my slavery, then slavery itself must go. If this life becomes all that there is, then there is no virtue in being the passive victim and no one will wait for tomorrow to end the oppression that can be ended today. The liberal principles of universal suffrage, one person one vote, graduated taxation, redistribution of wealth and land, the organization of labor unions to extract equitable wages from those who own the means of production, civil rights, the feminist movement, gay rights . . . these are the ideas of the twentieth century, created, I would assert, as a direct result of the decline in confidence about life after death. The various movements in European politics called by such varied names as Christian Socialism, Socialism, Marxism, and Communism, and the American political dreams known as The New Deal, The Fair Deal, The New Frontier, The Great Society, are all attempts to make fair an unfair world. This is precisely the issue previously addressed by the content of our concepts of life after death. The existence of an earthbound liberal passion for justice is eloquent testimony to the fact that in our century the sense of transcendence has been lost and the hope for life after death has waned.

In the process of focusing on life after death we discover that far beyond the theological issues this concept has vast personal, social, economic, and political connotations. In some ways the idea of life after death has been one of the most powerful, most influential ideas in all of Western civilization. But, is that concept forever lost? Some would surely say yes. Others would maintain that it is only the content with which we have surrounded the concept that has been lost. If that is so then perhaps we can examine the concept anew only after we have stripped away the traditional religious content which is no longer compelling. That is the task I submit that draws us to this subject. It is the task that draws me.

We address this issue in this book from many disciplines, from many perspectives. We examine this human question with all of the integrity we possess. We are united not in our answers but only in our humanity. We are inescapably self-conscious creatures who inevitably wonder about the meaning of life in a vast and impersonal universe. We wonder whether the created order has a personal center that we might call God to which our personal centers might relate. We wonder whether there is a spirit which animates us and the universe and which binds all life together in a way that an individualistic age disregards. We wonder if we might still hope to participate in that which, for lack of better words, we might term eternity.

This volume may arrive at no conclusions, but at the very least, the fact that we dare to address the subject is a compliment to the human spirit, for it is a subject worthy of our time and our thought.

I

SURVIVAL OF CONSCIOUSNESS AFTER DEATH: A PERENNIAL ISSUE REVISITED

Willis W. Harman

The question of survival of individual consciousness after physical death has been a crucial question for every human society ever since the evolution of self-consciousness. Most societies through history have answered in the affirmative. In some the entity was assumed to go "somewhere else"; in some it reincarnated; in some there was a merging with a vaster whole.

In modern Western society a skepticism developed, associated with the rise of scientific positivism. Within the scientific worldview as that developed through the first half of the twentieth century, it was hard to conceive of any meaningful way to answer the question affirmatively. As a result, more highly educated persons in the West tended to view the question as unworthy of serious consideration.

However, sometime after 1960 the cultural tide appeared to turn, and the topic of death and its meaning became fashionable again. Over the past quarter century interest in the survival question has shown signs of renascence. There is a developing sense that the question is indeed pertinent, that past answers—religious *and* scientific—have been inadequate. Perhaps the time has come for a reexamination

Why Is The Survival Question Important?

It is a significant commentary on our times that it is even necessary to argue the importance of the survival-of-consciousness question. In his *Critique of Pure Reason*, Kant affirms immortality, along with the existence of God and freedom of the will, as the three indispensable conditions of the moral life. The realization of happiness, the summum bonum, "is only possible practically on the supposition of the immortality of the soul".

Even if one assumes the question to be meaningless or null, the premises people hold with regard to it affect values and motivations, attitudes and behaviors—the very form and goals of society. As Nobel laureate neuroscientist Roger Sperry wrote recently:

> Beliefs concerning the ultimate purpose and meaning of life and the accompanying worldview perspectives that mold beliefs of right and wrong are critically dependent, directly or by implication, on concepts regarding the conscious self and the mind-brain relation and the kinds of life goals and cosmic views which these allow. Directly and indirectly social values depend . . . on whether consciousness is believed to be mortal, immortal, reincarnate, or cosmic . . . localized and brain-bound or essentially universal.[1]

Assuming the potential importance of the question, we propose to examine below why there may be some hope of dealing with it more satisfactorily than in the past.

Why Is It A Meaningful Question?

The survival question arises in the first place because people down through the centuries have had experiences which convinced them that consciousness exists somehow apart from the human body. Unless one assumes that all of these experiences have simply been conjured up to deal with the existential fear of death, they amount to a body of evidence requiring impartial examination.

On the other hand, despite many attempts to make research in such areas as the study of mediumship (or psychic research in general) meet well-accepted scientific criteria, on the whole this can hardly have been said to be successful. That may mean that the phenomena were never there in the first place—or it may mean that the methodology of investigation was not fully appropriate to the matter being explored.

The chief evidence usually cited in support of the survival hypothesis is in the following categories:

Near-Death Experiences

Persons who, through accident or illness, approach physical death, often report "threshold" experiences that assure them of their continued existence whatever may happen to the body. Common characteristics of these reports include experiencing of white light, "other-dimensional space", extreme peacefulness and nonattachment, and often some measure of choice as to whether to "die" or not. The experience typically leads to loss of fear of death. Cross-cultural studies seem to indicate that the characteristics of near-death experiences are independent of cultural beliefs about death.

Out-of-Body Experiences

"Out-of-body" experiences (experiences of consciousness existing outside one's physical body) seem to be a universal phenomenon in that they are reported as experienced in every time and culture; however, only some small fraction of people seem to have such an experience (or in any event to remember it). They sometimes are associated with severe illness or near-death, but more often not. The person's response to such experience is very frequently to develop a deep conviction that consciousness survives the death experience.

Mediumship

Probably the most fascinating and most confusing part of this evidence is the long history of research on presumed communication, via a "medium", with persons no longer existing alive on the Earth. The early work in the nineteenth century is summarized in the remarkable *Human Personality and Its Survival of Bodily Death* by F. W. H. Myers (1903). The example that is considered by some to be the most evidential is the so-called "cross-correspondences" wherein fragmentary messages purporting to come from Myers many years after his death, received by several mediums completely isolated from one another, were found to fit together like pieces of a jigsaw puzzle.

Memories Of "Past Lives"

Numerous studies have been made of persons experiencing memories of another lifetime than the present one. Some of these are extraordinarily evidential, particularly the investigations of Ian Stevenson of memories of children who spontaneously appear to recall persons and episodes from another life, a lifetime recent enough in some cases to allow quite thorough checking of the veracity of the recollections.

Parapsychology
The overall import of the voluminous research on psychic phenomena (unless one is prepared to dismiss it in its entirety) is that human consciousness is something other than and beyond the physical processes of the brain. Thus it is not unreasonable to think that it might outlive the death and disintegration of that brain.

Cultural Anthropology
This field of study has contributed the understanding that experiences and their interpretations, relating to the survival question, have a certain commonality across cultures.

Comparative Religion
Studies in this field have resulted in the insight that, although the exoteric (public) forms of religion differ tremendously, the esoteric, inner-circle understandings have much more commonality across the many spiritual traditions of the world. This common esoteric core, sometimes referred to as the "perennial wisdom", includes an assurance that conscious awareness transcends physical death.

Convincing as this evidence is to many, it simply doesn't reconcile with the picture of the world that has been built up through the centuries by objective scientific research.

Why Is The Survival Question Pertinent Now?
Why is the question receiving renewed attention now? Partly, no doubt, because of changes in the culture, and partly because of changing attitudes within science about the existence of the trans-physical.

We hardly need to be reminded of the kinds of changes that have taken place in cultural attitudes and values since the early 1960s. Manifest indications of growing interest in yoga and meditation, role of the mind in healing, Eastern philosophical religions, death and dying, astrology, channeling, and a host of related topics, all indicate an increased willingness to explore questions which a couple of generations ago may have seemed settled once and for all by positivistic, reductionistic science.

In the scientific community it has become acceptable to entertain the idea that consciousness "exists" in some sense, even though it remains unmeasurable. The idea is presented, in one form or another, by numerous high-ranking scientists including neurophysicist Roger Sperry, neurophysiologist Sir John Eccles, physicist David Bohm, biologist Rupert Sheldrake. In the same paper quoted above, Sperry asserts:

> Current concepts of the mind-brain relation involve a direct break with the long-established materialist and behaviorist doctrine that has dominated neuroscience for many decades. Instead of renouncing or ignoring consciousness, the new interpretation gives full recognition to the primacy of inner awareness as a causal reality.

Undoubtedly a contributing factor in this new humility before the great questions is the recognition of past arrogance. Whereas children were once taught that the destiny of humankind is to explain away mystery through science and to control nature through technology, there is now a new mood to establish a different quality relationship with nature and its life processes. The vexing global dilemmas, from the nuclear weapons threat to the serious examples of environmental degradation around the planet, give testimony to the problems inherent in the older ethic, based in a materialist scientific worldview.

Is The Question Answerable?

Despite the new tolerance and openness, the legitimate question remains: Are we dealing with a question which is in some sense empirical, yielding to systematic exploration, or is the question by its very nature "metaphysical" and open to speculative answers only?

It must be recognized that although competent scientists have been dealing directly with this question for over a century, there is little demonstrable progress beyond where Frederic Myers and his colleagues had brought matters by the turn of the century. And if we had twice as much research of the same kinds, the verdict would probably be the same. We must look elsewhere than conventional research for insight as to why the survival question seems so obdurate.

That elsewhere is the field of cultural anthropology. It is well known to anthropologists that people who grow up in different cultures literally perceive different realities. The phenomenon is basically the same as hypnosis. Accepting a suggestion from a hypnotist, I can be persuaded to perceive something that isn't there, or to fail to perceive something that is there. I can be led to experience limits that I normally don't experience (for example, the inability to lift a chair weighing a few pounds); or I can be led to transcend limits normally there (for example, to use my rigid body as a "human bridge" between two chairs and support someone's weight on my stomach). Similarly, people who are "hypnotized" by the suggestions implicit in one culture will perceive differently, experience different limits, etc. from those with a different "cultural hypnosis".

A pertinent example—one among many possible—is the current popularity of firewalking workshops. There was ample evidence, for many generations, that people in certain cultures find it traditionally possible to walk barefoot through burning coals without damaging their feet. Until the last couple of years, that possibility was not a part of reality in this culture. Within the past two years, thousands of well-educated professional and business types have demonstrated to themselves the powers of their minds by firewalking, after only a few hours' preparation.

Another example, even more pertinent to the subject of this paper, is the phenomenon of "remote viewing"—sending one's mind out as far as hundreds or thousands of miles to "see" what is going on at some remote location. Primitive tribes had long used this ability to check up on distant relatives or strayed cattle; only in the last two decades have military intelligence groups on both sides of the Iron Curtain put the phenomenon to their own uses. (As have archeologists searching for ruins buried under many feet of sand, and energy companies seeking where to drill for oil.)

It has been humbling for scientists to come to recognize, as they have been doing in increasing numbers over the past quarter century, that science is in a sense a cultural artifact: A different society with a different "cultural hypnosis" would have created a different science.

First of all, the science of any society is biased by the pattern of support—what research gets supported and what does not. A society will support research into areas that are deemed important by that society. Thus an industrializing society supported research into knowledge that would improve the abilities to predict and control and generate new technologies. Other areas might be quite neglected—as, for example, the area of human subjective experience.

Beyond that, we know from research in hypnosis and other areas of experimental psychology that once a person has an internalized picture of reality, reality tends to be experienced in accordance with that picture. Thus, for example, people of a certain ethnic origin tend to be seen to have characteristics expected of that ethnic group. The hypnotized subject not only sees reality in accordance with the internalized suggestions, but has very logical-sounding explanations as to why reality "really" is that way.

Thus we have the important dual relationship between the experienced world and the science that is developed. The scientific knowledge that has been gained influences the way we perceive the world. *But*, the way the world is experienced in our culture influences what kind of science gets developed.

Choose Your Metaphysic

This may be a profoundly disturbing thought as one pursues its implications—that a society's basic experiencing of reality shapes its science as well as the reverse. In the history of Western society, a fundamental shift took place at the end of the Middle Ages. The most basic premises about the nature of reality underwent profound change. No one knows "why"—if indeed one can ask such a question of history. In what sociologists term the "secularization of values", the implicit metaphysic of the society of Western Europe fundamentally changed. (One aspect of that change we call the "Copernican revolution".) From that change developed a comprehensive science that could never have developed from the medieval outlook.

Improbable as it may seem to many persons still, we appear to be going through another such profound change. The evidence so far is scanty. We can invite the reader to observe the pattern; we cannot claim it is demonstrable.

Oversimplifying somewhat for clarity, let us think in terms of three basically different kinds of implicit metaphysics:

• *M-1*

In the first of these, the basic stuff of the universe is matter-energy. We learn about reality from studying the measurable world. (The positivist assumption is that that is the *only* way we can learn.) Whatever consciousness is, it emerges out of matter (that is, the brain) when the evolutionary process has progressed sufficiently far. Whatever we can learn about consciousness must ultimately be reconciled with the kind of knowledge we get from studying the physical brain.

• *M-2*

An alternate metaphysic is dualistic. There are *two* fundamentally different kinds of stuff in the universe: matter-energy stuff and mind-spirit stuff. Matter-energy stuff is studied with the present tools of science; mind-spirit stuff must be explored in other ways more appropriate to it (for example, inner, subjective exploration). Thus there develop, in essence, two complementary kinds of knowledge; presumably there are areas of overlap (for example, psychic phenomena).

• *M-3*

Yet a third metaphysic finds the ultimate stuff of the universe to be *consciousness.* Ultimately reality is contacted, not through the physical senses, but through the deep intuition. The physical world is to the greater mind as a dream image is to the individual mind. Consciousness is not the end-product of material evolution; rather, consciousness was here first!

These three basic metaphysical perspectives are summarized briefly in the following table:

THREE METAPHYSICAL PERSPECTIVES

M-1 MATERIALISTIC MONISM (matter giving rise to mind)
M-2 DUALISM (matter plus mind)
M-3 TRANSCENDENTAL MONISM (mind giving rise to matter)

Although Descartes postulated a dualistic universe, by the twentieth century science was rather firmly committed to an M-1 metaphysic. Within the past decade or so some scientists, recognizing that the extreme positivist position simply doesn't square with human experience, have been writing and speaking about the need to rebase science on an M-2 metaphysic. (Roger Sperry and Sir John Eccles are two examples.) Quietly, a number of scientists find that when they take their total experience into account the M-3 metaphysic fits best; besides, that seems to be implicit in the esoteric "perennial wisdom" of the world's spiritual traditions. For the present that position seems a long way from the picture of the world that emerges out of our various sciences. However, in the long run it may very well be where science ends up.

It is important to recognize that although science in its present form essentially evolved within an M-1 Weltanschauung, it is perfectly compatible with either the M-2 or M-3 metaphysic—compatible but inherently incomplete.

When we now look at the question of survival of consciousness after death in the light of these alternate metaphysics, several interesting things stand out. First, in the framework of the M-1 metaphysic, the one which still predominates in conventional science, there is really no way to make the question meaningful. In a conceptual framework based on an M-2 metaphysic, on the other hand, there is no problem with the spirit surviving—somewhere. It is not terribly clear what kind of research one might do to find out more.

Within the M-3 metaphysic the situation is quite different. In this picture of reality consciousness never nonexisted. Survival is not an issue. The concept of knowledge is basically different—there is not a need to discover so much as to remember.

Thus it would appear that the reason research on the survival question has been relatively unfruitful is because the research was essentially attempting to resolve the survival question *within the M-1 metaphysical framework.* Within that framework it has no answer, because the matter has been essentially prejudged. The more pertinent question to be asked is: *Which of the three metaphysical premises best fits with the totality of human experience?*

Can research help answer that question? Not directly perhaps. But indirectly it can help a great deal. (Research findings never prove a pattern, but they can help determine whether the pattern gives a useful fit.) The more that is found out, documented and systematized about all dimensions of human experience, the better position we are in to decide that M-1, or M-2, or M-3 seems most capable of dealing with the totality of that experience.

Research findings cannot test or "prove" a metaphysic. The basic reason is that *the research methodology itself grows out of a metaphysic,* so the research tends to lead us full circle, back to that metaphysic.

Recognition of this limited bearing of research findings to resolve the metaphysical issue might seem to lead one to a counsel of despair. Is it, after all, meaningful to assume a cultural evolution toward increasing knowledge? Or are we forever caught in this basic uncertainty of not knowing which metaphysic is "right"? Perhaps the best position to take is that of freely interpreting the research from the standpoints of all three metaphysics, honoring them all and exploring which is useful for what.

That may solve the problem very well for science, which can afford to remain tentative indefinitely. But it is a different matter for the individual. *Ultimately, each of us bets his life on some picture of reality,* recognizing (perhaps) that in a scientific sense at least, we can never know. What is the best way to make that bet?

The Roman Catholic scholar Poulain gave three tests for transcendental experience, which will also suffice to test the choice of metaphysic: 1) Does it lead to sound ethical and moral values, to wholesome behavior and attitudes? 2) Is it in accord with the best of tradition—with the deepest wisdom of human experience down through the ages? 3) Does it feel deeply, intuitively "right"—and does it continue to feel so as time goes on?

Perhaps we are at a point in history where vast numbers of individuals are making that choice, and betting their lives—in a way that in the end amounts to a new choice for society.

Footnote

1. "Changing Priorities", 1981 *Ann. Rev. Neuroscience.*

II

THE CARTESIAN PRESUPPOSITIONS OF THE SURVIVAL HYPOTHESIS

Antony Flew

Nowadays, I am told, many popular novels have anti-heroes, not heroes. So perhaps it accords with the spirit of the times for my sermon to have not a text but an anti-text. This is taken from the first chapter of *Our Knowledge of the External World* by Bertrand Russell.

> All the questions which have what is called a human interest—such, for example, as the question of a future life—belong, at least in theory, to special sciences and are capable, at least in theory, of being decided by empirical evidence . . . a genuinely scientific philosophy cannot hope to appeal to any except those who have the wish to understand, to escape from intellectual bewilderment . . . it does not offer, or attempt to offer, a solution to the problem of human destiny, or the destiny of the Universe.[1]

Here this becomes an anti-text because my project is not to expound or expatiate upon a proposition assumed or even known to be true, but to argue that one widely taken for granted is in truth false. The heart of the matter is that in discussing the question of a future life, if nowhere else, everyone, or almost everyone, takes as given a Platonic-Cartesian or, more specifically, a Cartesian view of the nature of man. But, until and unless such a view can be vindicated, that question, most emphatically, is not an open question "capable, at least in theory, of being decided by empirical evidence".

On the contrary, if, as is maintained in the opposing Aristotelian tradition, [2] we are wholly (or even in the main) creatures of flesh and blood, then it is the most truistic of universally known universal truths that "all men are mortal". For did not even (or especially) the Scholastics, forgetting the privileged cases of the alleged translation of the prophet Elijah and of the supposedly ever-Virgin Mother of Jesus, accept this as the incontestable first premise for an exemplary syllogism? Similarly, "we all survive death" is accepted as self-contradictory by everyone who divides those involved in a disaster into two mutually exclusive and together exhaustive categories of "dead" and "survivors", with no second or third columns for "both" or "neither".

Once Cartesian presuppositions are recognized to be the contentious, paradoxical, and perhaps ultimately incoherent claims which they in fact are, then it becomes clear that there are possibly insoluble philosophical problems to be treated before an open "question of whether self-conscious life survives physical death" can be passed to the scientists to be "decided by empirical evidence".[3] The problems are philosophical inasmuch as they arise from a sophisticated challenge to the meaningfulness of any survival hypothesis not already known to be false.

That qualification "not already known to be false" is vital. For the main reason, surely, why this semantic challenge is so often either not recognized or, if recognized, not treated very seriously is that the semantically impeccable but of course falsified hypothesis that flesh and blood people will survive, perhaps forever, is unwittingly confounded with a doubtfully coherent survival hypothesis, this time construed in Platonic-Cartesian terms.

It is, I imagine, no secret that I myself am inclined to believe that the philosophical problems simply cannot be solved, that it is altogether impossible to justify the crucial Cartesian presuppositions. I should, however, have considerably more confidence in this negative verdict had my now nearly thirty-five-year-old campaign to bring out the nature and seriousness of the problems been more successful[4]; had more of our contemporaries been by it provoked to try to solve them; and had they too, like some of our greatest predecessors, failed. Certainly, unless these tricks can be turned, the inescapable conclusion must be that of a very ancient Chinese poem, sung, the translator tells us, only at the burial of kings and princes:

> How swiftly it dries,
> The dew on the garlic-leaf,
> The dew that dries so fast
> Tomorrow will fall again.
> But he whom we carry to the grave
> Will never more return.[5]

So just what are these crucial Cartesian presuppositions, assumptions in the present context often taken absolutely for granted, yet rarely either stated or challenged or defended? The most dramatic answer is to be found in the first two paragraphs of Part IV of the *Discourse on the Method*. It is there, after a smoothly discursive buildup in three gentle and apparently innocuous initial parts, that Descartes suddenly releases his most shattering salvo of almost all-destroying doubt:

> Thus, because our senses sometimes deceive us, I wished to suppose that nothing is just as they cause us to imagine it to be, and because there are men who deceive themselves in their reasoning, and fall into paralogisms, . . . judging that I was as subject to error as was any other, I rejected as false all the reasons formerly accepted by me as demonstrations. And, since all the same thoughts and conceptions which we have while awake may come to us in sleep, without any of them being at that time true, I resolved to assume that every-thing that ever entered into my mind was no more true than the illusions of my dreams.[6]

Next, as everybody knows, Descartes picks out the only things of which he feels sure that he can be rock-solid certain: "But immediately afterwards I noticed that whilst I thus wished to think all things false, it was absolutely essential that the 'I' who thought this should be somewhat . . ." Hence "this truth, *'I think therefore I am'*," became "so certain and so assured that all the most extravagant suppositions brought forward by the skeptics were incapable of shaking it."

Then, "examining attentively that which I was, I saw that I could conceive that I had no body . . . but yet that I could not for all that conceive that I was not." Descartes therefore concludes that he is "a substance the whole essence or nature of which is to think, and that for its existence there is no need of any place, nor does it depend on any material thing; so that this 'me', that is to say, the soul by which I am what I am, is entirely distinct from the body. . . ." So, "even if body were not, the soul would not cease to be what it is."[7]

For us it is vital to grasp a pair of points: First, that the two elements in this Cartesian framework are complementary; and second, how enormously influential it has been, and remains. The second, more obviously relevant, of these two elements is the contention that the core person, the principle of personality—the that-by-which-the-person-is-that-which-the-person-is—is supposed to be an incorporeal substance. In this sense a substance is what can significantly be said to survive separately, unlike the grin on the face of the vanishing Cheshire Cat or the dog's lost temper in the Red Queen's subtraction sum.[8] The mind or soul has to be such a substance if the suggestion of its survival is even to make sense. It is said to be incorporeal, inasmuch as it is supposed to lack all material characteristics, to be independent of "any material thing", and even to have no dimensions or position. It has to be all this in order to account for our failure to detect its departure at the time of death.

The first element in the pair is the contention that these supposed incorporeal substances are essentially subjects of thoughts, in an extremely comprehensive, made-to-measure sense.   The word "thought" thus comes to cover every kind of purely subjective consciousness.   It is, therefore, roughly equivalent to "ideas" in Locke or "perceptions of the mind" in Hume. In resolving "to assume that everything that ever entered into my mind was no more true than the illusions of my dreams" Descartes was proposing that we are never immediately and non-inferentially aware of anything outside, in what his successors dubbed the External World. We are instead immediately aware only of successive moments of our own necessarily private consciousness. Yet, if this is right, then no subject confined to such cognitively restricted "thoughts" can ever be in a position to know without inference even that it possesses a body. (Nor, consequently, whether it is a he, or a she, or an it, or even perhaps none of the above!)

The two elements in this Cartesian framework are, as was said before, complementary. So to the question, "What is the External World external to?" the perfect answer would begin, "The Ghost in the Machine".[9] This Cartesian framework embraces the two constituents of the Platonic-Cartesian view of the nature of man. One is the contention that men and women consist of two components, the corporeal body and the incorporeal (yet substantial) mind or soul. The other is the contention that this mind or soul truly is the real, core person.

The force and fascination of all this comes out most strikingly when we consider how many of the most formidable philosophical successors of Descartes adopted the same or similar starting points. Locke and Berkeley, Hume and Kant, all ended in very different places— different both from Descartes and from one another. Yet upon these fundamentals they could not, it seems, help agreeing. Hume, for instance, in Part I of the final section of his first *Enquiry*, speaks of

> the obvious dictates of reason . . . no man, who reflects, ever doubted, that the existences which we consider, when we say *this house* and *that tree*, are nothing but perceptions of the mind.[10]

More remarkably still, although he, alone of them all, wanted eventually to defend mortalist conclusions,[11] Hume incongruously persisted in taking it that persons are essentially incorporeal. In *A Treatise of Human Nature*, a work offered as a contribution to the moral sciences, he is in the present context the radical only in arguing that we wholly and solely consist in collections of (logically) private experiences, without any substantial selves to have, enjoy, or suffer what are supposed to be inherently "loose and separate", purely subjective "perceptions of the mind".[12]

In a nutshell, the great objection to all this is that while, where these words are not to be construed as referring to sorts of substances, sense has been duly given to talk of minds or souls or even selves; no similarly satisfactory account either is or can be provided of how such putative supposedly incorporeal substances are to be either first identified or later reidentified through time. Of course we can all understand what it means to say that in Finals her papers showed that she has a first-class mind, or that his performance in the Marathon constituted a triumph of mind over body. All such sometimes misleadingly picturesque idioms, however, can without difficulty be cashed into more pedestrian statements about the abilities and achievements of (flesh and blood) persons.

When the words "mind", "soul" or "self" are to be construed in this everyday, commonsensical, Rylean[13] sort of way, it becomes easy to see how they are to be introduced, and their senses explained. This is and has to be by reference to the (wholly or predominantly) flesh and blood creatures whose minds or souls or selves we wish to discuss. Although his characteristic approach from the subjective conceals this from him, Descartes implicitly does precisely this when he speaks of his soul as "that by which I am what I am".

For the soul of Descartes is here being identified by reference to Descartes, while both "Descartes" as a personal name and "I" as a personal pronoun are paradigmatic person words. Another sub-class is that of words for persons playing particular roles—words such as premier, bogeypersons, spokesperson, aviator, referee, and so on. Person words, therefore, are words the use of which is to refer to people; while people, as all native speakers of English must know, are members of that most peculiar class of creatures corporeal to which we one and all belong.

These simple, familiar, fundamental truths once grasped, we are in a position to appreciate how preposterous it is to think of minds or souls or selves as substances—entities, that is, which "can significantly be said to survive separately" and to exist, as it were, in their own right and independently. For Descartes to maintain that his soul, by which he is what he is, "is entirely distinct from the body" in such a way that "even if body were not, the soul would not cease to be what it is", is as if he were to insist that a character or a personality might survive the dissolution of the person whose character or personality it was. We are by this got into Wonderland—where grins are said to survive the disappearance of the faces of which they are a sort of configuration, and lost tempers may remain after their losers have departed.[14]

Suppose now that someone claims to have found hard scientific evidence for the existence of substantial, and therefore in principle separable, minds or souls or selves. People, they allege, have been found to consist in two radically disparate yet subtly integrated elements, the one physical and corporeal, the other non-physical and incorporeal. It is, they usually continue, to the latter that we should more properly attribute those powers, actions, and affections which both the uninstructed laity and philosophers in the Aristotelian tradition wrongly see as the powers, actions, and affections of the whole person.

About these assertions three points, deployed in ascending order of contentiousness, need to be made at once. First, no such factual discovery, important and remarkable though it would most certainly be, could falsify our theses about the presently established meanings of person words. For it is, or would be, not a discovery that it is according to established usage incorrect to employ person words to refer to members of that class of creatures to which we all belong, but a discovery about their—that is—our—internal composition and construction, and about the mechanisms which enable us to do and suffer what it remains so far correct to say that we, rather than any of our organs or parts, do do and suffer.

Second, we must resist the temptation to infer from the premise that it is possible, or even most natural, to describe certain surprising phenomena in terms of a Platonic-Cartesian view, the conclusion that the occurrence of those phenomena provides support, perhaps decisive support, for such a position. Throughout the entire history of psychical research this has been a besetting error. Most if not all the British founding fathers were attracted into the field because of their belief that, whereas all the other and established sciences were constantly providing further support for what I should call an Aristotelian view of man, the putative phenomena of this new area would, if they really occurred, be incompatible with any but a Platonic-Cartesian view. Many of these founding fathers were also excited by the prospect that to establish the genuineness of these phenomena would be to make "the question of a future life . . . capable . . . of being decided" by one of the "special sciences": namely psychical research itself.[15]

Although not himself so obviously involved in that great question, J. B. Rhine in his popular presentations always attributed any putative psi-phenomena to the activities of the supposedly substantial albeit not directly detectable minds or souls or selves of his successful experimental subjects.

Quite apart from the difficulties of giving sense to any notion of an incorporeal and non-physical substance, such descriptions are arbitrary and uneconomical. Take, for instance, those out-of-body experiences which are so much discussed nowadays. Suppose the subjects really do come up with information not normally accessible to them about the destinations of their alleged journeyings. Then it certainly looks as if we shall have to postulate powers of ESP or, better, psi-gamma. But why say that these are powers not of the actual and observed person but of a hypothesized and unobservable "spiritual substance"? What we cannot do on present assumptions is to avoid postulating powers of psi-gamma. For there could, surely, be no other way for incorporeal beings to acquire information.[16] But we can and should eschew the hypothesizing of such semantically dubious entities.

The third thing to be said about claims to have discovered empirical confirmation of a Platonic-Cartesian account of human nature is that no such discoveries can be made until and unless the hopeful discoverers have either themselves supplied or have been by others furnished with means by which their putative entities could, at least in principle, be first identified and then later reidentified as the same through time. One reason why so many philosophers and scientists fail to recognize this need is confusions: between the words "minds", or "souls", or "selves" construed as referring to a peculiar kind of substances; and the same words interpreted as referring to aspects or capacities or dispositions of quite ordinary people.

Another reason is that they succumb to the temptation to misread such wholly negative words as "immaterial", "non-physical", and "incorporeal" as positively descriptive.[17] But immaterial, non-physical, or incorporeal persons are no more a kind of person than are imaginary, fictitious, or otherwise non-existent persons. "Incorporeal" in that expression is, if you prefer to be modestly and discreetly technical, an *alienans* adjective, like "positive" in "positive freedom" or "Soviet" in "Soviet democracy". To put the point more harshly, and thus to provide an always welcome occasion for quoting "the Monster of Malmesbury", for you to assert, in that ordinary everyday understanding, that somebody survived death, but disembodied, is to contradict yourself. Hence, in Chapter V of *Leviathan*, the incorrigible Thomas Hobbes was so rude as to say that

> If a man talks to me of 'a round quadrangle'; or 'accidents of bread in cheese'; or 'immaterial substances'; . . . I should not say that he was in error, but that his words were without meaning: that is to say, absurd.

In the above text, I deployed a challenge to Platonic-Cartesian assumptions. Now I propose to deal with some of the rather few attempts which have been made to meet this challenge. Consider, for a start, the long succession of staunchly godless mortalists who have claimed to be able not merely to conceive but also to imagine (image) their own disembodied survival. Were this claim true it would decisively dispose of all the "strange perplexities" which I previously raised.[18] But it is not. The latest such claimant to attract my own attention was the late J. L. Mackie. He made his claim on the very first page of a book in which he set out to reach atheist and presumably also mortalist conclusions.[19] The correct response is that, whatever the truth about what can or cannot be conceived, no one, surely, can distinguish an image of their own funeral from an image of themselves (but disembodied!) witnessing that funeral.[20] It would be hard to find a more impressive index of the stubborn strength and widespread persistence of Platonic-Cartesian assumptions than Mackie's claim.

Just because we can indeed understand hopes or fears of survival or immortality it does not follow that we can conceive, much less image, existence as persons, but disembodied. No one has ever emphasized and commended incorporeality more strongly than Plato. Yet when, in the Myth of Er, Plato[21] labors to describe the future life awaiting his supposedly disembodied souls, everything which even that master craftsman of the pen has to say about them presupposes that they will still be just such creatures of flesh and blood as we now, and he then.

Again, my respected Keele successor, Richard Swinburne, recently thought to deflect the ferocity of Hobbist onslaughts by making the emollient point that no one has any business to argue, just because all the Xs with which they happen themselves to have been acquainted were Ø, that therefore Ø is an essential characteristic of anything which is to be properly rated an X.[22] This is, of course, correct. Certainly it would be preposterous, and worse, to argue that because all the human beings with whom you had so far become acquainted had had black skins, therefore anyone with any other skin pigmentation must be disqualified as a human being. But, as I contended earlier, incorporeality is a very different kettle of fish; or perhaps we should say, no kettle and no fish. For to characterize something as incorporeal is to make an assertion which is at one and the same time both extremely comprehensive and wholly negative.

To the challenge to provide a substance sense for the key words "mind" or "soul" or "self", Paul and Linda Badham would respond by asserting that such a sense is already available in our colloquial vocabulary. For to the claim "that words like 'you', 'I', 'person', 'Flew', 'woman', 'father', 'butcher', all refer in one way or another to objects," they respond with what they rightly insist is more than "a purely grammatical point . . . that the word 'I' can never be so used, but must always relate to the subject."[23]

From this they proceed to infer that "What makes me 'me' is not my external appearance . . . rather it is that I am the subject of the thought, feelings, memories, and intentions of which I am aware."[24] This subject, it is assumed, could significantly be said to change bodies or even to continue to exist—and to have "thoughts, feelings, memories, and intentions", without any body at all: "The flames of the crematorium will not torture 'me' for 'I' shall not be there. Either I will cease to exist with my body or I shall continue to exist without it."[25]

Now this, as British rally drivers used to say, is going a bit quick. In so doing the Badhams have surely run out of road? Certainly, as Shakespeare realized, it is primarily because we are creatures endowed with conscience, in the sense of consciousness, that we are so strongly inclined to believe that talk of our disembodied survival is coherent:

To die, to sleep
No more; and by a sleep to say we end
The heartache, and the thousand natural shocks
That flesh is heir to; 'tis a consummation

Devoutly to be wish'd. To die, to sleep.
To sleep: perchance to dream: ay, there's the rub;
For in that sleep of death what dreams may come,
When we have shuffled off this mortal coil,
Must give us pause...

Yes indeed. If it truly did make sense to say that the same person might survive as an incorporeal dreamer, disentangled from the mortal coils of flesh and blood, then it must be altogether reasonable to speak of death as the still undiscovered country. So, Hamlet continues:

The undiscover'd country from whose bourn
No traveller returns, puzzles the will,
And makes us rather bear those ills we have
Than fly to others that we know not of.
Thus conscience does make cowards of us all... [26]

Yet in the end, after the play is over, the prosaic objection must once more be put. After the death of Hamlet, where or what could Hamlet be? Who or what is the future dreamer—the putative he, or she, or it—whose possible nightmares—or should it be the possible nightmares of which?— the Hamlet of "too, too solid flesh" was anticipating with such trepidation? How is the subject "I" to be identified, if not always and only by reference to the sensations, desires, and thoughts of the object person who is at the same time the subject of those sensations, desires, and thoughts? However could it be identified thus separately, and hence as being presumably separable any more than mental images and bodily sensations, or "ideas and impressions", can be identified "loose and separate", and without reference to the people who are the subjects of such moments of consciousness?

The difficulties of re-identifying a particular substantial mind as one and the same with another first identified at an earlier time are, if possible, even more intractable than those of giving an account of such first identifications. This is of course another aspect of, and just as unmanageable as, the traditional problem of personal identity, when that problem is misunderstood, as it usually is, to be one of re-identifying an essentially incorporeal subject or collection of Humean "perceptions of the mind".[27] It is, therefore, not surprising that Swinburne, while engaged in the uphill task of defending *The Coherence of Theism*, is very quick to conclude "that the identity of a person over time is something ultimate, not analyzable in terms of bodily continuity or continuity of memory or character."[28]

This is wrong. For what we do actually use bodily criteria for is to establish bodily continuity. Yet that is not just a usually reliable criterion for, but a large part if not the whole of what is meant by, personal identity. It would be if persons just are, as I maintain that we all know that we are, a very special sort of creatures of flesh and blood.

Hence, like so many others, Swinburne not only overlooks the theoretical possibility and actual frequency of honest yet mistaken claims to be the same person as did this or suffered that, but also fails to appreciate the decisive force of Butler's refutation of any analysis of "being the same person as did that" in terms of "remembering being the same person as did that". In consequence Swinburne is inclined to assume that whatever difficulties other people might confront in trying to re-identify some putative person as the same as the one who did that particular deed, or who enjoyed or suffered that particular experience, the putative person in question must be in a position to know the true answer.

Of course, if there is or even could be a true answer, then the question to which it is a true answer must already have sense. So, believing as he does that there either is or always could be, it must seem to Swinburne that he has succeeded in deflecting the impetus of Penelhum's objections to the suggestion that disembodiable and disembodied persons can be thought of as incorporeal substances:

> Beyond the wholly empty assurance that it is a metaphysical principle which guarantees continuing identity through time, or the argument that since we know that identity persists some such principle must hold in default of others, no content seems available for the doctrine. Its irrelevance . . . is due to its being merely an alleged identity-guaranteeing condition of which no independent characterisation is forthcoming.[29]

Arguing against Penelhum, Swinburne mistakes it that the objection to giving an account of the identity of disembodied persons in terms of memory claims is that such claims could not be checked, which he contends they could be. But the decisive objection, put first and perfectly by Bishop Butler, is that true memory presupposes and therefore cannot constitute personal identity: When I truly remember my doing that, what I remember is that I am the same person as did it.[30] So, until and unless sense has been given to the expression "disembodied person", no problem of discovering whether in fact X at time one was the same disembodied person as Y at time two can arise, and hence no consequential problem of whether any such putative discovery could be checked.

Swinburne's second mistake here, and again it is an error in which he has a host of companions, is a matter of method. In a word, this seductive and popular mistake consists in the misuse of possible puzzle cases; cases which if they actually occurred, and were thought likely to recur, would require us to make new decisions as to what in future correct verbal usage was to be. The mistake is to assume that decisions, even the most rational decisions about responses to purely hypothetical challenges, and usually challenges which we have no reason or less than no reason to expect to have to face in real life, must throw direct light upon the present meanings of the words concerned. For these present meanings are, of course, determined not by hypothetical future but by actual present correct usage; while our ordinary language provides us with the concepts with which it does provide us because these were those which were evolved in and adapted to the worlds in which our ancestors lived.

It is, therefore, all very well to introduce bizarre puzzle cases in order to stimulate a mind-flexing realization that in a very different world we might evolve a very different concept of what would there be called a person along with correspondingly different criteria of personal identity. Such speculations can also help us to see what are those actual features of the world as it is to which our present concepts are well adapted. But these puzzle cases, and the speculations which they provoke, cannot legitimately be employed to prove that our present concept of a person, and our present and corresponding criteria of personal identity, are other than they are. That present concept, as has been argued throughout, is a concept of a special kind of creatures of flesh and blood; while, as I have argued more fully elsewhere, our present criteria for personal identity are, correspondingly, criteria for the reidentification of particular specimens of this kind—criteria, that is, for discovering whether this specimen here at time two is physically continuous with that specimen there at time one.[31]

The truly disturbing conclusion to be derived from a proper employment of puzzle cases is one to which Swinburne seems to have blinded himself. It is that it is possible to conceive, and even to imagine (image), situations giving rise to questions about personal identity to which, in the present meanings of the key terms, there could be no unequivocally true or unequivocally false answer. So not even the person or persons themselves could know that answer. Consider, for instance, the questions which would arise if someone were told that they were going to split like an amoeba—and did.[32]

Footnotes

1. B. A. W. Russell, *Our Knowledge of the External World* (London: G. Allen and Unwin, 1914), p. 28.

2. For a vindication of this form of historical representation see the Introduction to Antony Flew (Ed.), *Body, Mind and Death* (New York: Macmillan, 1964), and compare *A Rational Animal* (Oxford: Clarendon, 1978), passim.

3. The formulation of the first quotation in this sentence is that of my letter of invitation to participate in the present Symposium on Issues of Consciousness and Survival.

4. This campaign started with the first publication in *Philosophy* for 1951 of "Locke and the Problem of Personal Identity", and later in the same year in the long since defunct and always purely local journal, *University* of "Death". This latter, with a note of other previous publications, was reprinted in Antony Flew and Alasdair MacIntyre (Eds.), *New Essays in Philosophical Theology* (London: SCM Press, 1955). Most material fit for salvage from these earliest papers was recycled into Chapters 8-11 of *The Presumption of Atheism*, recently reissued as *God, Freedom and Immortality* (Buffalo: Prometheus, 1984).

5. Arthur Waley, *170 Chinese Poems* (London: Constable, 1918), p. 38.

6. *The Philosophical Works of Descartes*, translated by E. S. Haldane and G. R. T. Ross (Cambridge: Cambridge University Press, rev. ed. 1931), Vol. I, p. 101.

7. Ibid., p. 100: Compare on "Descartes on 'Thought' ", John Cottingham in the *Philosophical Quarterly* for 1978.

8. See *Alice's Adventures in Wonderland*, Chap. VI and *Through the Looking Glass*, Chap. IX, pp. 67 and 223 in the *Complete Works of Lewis Carroll*, Ed. by Alexander Woolcott (London: Nonesuch, 1939).

9. I remember discussing this question with Gilbert Ryle after some examiner had set it in Finals. But I cannot now recall which of us was the first to suggest how a first class answer should begin.

10. *Enquiries Concerning Human Understanding and Concerning the Principles of Morals*, L. A. Selby-Bigge (Ed.), (Oxford: Clarendon, Third Ed., 1976), p. 152.

11. See especially the originally suppressed essay "Of the Immortality of the Soul".

12. *A Treatise of Human Nature*, Ed. by L. A. Selby-Bigge (Oxford: Clarendon, rev. ed., 1977), I (iv) 6. Respect and affection for "the good David" shall not inhibit us from commenting that such talk is, of course, utterly preposterous. Perceptions of the mind cannot be "loose and separate". Pains, sense data, and the rest can be identified only by reference to those experiencers whose (logically private) experiences they are.

13. See Gilbert Ryle, *The Concept of Mind* (London: Hutchinson, 1948).

14. See Note 8 above.

15. For evidence of these assertions see my "Parapsychology: Science or Pseudo-Science" in M. P. Hanen, N. J. Osler, and R. G. Wayant (Eds.), *Science, Pseudo-Science and Society* (Waterloo, Ontario: Wilfrid Laurier UP, 1980); reprinted in the *Pacific Philosophical Quarterly* Vol. LXI (1980) and again in P. Grim (Ed.), *The Occult, Science and Philosophy* (Albany, NY: SUNY Press, 1982). Or compare my *A New Approach to Psychical Research* (London: C. A. Watts, 1953), passim. A more accessible source will be Antony Flew (Ed.), *Philosophical Issues in Parapsychology* (Buffalo: Prometheus, 1986).

16. I have, in the article mentioned above in Note 15 and elsewhere, argued that this too must be impossible for such, as I believe, nonentities.

17. See Irving Thalberg, "Immortality" in *Mind*, 1983, pp. 105-13.

18. In his Dissertation "Of Personal Identity", Bishop Butler wrote: "Whether we are to live in a future state, as it is the most important question which can possibly be asked, so it is the most intelligible one which can be expressed in language. Yet strange perplexities have been raised about the meaning of that identity or sameness of person, which is implied in the notion of our living now and hereafter, or in any two successive moments."

19. John Mackie, *The Miracle of Theism* (Oxford: Clarendon, 1983).

20. See my "Can a Man Witness His Own Funeral", in the *Hibbert Journal* for 1956; reprinted in J. Feinberg (Ed.), *Reason and Responsibility* (Belmont, Ca: Dickenson, 1971), W. J. Blackstone (Ed.), *Meaning and Existence* (New York: Holt, Rinehart and Winston, 1972), F. A. Westphal (Ed.), *The Art of Philosophy* (Englewood Cliffs, NJ: Prentice-Hall, 1972), and P. A. French (Ed.), *Exploring Philosophy* (Morristown, NJ: General Learning Press, 1975). P. A. French also includes a remarkably similar piece under his own name in another of his collections, *Philosophers in Wonderland* (St. Paul, Minn: Llewelyn, 1975). For final good measure I myself added my own improved rewrite for my *The Presumption of Atheism* (London: Pemberton/Elek, 1976), a book reissued in 1984 by Prometheus as *God, Freedom and Immortality*.

21. *Republic*, 614B ff.

22. Richard Swinburne, *The Coherence of Theism* (Oxford: Clarendon, 1977), p. 54

23. Paul and Linda Badham, *Immortality or Extinction* (London: Macmillan, 1982), p. 7.

24. Ibid., p. 10.

25. Ibid., p. 11.

26. *Hamlet*, III (i).

27. On this and related issues see my "Locke and the Problem of Personal Identity", first published in *Philosophy* for 1951; reprinted in variously revised versions, in C. B. Martin and D. M. Armstrong (Eds.), *Locke and Berkeley* (New York: Doubleday, 1968), in B. Brody (Ed.), *Readings in the Philosophy of Religion* (Englewood Cliffs, NJ: Prentice-Hall, 1974), and in my *The Presumption of Atheism*. (See Note 4 above.) This is the article which in his book *Personal Identity* (London: Macmillan, 1974) Godfrey Vesey said "Marks a turning point in discussions of personal identity" (p. 112). I will not resist the temptation to add my own opinion that many of the other contributors to those discussions might have avoided various recurrent errors had they attended, or attended more carefully, to that now ancient article. At the least they might have found it a relatively painless way of acquainting themselves with the relevant key sentences from the writings of such great men of old as Locke and Butler, Hume and Reid.

28. *The Coherence of Theism*, p. 110.

29. Terence Penelhum, *Survival and Disembodied Existence* (London: Routledge and Kegan Paul, 1970), p. 70.

30. Compare, in the Dissertation mentioned above in note 18, Butler's contention that "though consciousness of what is past does . . . ascertain our personal identity to ourselves, yet to say, that it makes personal identity, or is necessary to our being the same persons . . ." is a "wonderful mistake". For "one should really think it self-evident that consciousness of personal identity presupposes, and therefore cannot constitute, personal identity, any more than knowledge, in any other case, can constitute truth, which it presupposes." There is little, if anything, which can usefully be added to a refutation so terse, so elegant and so decisive.

31. We must not fail to distinguish primary from secondary senses of "same person". For it is only when we are sure that someone is in the primary sense the same person as, say, joined the French Foreign Legion that we can go on to assert that he is as a result of this now quite a different person!

32. Compare, again, the article mentioned above in Note 27.

III

ALTERED STATES OF CONSCIOUSNESS AND THE POSSIBILITY OF SURVIVAL OF DEATH

Charles T. Tart

The essence of the ideas I want to share is expressed in the following two sentences: First, after some initial shock and confusion resulting from the process of dying, I will not be too surprised if I regain consciousness. Second, I will be quite surprised if "*I*" regain consciousness.

To put it more precisely, I will not be too surprised if I regain some kind of consciousness after death, but that consciousness may be of a quite different sort than the ordinary state of consciousness I am accustomed to. Further, I doubt that "*I*", in the sense of my ordinary self, will be the self that regains some sort of consciousness.

By thinking about survival in terms of our ordinary, taken-for-granted "I" surviving, we have inadvertently confused the issue, so it is no wonder that we do not have a clear answer about the possibility of survival.

What we call "I" is actually quite changeable from minute to minute, rather than being as fixed as we like to think it is. Some of these forms of "I" occur often, so it is useful, especially if we are interested in personal growth, to speak of our many "I"s or subselves.[1] Consider that many of these ordinary "I"s often do not long "survive", in the sense of maintaining their presence and integrity, many of the small changes of ordinary life, like strong emotions, hunger, sexual desire, fatigue, alcohol and multitudes of other mind-altering drugs. If ordinary "I"s cannot survive these minor shocks, how could ordinary "I"s survive the vastly greater shock of death?

The question "Will I survive death?" cannot really be satisfactorily answered except as a subset of the larger question, "Who and what am I?" This is the central question I will address as we explore the issue of survival of death.

The Nature Of Ordinary Consciousness

The nature of ordinary consciousness (and the ordinary "I"s associated with it) and the nature of altered states of consciousness provide background for examining the survival question.

Figure 1 is a diagram taken from my systems approach to understanding altered states of consciousness which we will use here to illustrate the major processes constituting consciousness as are now recognized by contemporary psychology. The named blocks represent processes or subsystems of the overall system of consciousness. The arrows represent major channels of information flow. The heavier the arrow, the more the information flow.

FIGURE 1

SYSTEMS APPROACH TO UNDERSTANDING STATES OF CONSCIOUSNESS

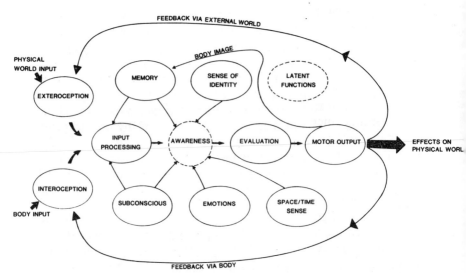

Subsystems Of Consciousness

Exteroception refers to the receptors we have for sensing the world external to our body, our ordinary senses. You read right now with an exteroceptor, your eyes.

Interoception is the class of processes that give us information about the internal state of our bodies. Noticing a cramped muscle, sensing your balance or your posture are examples of interoception.

Input Processing refers to the fact, amply documented by modern psychology, that our perception is not just given by the nature of the sensations reaching our exteroceptors and interoceptors. It is a construction, a complex process whereby the input from our receptors is shaped, modified, added to, and subtracted from, until it becomes a percept of something familiar. The beliefs and prejudices of our culture result in many semi-arbitrary habits of perception. These complex processes have all become fully automated in the course of enculturation, so we normally aren't aware of the steps in the process; it seems as if we just naturally see, hear, feel and so on.

Memory refers to the many ways in which information about previous experiences, thoughts, and feelings is stored. Input processing relies heavily on memory for direction in its construction process.

Awareness is really beyond definition in words, as words are only a small subset of the total functioning of mind. It loosely refers to our ultimate ability to know that something exists or is happening. In ordinary consciousness, awareness is usually almost totally wrapped up in words, internal talking to ourselves (which is what we usually mean by thought), but it is far more basic than words. To jump ahead of my discussion for a moment, if something survives death, it is going to be more closely connected with the nature of basic awareness than with ordinary consciousness. The systems diagram shows information from input processing feeding into awareness, as does information from most of the other processes shown in Figure 1.

Sense of Identity refers to a special quality of information that is added to certain contents of awareness, a feeling as well as a cognitive quality that "This is me!" an "I" quality that gives whatever it is added to special priority for awareness and energy. The perception that "John Smith has a spider crawling toward his leg" doesn't have the feeling quality of the perception that "I have a spider crawling toward *my* leg!" Input from your body, via the interoceptors, is normally an important part of your sense of identity.

Emotions are the various ordinary (and not so ordinary) feelings that we experience, such as excitement, fear, anger, love, contentment and so on.

Space/Time Sense is part of the process of constructing our perceptions of our self and our world. It provides a space and time reference. Experiences usually don't just happen, they happen *now*, at *this place*.

Evaluation refers to the various processes of evaluating information. Given what I am perceiving and what I already know, what does it mean? What should I do? Evaluation includes relatively formal, conventionally logical reasoning processes and *alogical* as well as *illogical* processes. The emotional processes have an evaluative function also, but they have been separated out because of their unique quality.

Subconscious processes are the normally invisible intelligent processes we invoke to explain organized experiences and behavior that don't make sense in terms of what a person consciously experiences. When someone claims to be quite calm, for instance, yet shows classical signs of fear, we suspect an unconscious process. I include positive processes here as well as the conventionally negative, Freudian ideas of the unconscious.

Finally, *Motor Output* refers to the processes used for controlling our muscles and our bodies that take the results of evaluations and decisions and allow us to act on them.

Now this is far too static a view of what is really an interlocking, mutually supportive collection of dynamic processes. Ordinarily the overall outcome of this dynamically interacting system is what is called "I" or "my state of consciousness". To the extent that some of these processes are primarily functions of the physical body and nervous system rather than inherent qualities of the mind (Motor Output, for example), they will not survive death and so we can anticipate that the quality of what might be perceived as "I" after death must be quite different.

Stabilization Of A State Of Consciousness

An especially important quality of the system of functioning that makes up our state of consciousness is that it is stabilized. It generally maintains its overall pattern, its integrity, in spite of constant changes in both our external and internal world. A sudden noise can occur; I can have a mild stomachache, and still remain me. Like any well-engineered system, changes produce their own compensation, so that the system is not pushed out of its range of optimal functioning. If one goes into a state of mystical ecstasy whenever there was a flash of light, it might be enjoyed for a moment, but the responder might not stay alive for very long. The sunlight glancing off the grill of the truck bearing down on its victim should not send the person into ecstasy. Rather the quite ordinary state standards become a warning to get out of the street! Much of the stabilization of ordinary consciousness comes about through the load, the work, that all these processes impose on awareness. Because doing this work is almost completely automated, we do not normally feel like we're working hard to maintain our ordinary state; we just seem to be in it. When a lot of that load is removed, as is typically done in inducing altered states of consciousness, the nature of conscious experience can change drastically. To the extent that much of this loading stabilization of ordinary consciousness depends on bodily and nervous system processes, it is removed at death. This argues that the post-death appearance will be of altered states.

Another major source of the stabilization of a state of consciousness (ordinary or altered) occurs through feedback. Information is sent back to processes. For example, if I want to push a heavy box across the room without hitting the furniture, I don't just throw all my muscle power into a shove. Rather I shove gradually, while perceiving how well the box is moving. Is it too slow? Can I shove a little harder? Is it too fast? Will I lose control and run into something?

Figure 1 shows two major feedback loops which are essential in stabilizing our ordinary consciousness. The upper one, feedback via the external world, refers to the fact that we use our exteroceptors to monitor the results of our actions, as with the example of shoving the box. The lower one, feedback via the body, refers to the fact that sensations in our body also tell us about the results of our actions. If I feel a pain starting in my lower back as I begin shoving the box, I need to heed that feedback and work out a different way for moving the box without injury to myself.

Ordinary consciousness is thus a semi-arbitrary construction. In the course of growing up we have built up huge numbers of habits of perceiving, thinking, feeling, and acting. The automated functioning of these habits in our ordinary environment constitutes a system called consciousness. Ordinary consciousness is stabilized, so it holds itself together in spite of varying circumstances. Forgetting the work that went into constructing this and not realizing the cultural relativity and arbitrariness of much of it, we take it for granted as "ordinary" or "normal" consciousness.

We think of survival in terms of the survival of personality, the set of characteristics that distinguishes each of us from another. This personality is manifested through our state of consciousness. Thus I will use "personality" and "state of consciousness" as largely synonymous terms.

Altered States

Each one of the psychological processes sketched above can undergo drastic changes. An ordinary face can be seen as that of an angel or a devil. Your heart can be felt as a glowing mass of radiant energy instead of only a barely perceptible pulsation in your chest. Your memories can seem like those of someone else, or you may "remember" things that intellectually you know could not be known to you; yet they are "obviously" your memories. Totally new systems of thought can come into play for evaluating reality. What is most dear to you may change drastically. Space and time can function in whole new ways, as in experiencing eternity. Even muscles may work in quite new ways.

When many of these changes occur simultaneously, we talk about experiencing an "altered state of consciousness". The change is too radical for it to be a variation of your ordinary state; it is both qualitatively and quantitatively different.

Consider the following example of an altered state reported by P. Stafford.

> At one point the world disappeared. I was no longer in my body. I didn't have a body. . . . Then I reached a point at which I felt ready to die. It wasn't a question of choice, it was just a wave that carried me higher and higher, at the same time that I was having what in my normal state I would call a horror of death. It became obvious to me that it was not at all what I had anticipated death to be, except it was death—that something was dying. I reached a point at which I gave it all away. I just yielded, and then I entered a space in which there aren't any words. The words that have been used a thousand times—starting with Buddha. I mean at-one-with-the-universe; recognize your Godhead; all these words I later used to explore what I had experienced. The feeling was that I was 'home'. . . . It was a bliss state of a kind I never experienced before.[3]

This kind of altered state experience is particularly relevant to the question of survival, and we shall return to it later.

The Dream State

To further our understanding of altered states, let us look at the most commonly recurring one, nighttime dreaming. Modern sleep research has shown that we all spend about 20% of our sleep time in a specific brain wave state, Stage 1, associated with the mental activity of dreaming, whether we remember it or not.

Figure 2 illustrates major variations in the functioning of the subsystems of consciousness that occur in nighttime dreaming. The irregular lines indicate that a process functions significantly differently from ordinary waking consciousness. We will examine the subsystems of consciousness in the same order as before, and focus on the changes that an after-death state of consciousness might involve. Nighttime dreaming while alive might well prove to be like the after-death state.

FIGURE 2

MAJOR VARIATIONS IN FUNCTIONING OF SUBSYSTEMS OF CONSCIOUSNESS IN NIGHTTIME DREAMING

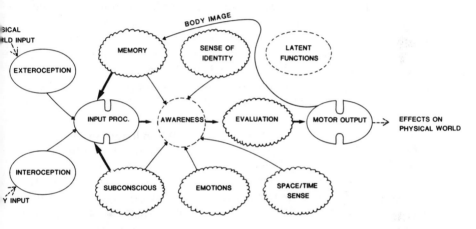

In order to dream, we must go to and remain asleep, that is, we must induce an altered state of consciousness. Usually this means reducing exteroception and interoception to very low levels. We turn out the lights and close our eyes, eliminating visual input, for example; we relax our bodies, eliminating interoceptive kinesthetic input. Thus Figure 2 shows little input, represented by small arrows to the extero- and interoceptors. If we survive death in some form, we will certainly not have the physical exteroceptors and interoceptors we had during life, so this customary input would be drastically reduced, as in dreaming.

We now know that there is a very active inhibition of what input does reach our receptors. Thus, input processing is shown as squeezed tight in the middle. If you deliberately stimulate a sleeper, but not intensely enough to wake him or her, and then awaken the subject to get a dream report, you'll find most stimuli do not make it through into the dream world. The few that do are usually distorted so they fit in with the ongoing dream. Calling the dreamer's name, for example, could become another dream character asking him about the state of his health!   If an after-death state is like a dream state, might similar distortions of our questions to the deceased occur?

Memory functions in a different way in dream consciousness. In our waking state we normally know when we are drawing information from storage. There is a non-verbal "This is a memory" quality attached to it. This quality disappears in dreams. The conventional view of dreams is that all the objects in the dream world are constructed from memory images, yet dreaming is experienced as *perceiving*, not as *remembering*.

Similarly our sense of identity, our emotions, and our evaluation processes can operate quite differently, as if the dream were of someone else with different emotional reactions and styles of thinking. What is sensible by dream standards may be outrageous by waking state standards. The space-time sense is totally changed: Instead of accurately putting our experiences in their "real" context of our lying in bed at night, we may be at a palm-lined oasis in the next century. If such alteration of the processing styles of emotion, evaluation, sense of identity, and space/time sense occurs routinely in dreams while alive, why couldn't these and other alterations occur after death? Suppose the after-death state is more like a dream state than an ordinary conscious state? Would someone who knew our personality in its ordinary state recognize our personality in something closer to its dream state?

Another common characteristic of dreams is that they usually seem to *happen* to us, rather than feeling like our active creations. Who is creating this world and these actions? Where does the scenery come from? How do the various actors know when to come on stage? If the after-death state is like nighttime dreaming, will it be so passive? Will we care from the after-death side of things about helping to prove our survival?

The subconscious is given the credit for the intelligent and active creation of dreams, since the dreamer declines credit. This is not a terribly good explanation, of course, but it is the best we have at this time—and a good reminder of how little we understand about our minds. If such a potent source of experience as dreams is controlled by mental processes we hardly understand at all, it reminds us of how careful we must be in extrapolating the characteristics of waking consciousness to the possible after-death state.

Finally, note that the motor output processes are shown as squeezed tight in the dreaming state of consciousness, as input processing is. This reflects the fact that you perform all sorts of physical actions with what you take to be your physical body in your dreams, yet an outside observer sees that you lie still. Modern research has now shown that neural signals for movement are indeed sent to our muscles during dreaming, just as when we are awake. If you dream of lifting your arm, all the necessary signals are sent to make your arm move that way. But, there is an active paralysis of our muscles during nighttime dreaming. Inhibitory signals are sent down the spinal cord to the muscles themselves so they will not respond. A good thing, too: It would be very dangerous to be physically moving about while our consciousness was in dreamland! The major exception to this overall inhibition is our eyes, which do move to follow the dream world imagery, just as if we were awake and actually looking at it. There is no practical danger in moving our eyes around while we sleep, so no inhibition is needed here.

No External Feedback In The Dream State

I emphasized earlier that a state of consciousness is a dynamically interacting and *stabilized* system. Ordinary waking consciousness is especially stabilized by two major routes, feedback via the external world and the exteroceptors, and via the internal world, the body, through the interoceptors. In dreaming, these major stabilization routes are lost, and so are shown as light, dotted lines in Figure 2, in contrast to their importance in Figure 1. In your dream you raise your arm and move a gigantic boulder, weighing tons. There is no actual input from the interoceptors in your physical arm to contradict the idea of your doing this. There is no actual perception via your physical eyes that there is no boulder there to contradict the idea of moving a gigantic boulder. What little "feedback" there is is from your body image, rather than your actual physical body. The *idea* thus has far more power to affect your construction of "reality", the experience you realize in the dream state, because there is almost no input from a fixed, lawful, external reality with which your internal idea must be consistent.

Might there be a similar lack of "reality checking" in an after-death state? Indeed some mediumistic communications suggest that the experienced reality of the ostensible surviving entities is largely one where their ideas and beliefs do construct the world they experience without the sorts of restraints that we have in the physical world because of the need to harmonize what we perceive about the world with our ideas about it. This would make for a highly variable state of consciousness and make personal identity much less stable.

In looking at dreams I have taken a conventional position: The dream is just a set of mental processes, based on physical brain and physical nervous system functioning, and nothing more. That is, a dream is all imaginary—unreal, isn't it?

Altered States Knowledge Of Survival

To be quite precise, we must accept the fact that usually a dream is perfectly real at the time it is occurring (I exempt lucid dreams, in which you know that you are dreaming while dreaming). For me, dream reality is just as "real" as ordinary reality, if not more so. So where do we get the idea that it is imaginary? Let us look at the nature of experience.

Three Categories Of Experience:

Most of my experience readily falls into three general categories that I shall call worlds. (We could just as well call them states of consciousness, but I want to stress the apparent "externality" of them here.) World 1 takes up most of my experienced life. It is a very rigid set of experiences; that is, its reality seems to be governed by some inflexible laws, such that most situations in it cannot be altered directly by my desires or will. I have to do things according to laws which seem external to me. If I want to move a heavy boulder, for example, I have to get long levers or a block and tackle and exert my muscles.

While World 1 is rigid, it is also very reliable. The boulder will not move by itself or do anything unexpected unless quite specific events happen, such as someone else using a block and tackle on it, or an earthquake occurring. For normal conversational purposes, I, like the independently existing entities I meet in it, call this World 1 reality of experience my "waking consciousness".

World 2 of my experiential reality takes up the least amount of experienced time by the yardstick of my direct experience, but the second largest amount of time by some of the regular experiences of my World 1 reality. My usual direct experience of World 2 is of nothing happening at all, but a feeling of some unknown amount of time having passed occurs right at the end of World 2 experience. By World 1 standards, *insofar as they are appropriate to apply outside their own experiential realm*, World 2 occupies almost a third of my life. When I am in the midst of World 1 experience I call my World 2 experience "dreamless sleep". When I am in the midst of World 2 experience, I generally do not call it anything at all.

My World 3 experiential reality is like my World 1 reality in many ways. I see, taste, touch, and smell. I feel pleasure and pain; I reflect on things and reach conclusions; I plan and carry out actions. World 3 experience occupies only a small amount of my total experience by World 1 standards, but in its own terms, it sometimes is brief, sometimes quite long. The apparently external laws and regularities that operate in World 1 experience make their appearance here, but generally are much more loosely applied. Sometimes I can move that boulder just by thinking about it; other times it may move by itself for no apparent reason. Sometimes I find principles or laws that only work for World 3 experience. I can fly by an act of will in World 3 experience, for example. It is a special mental act that must be done correctly, and this act of will has no effect in World 1.

When in the midst of World 1 experiences, I generally call my World 3 experiences "dreams". In the midst of World 3 experience, it is usually just as real as anything else I experience in any World.

World 1 Invalidation Of World 3:

The really curious thing is that in World 1, I and the other ostensibly independently existing beings have convinced themselves that only World 1 experience is real and worthwhile, and that World 3 experience, dreaming, is useless, unreal, and totally delusory! Why? Because it is not consistent in the way that World 1 experience is, and because it does not accurately mirror the regularities and events of World 1. I, a being who knows nothing directly but my own experience, have convinced myself that part of my direct knowledge, direct experience, which I know just as directly when I experience it as any other kind of direct experience, isn't real.

This dismissal of dream experience as unreal and delusory is, of course, culturally relative. Some cultures still accept dream reality as real and important, even if it isn't an accurate mirror of ordinary reality. Indeed it is only a historically recent development in our own culture to reject dreams so thoroughly. The rejection of the reality of dreams goes hand-in-hand with a mainstream rejection of the reality of altered states in general.

State-Specific Knowledge

We have been skirting around one of the most important qualities of knowledge, namely that it is *state-specific. What you can know depends on the state of consciousness you are in.*

A simple analogy is using a net to troll through the ocean. If your net has one-inch mesh, it will not pick up anything that is smaller than one inch, thus excluding an enormous amount of life. If you understand this property of your net, your "data collection system", there is no problem. If you are too enamored of it, you are likely to think that ocean life is all bigger than one inch. You cannot study small life with your net.

Altered state of consciousness research has shown us that some kinds of human knowledge are *state-specific.* If you are not in a particular state of consciousness, certain things cannot be known.

Some knowledge is only partially state-specific, in that it can be known in two or more states of consciousness. If you ask someone the street address of his home, for example, he will probably give you a correct answer in his ordinary state, in a dream state (assuming you are some dream character asking the question), in a sexually aroused state, in a depressed state, and in a state of alcohol or marijuana intoxication. But there are things you can know in altered states of consciousness that you cannot really remember in your ordinary state, much less tell others about in any adequate way.

If we want to know all that a human being can know, we must study some things in an appropriate altered state of consciousness. If we do not enter that state and work appropriately with it, we will never really know the answers. One of the tragedies of our times is that we have forgotten about the state-specificity of knowledge in regard to many vital spiritual questions. Thus, we approach them only from an ordinary states perspective and get answers that are distorted and pale reflections of reality. We have traded, as it were, direct knowledge of something like Unity of Life for abstract verbal statements and theories about unity. It doesn't satisfy, and it doesn't work very well.

Altered States And Survival: The Denial Of Experience

What does this have to do with survival? Just this: *The direct experience of existing and experiencing in some form that seems partially or fully independent of the physical body is relatively common in various altered states of consciousness and this kind of experience constitutes the most direct knowledge of survival an individual may have.* There is nothing wrong with indirect forms of evidence, of course, but by this wholesale rejection of direct altered states of consciousness experience, we force the survival issue to be solely one of *indirect* experience, of abstraction and deduction instead of direct experience. This also amounts to throwing away some of the most relevant evidence about survival, and may make it impossible to get a *personally* satisfactory answer.

Further, contemporary research in humanistic and transpersonal psychology has shown that the wholesale rejection of dream and other altered states of consciousness experience has strong and largely pathological consequences for our happiness and our full development as human beings.

There are many personal and cultural roots for the rejection of altered states of consciousness. We will focus now on the dominance of materialism as a philosophy of life.

The Materialist Position
   In the materialistic view of man, so widespread today, consciousness is regarded as essentially a discussion about computer circuits—biocomputer circuits to be specific, but *nothing* more than this. Consciousness is like an actively running program in the biocomputer; altered states are simply different programs. The various aspects of consciousness discussed above are merely subprograms of the larger program, which is *nothing but* the totality of one's biological, material self. The programs and subprograms may produce all sorts of outputs and experiences. Many of them are very useful to our pleasure and biological survival, but many of them are quite arbitrary or even nonsensical.
   I have programmed one of my laboratory's computers, for example, to print out the statement, "I have just achieved ecstatic transelectrical fusion with the great Chip in the Sky, experiencing all binary knowledge and the depths of mystical electro-ecstasy!" We know that the logical content of this statement is nonsense, of course. Computer chips don't have "experiences" and do nothing but what the physical nature of the computer allows them to do. In the materialistic reduction of consciousness to a set of programs running in the human biocomputer, we know that the program is totally dependent on the hardware, the "bioware", the physical existence and state of the material components the biocomputer is built from. In my computer if the hardware's state is greatly changed, by turning off the power or physically destroying a component, the program dies. When the brain and the body dies, the hardware of human consciousness dies with it. No belief or even mystical experiences of being more than the body mean a thing in this view: When the brain/body dies, you die. Period.

   To put it simply, the materialistic equation is:
   Mind = Brain
   And this is considered to be the complete story.

Why Has Materialism Become So Dominant?
   Why has materialism become the dominant view of this century? One reason is that it works exceptionally well for a very wide range of situations in life. For example, it has made us materially richer than ever before, given us enormous power over the physical world, and alleviated pain and illnesses that once killed those who contracted them.
   On an intellectual level, materialism appears to give us a consistent and straightforward understanding of the universe. This consistency is very intellectually satisfying.

Another reason is that materialism gives us protection against many "things" and "powers" that people were afraid of in the past. When belief in capricious, supernatural forces and malicious demons was widespread, it was a matter of great practical concern to protect yourself, and frequently it seemed that you had failed. Fear of the nonmaterial unknown was very real. But if you gave total acceptance to a belief system that said there were no supernatural forces or beings to begin with, then there was nothing to fear! Many apparent problems were thus resolved at once.

As a psychologist I suspect that materialism is not actually very solid as a belief system for many or most of the people who think they accept it; on a deeper level they have many unresolved fears of the supernatural. Their passionate advocacy of materialistic philosophy may be of the nature of a psychological defense, a reaction formation that tries to avoid conscious awareness of conflict.[4]

A materialistic philosophy, by invalidating vital aspects of human nature, creates a dismal outlook on life, an outlook that is usually not explicitly acknowledged because of its dismalness. When hope, love, and joy, to say nothing of intellect and the materialist philosophy itself are reduced to their "ultimate reality" there is nothing but electrochemical impulses in a biocomputer that originated by chance in a dead universe.

As a workshop exercise, I have been able to guide people to useful insights by having them go through a "belief experiment". I ask them to give to something called the Western Creed as much attention and belief as possible for 15 minutes or so, observing their emotional reactions. This experiment is designed to help people realize how much of the prevailing materialistic philosophy they have implicitly and unconsciously accepted, in spite of their conscious beliefs. This concise statement of the prevailing materialist view has practical consequences on the human spirit.

The Western Creed

I believe in the material universe as the only and ultimate reality, a universe controlled by fixed physical laws and blind chance.

I affirm that the universe has no creator, no objective purpose, and no objective meaning or destiny.

I maintain that all ideas about God or gods, supernatural beings, prophets and saviors, or other nonphysical beings or forces are superstitions and delusions. Life and consciousness are totally identical to physical processes, and arose from chance interactions of blind physical forces. Like the rest of life, my life and my consciousness have no objective purpose, meaning, or destiny.

I believe that all judgments, values, and moralities, whether my own or others, are subjective, arising solely from biological determinants, personal history, and chance. Free will is an illusion. Therefore, the most rational values I can personally live by must be based on the knowledge that for me what pleases me is good; what pains me is bad. Those who please me or help me avoid pain are my friends; those who pain me or keep me from my pleasure are my enemies. Rationality requires that friends and enemies be used in ways that maximize my pleasure and minimize my pain.

I affirm that churches have no real use other than social support; that there are no objective sins to commit or be forgiven for; that there is no retribution for sin or reward for virtue other than that which I can arrange, directly or through others. Virtue for me is getting what I want without being caught and punished by others.

I maintain that the death of the body is the death of the mind. There is no afterlife, and all hope of such is nonsense.

Please note that this Western Creed does *not* reflect my personal beliefs, or my scientific opinion about the nature of reality. It is a parody of genuine religious creeds, created in order to illustrate the degree to which a distorted form of science, intermixed with naive materialism, which leads to the implicit religion of "scientism" that has greatly affected our Western beliefs and values. By experimentally believing this creed and reciting it aloud, preferably with a group of friends, and then discussing how it makes you feel and what it reveals about your deeper beliefs, much can be learned.

The ideas expressed in the Western Creed are generally claimed to be accurate representations of the best scientific *fact*, though, not just a belief system. If they are indeed facts, then we must accept them, whether or not we like them. I certainly don't like them, but I must divorce my liking or disliking ideas from my scientific investigation of their truth value. Are they well-proven facts?

The Inadequacy Of Materialism

If materialistic science and philosophy simply claimed to be a specialized branch of knowledge, useful in its own area but not too relevant to things outside its area, it would lose most of the power it claims by virtue of being all-embracing. Plumbers have very useful knowledge about a very material subject, but I do not know of anyone whose spiritual outlook on life was deeply disturbed because plumbers are so good at the material things they do.

Because the practical and intellectual results of modern science are so powerful, we (including almost all scientists) are too impressed with the materialistic philosophy intermixed with it. We can consciously reject materialism because of the loss of vital spirit it leads to, but it is hard to reject effectively the cultural conditioning and emotional involvement that we as Westerners almost invariably have in the scientistic outlook. Thus, it is important for us to be able to deal rationally with the intellectual claim of comprehensiveness of materialism, not just take a position like "I don't like the way materialism feels, so even if I have to ignore my intellect, I'm going to reject it."

The good news is that you don't have to be ignorant or unscientific in order to argue reasonably that the scientistic position is far from complete and thus is not an all-powerful set of reasons for rejecting the possible reality of the spiritual. I am not arguing the opposite and encouraging you to believe everything that is labeled "spiritual". There is a lot of nonsense under that label that should be sorted out and rejected, but not everything.

Scientific Parapsychology As An Underminer Of Materialism

The good news is based on the findings of scientific parapsychology, a collection of thousands of naturalistic observations and at least 700 laboratory experiments in the last six decades that, to my mind, conclusively demonstrate that there are aspects of the human mind that simply cannot be reduced to materialistic explanations. Thus, the equation "Mind = Brain" is woefully incomplete and should not be used to rule out spiritual realities or the possibility of survival on an a priori basis.

Briefly, parapsychological research has firmly demonstrated the existence of four major psychic abilities. "Psychic" means that we are sensitive to and experience transfer of information from beyond the physical world. There may be other psychic abilities—I think there are, but they have not been investigated and established to the degree that these four have. Therefore, I focus on them as the foundations of parapsychology. They are telepathy, clairvoyance, precognition, and psychokinesis.

Telepathy is the transmission of information from mind to mind after we have ruled out ordinary physical means such as talking to one another, or sign language, and inference from physically known data. The laboratory studies that firmly established telepathy were mostly card-guessing studies. A sender, isolated in a room, looked at one card after another from a thoroughly shuffled pack of cards, and tried to send his or her thoughts. A receiver, isolated in another room, wrote down his or her impressions of the cards. Perfect scores were extremely rare, but enough studies showed more hits than could be reasonably expected by chance to establish telepathy.

Clairvoyance is the direct extrasensory perception of information about the physical world without the intervention of another mind which already knows the information by ordinary sensory means. The classical card test studies involved a participant giving impressions of the order of a deck of randomized cards, when no living human being knew what the order of that deck was. Many studies showed enough accuracy to establish clairvoyance. The information transmission rate is about the same as in telepathy studies.[5] Both telepathy and clairvoyance seem unaffected by physical factors like spatial distance or physical shielding.

Precognition is the prediction of the future when the future is determined in a random way, such that inference from present knowledge would not be helpful. The classic experimental design is to ask a percipient to predict the order of a target deck of cards. The cards will be randomly shuffled at some future date. Precognition of this sort has been successful at intervals of up to a year. Curiously, the average information transfer rate is much lower than in present-time telepathy or clairvoyance studies.[6]

Collectively, telepathy, clairvoyance, and precognition are known as extrasensory perception (ESP), as they all involve information gathering.

Psychokinesis (PK) is the fourth well-established psychic phenomenon. It is popularly called mind over matter. The classic tests involved wishing which way machine-thrown dice would turn up, although the target object is now usually an electronic random number generator. The frequency of PK appearance is about the same as precognition.[7]

The importance of these psi phenomena, as the four are now collectively called, is that they are manifestations of *mind* that have resisted all attempts to reduce them to known physical forces, or straightforward extensions of known physical forces. I exempt some of the speculations on the frontiers of quantum physics to explain psi as "straight-

forward" extensions of physics for they are controversial ideas in physics, and involve such a radically different view of what is "physical".
They should not be linked with the old materialistic physics. There
has not been a significant degree of understanding and controlling psi
phenomena in the scientific community.

The psi phenomena are examples where we must say:

Mind ≠ Brain

Certainly some aspects of mind and consciousness are partially or
wholly based in brain and nervous system functioning, but psi phenomena are not, and so openly demonstrate the need to investigate mind on
its own terms. These psi phenomena do not "prove" survival, but insofar as mind has aspects which do not seem limited by space or time,
such aspects of mind are the sort we might expect to survive bodily
death.

Scientific Research On Survival

Modern parapsychological research has focused on the four aspects
of psi mentioned above, but historically parapsychology, originally
called psychical research, focused specifically on the question of survival of death.

Modern spiritualism was born near the end of the last century when
mysterious rappings in the home of the Fox sisters were interpreted as
PK-like effects of departed spirits who were trying to communicate
with the living. In a short time, Spiritualism was a world-wide religion. Its basic message was very appealing and scientific in style.
Spiritualism accepted the fact that much that was called religion,
based on authority, was indeed just superstition. Scientists were right
who said that experience, data, and facts were more important than
belief or dogma. "Don't *believe* in survival," said the spiritualists;
"*test* the idea of survival against the facts!"

Spiritualist mediums claimed that this is just what they were: mediums of communication, channels between the living and the deceased
for exchanging messages. If you wanted to know if your Aunt Matilda
had survived death, you sat down with a medium at a seance and
asked to speak to Aunt Matilda. When the spirit who claimed to be
Aunt Matilda was contacted, you spoke through the medium and asked
her questions about herself until you were convinced that it was indeed
Aunt Matilda speaking.

Many, many people carried out this experiment. Some were not convinced of survival. As the early psychical researchers noted, many of
the ostensible spirits gave only the vaguest details of their earthly
lives, or were just plain wrong in what they said. Some seance commu-

nications from the ostensible spirits were of a very high quality, though, and convinced sitters of the reality of survival. Here is an example of the kind of high quality sitting that has been reported, this one from after World War II by the British investigator, Rosalind Heywood:

> . . . I went to a Scottish medium to see if she could pick up something about a friend, a German diplomat who I feared had been killed either by the Nazis or the Russians. I simply didn't know what had happened to him. The medium very soon got onto him. She gave his Christian name, talked about things we had done together in Washington, and described correctly my opinion of his character. She said he was dead and that his death was so tragic he didn't want to talk about it. She gave a number of striking details about him and the evidence of personality was very strong. . .

I believe any of us would be strongly impressed by this kind of evidence for the survival of death, and it has convinced a few parapsychologists.

Complexities Of Survival Research

Survival research is now a very small part of parapsychology (itself a miniscule field).[8] Compared to the central role it once had, survival research has been almost abandoned for a half century. The reason is quite interesting.

When psychical researchers first began investigating mediums, the idea that living people had extraordinary psychic abilities was not generally accepted. If information from an ostensible surviving spirit was in accord with what the investigator knew about the deceased, he was inclined to accept it as evidence of survival. Who but he and the deceased knew it? As researchers gradually established that ordinary people sometimes showed telepathy, clairvoyance, and precognition, however, the picture became more complicated. The validating information *might* have come from the deceased, but it might also come from the medium's unconscious telepathic reading of the investigator's (or some friend's of the deceased) mind, or from a clairvoyant pickup of information from surviving documents and records. If *pre*cognition existed, how about the possibility of *retro*cognition, where the medium's unconscious psychic abilities went back in time to get information about the deceased when he was still alive?

Added to these psychic complications were the facts arriving from the study of hypnosis and of abnormal mental states like those involved in multiple personality that showed that the subconscious part of a person's mind could do marvelous imitations of people. Further, add the fact that subconscious processes could distort a person's mental functioning to alter experience so it supported deeply held beliefs, and the grounds were established for a powerful alternative explanation of the best data for survival.

Data: Sometimes ostensible spirits, communicating through mediums, give very specific and characteristic information that was known to the deceased but could not have been known to the medium through normal, sensory means.

Survival Theory: This means that the deceased has indeed survived and is sometimes able to communicate with the living.

Unconscious Impersonation Theory: Because the medium believes in survival and has a need to have experiences which reinforce her belief system, an unconscious part of her mind *imitates* deceased people. Because of occasional use of ESP abilities by this part of the subconscious mind to come up with information about the deceased that could not be normally known to the medium, these imitation personalities are very convincing. Because of the dissociation of the subconscious mind, the medium consciously feels like she is indeed simply a channel for personalities outside herself.

The Undead Deceased

To illustrate the complexities of survival research, let us continue the case cited above:

> If I had never heard any more, I would have thought it very impressive. But after the sitting, I set about trying to find out something about him. Finally the Swiss Foreign Office found him for me. He was not dead. He had escaped from Germany and had married an English girl. He wrote to me that he had never been so happy in his life. So there I think the medium was reading my expectations. She was quite wrong about the actual facts, but quite right according to what I had expected.

Most parapsychologists abandoned survival research and focused on the psi abilities of the living because cases like this made it look just too difficult to decide between the survival hypothesis and the unconscious impersonation theory. The abandonment is probably premature, and a few parapsychologists are still actively working to devise better tests of survival that could distinguish between these two explanations. Ian Stevenson, for example, a psychiatrist at the University of Virginia, has proposed that subconscious ESP on the medium's part might account for factual knowledge shown by an ostensible surviving spirit, but would not account for complex skills if they were shown. To speak responsively a foreign language you were sure was unknown to the medium, for example, rather than just to mention isolated words or phrases from that language, would be very convincing. Unfortunately, we do not have good cases of that type yet. Perhaps we will.

I stated at the beginning of this chapter what little survival research has been done was implicitly about the survival of ordinary consciousness—the ordinary "I". We have seen how ordinary consciousness and ordinary "I"s are just one manifestation of whatever our more basic nature is. Let us now look at possibilities of survival that include some of the realities of altered states of consciousness.

Models Of Survival

Ordinary Consciousness, Equivalent Body Survival:

This model assumes that existence after death would be rather like permanent exile to a foreign land, but with consciousness and "external" reality much like they were before death. Given how much the structure of the body and brain shape the pattern of consciousness, we would expect some sort of nonphysical structure or process that mimicked most of the physical body's effects on consciousness in this sort of survival if consciousness was to be like it was when the physical body was still present.

Stable Altered State Of Consciousness Survival:

This model would assume that there is a primary, "ordinary" (for the after-death state) state of consciousness after death, with stable and comprehensible (at least from within) qualities. It would be an altered state of consciousness compared to pre-death embodied ordinary consciousness. We would have to learn the qualities of this after-death state in order to comprehend fully and communicate with the deceased.

Multiple, Stable Altered State Of Consciousness Survival:

There may be several altered states of consciousness that the surviving person exists in from time to time. Communications from the same deceased person, but originating from different states, might seem contradictory or disjointed. The confusion could be lessened if either the surviving individual discriminated between such states and indicated which state they were in and its characteristics, or if we could make such discriminations. Then by learning the characteristics of each state we would synthesize a coherent whole from the various communications.

To gather evidence in favor of the possibility of survival, we have to make an assumption in this and the previous model, namely that at least some of the altered states of consciousness the deceased can communicate from bear a clear enough resemblance to the pre-death personality and state of consciousness so we can see the connection. It may be that people survive death in an altered state of consciousness that is so drastically different from their former state and personality that we can see no connection at all. But we can never gather evidence for survival from such a reality. Or, as suggested by some research and spiritual tradition, relations to the ordinary pre-death state may persist for a while after death but gradually fade, making it possible to gather evidence for survival for recently deceased persons but not for long deceased ones. I personally incline toward a model of continual evolution of consciousness, and would hope that I would not remain too fixed for too long after death.

Unstable, Transmitting States Of Consciousness Survival:

I have theorized elsewhere[2] that the most comprehensive explanation for some of the altered states of consciousness phenomena we see, especially those induced by powerful psychedelic drugs in untrained individuals, is to recognize that we are not dealing with a single, stabilized, altered state of consciousness but with continuous, unstable transitions from momentary configuration to momentary configuration. The colloquial term "tripping" illustrates the flavor of this. A person's condition, whether induced in life by a powerful destabilizing force like a drug or by the nature of the after-death state, is a lack of stability, a rapid shifting from one momentary configuration of conscious functioning to another. Such a condition would be rather like delirium. To both the person experiencing it and to outsiders, there would be moments of sense and lucidity, perhaps moments of even greater lucidity than normal, but overall, it is confused rambling.

The Body As A Stabilizer Of Consciousness

Given the importance of the body and brain as stabilizing mechanisms for both ordinary and altered states of consciousness, the lack of a body and brain in an after-death state might well mean that it would be characterized by great instability. If we would investigate what happens to mental functioning in life when body awareness is greatly reduced or temporarily eliminated, we might have a better understanding of what an after-death state might be like.

Our discussion of dreaming earlier is quite relevant to this idea, for in dreaming we have almost no awareness of our actual physical bodies, only of our mentally constructed dream bodies. Sensory deprivation studies also shed some light on this question. Ketamine intoxication might also be an excellent analogue for studying the qualities of mind when no body is perceived in life. Used as an analgesic in surgery, it has also been used in much lower doses (about one-tenth the surgical dose) as a psychedelic drug, with a major effect in some users of making the physical body effectively disappear from consciousness. The experience cited from Stafford near the beginning of this chapter to illustrate an altered state of consciousness was one that was induced by Ketamine.

Interoceptive input from our physical bodies is not the only major source of stabilization of consciousness in physical life, of course, so it may be possible for stable states of consciousness to develop in an after-death state based on other kinds of stabilization processes.

The Noisy Telephone Line Model

Another way of looking at the survival question involves a focus on the quality of the communications from the ostensible deceased spirits. Almost all survival research carried out to date has implicitly been based on what we might characterize as the noisy telephone line model. This assumes the "ordinary consciousness, equivalent body" model of survival: The deceased's mind and personality still function pretty much like normal, and includes a desire to communicate with surviving loved ones and convince them that he or she has survived death. The obvious inconsistencies, irrelevancies, and errors in mediumistic communications then call for a further step in modeling to explain the usually poor quality of communication.

Suppose you receive a long distance telephone call, the essence of which is that the caller claims to be your long missing sister. She says she was kidnapped, but will be released if you leave a very large sum of money (essentially all of your savings) in a certain place. Otherwise they will torture and kill her.

Naturally you want to save your sister, even if it means a great sacrifice. Unfortunately the quality of the connection is very bad. There is not only hissing, crackling, and periods of silence, the voice quality is badly distorted, so you're not sure it is really your sister's voice. Sometimes there is cross talk, and other phone conversations are picked up. But, with the bad quality on the line, you are not always sure when something was said by your sister and when it was a fragment of a conversation by other people.

You naturally want to be sure this is your missing sister before you part with your life's savings. You want to ask questions about physical life events, which are only known to you and your sister, such as the name of a pet dog she had when she was six years old. Sometimes you get answers that seem to make sense, but other times your sister claims she can't hear and understand you properly, or her answer is distorted or too general to be satisfying. Sometimes she claims she can't answer for reasons that aren't really satisfactory—such as "they" won't let her answer that one. All in all, this would be a very unsatisfactory state of affairs.

The analogy is a good parallel to the quality of most mediumistic communications with the ostensibly surviving deceased. The problem is assumed by most Spiritualists and most investigators to be in the "telephone line", in the psychology of mediumistic communication: Your kidnapped sister is still pretty much who she was. There is an implicit faith that if we could just get better telephone connections, the question of whether this was really your sister would receive an unequivocal answer.

The Delirious Phone Conversation Model

I believe the noisy telephone line analogy is useful. If people do survive, there may indeed be massive problems with the medium as communications channel, or problems with whatever kind of psi the medium uses to communicate with the deceased. Some information may not be transmitted at all or may be distorted in transmission (as in trying to get external stimuli into nighttime dreaming), and noise (generalizations, guesses, unconscious impersonation) may be added by the medium's unconscious mind. Hypothesizing all of the problems of the inconsistency and error of communication from the deceased as a communications problem is probably inadequate, however.

Suppose the reality of survival for many individuals is closer to what we called the unstable transiting states of consciousness model. Yes, the deceased has survived, but the state of her consciousness is constantly changing, as in delirium. Imagine a telephone call from your kidnapped sister on your noisy telephone line while she is alive; but she is drugged or delirious. Indeed, she may never return to what used to be "normal" consciousness for her. What kind of conversation will you have now? Will the occasional moments of lucidity (that is, momentary configurations of states of consciousness that are like her ordinary state, so that ordinary sorts of information can be exchanged) produce sufficient evidence of your kidnapped sister's identity to counter the confusions, errors, and changed points of view that may dominate the communication?

The Altered States Phone Conversation Model

Suppose your kidnapped sister is permanently in an altered state of consciousness, changed forever by the experiences she has gone through, but is in one that is stable. While we still have the problem of the noisy communication channel to deal with, we at least have a stable source of communications. Your sister may not be who she used to be, but she is an identifiable person, and that person has a definite relation to who your sister used to be.

Now we need to understand the nature of the state of consciousness she is in so as to ask her questions that will make sufficient sense in her altered state of consciousness to elicit relevant and intelligent responses. Similarly, if the after-death state involves a stable consciousness, even if it is altered by ordinary living-state criteria, we need to learn how to speak the "language" of that altered state of consciousness if we want to learn whether someone has survived death.

Inappropriateness Of Tests

If a person who survives is in a quite different state of consciousness than he or she was before death, the kinds of tests we use to establish identity might be quite inappropriate. They might give false negative results, that is, say this is not the person when they should say it is, or give inconsistent and confusing results.

I am reminded of some experiences I had that illustrate this problem. When I was a graduate student I served as a subject in some studies of psychedelic drugs. One of the questions of interest was what such drugs did to color perception. Subjects uniformly reported that color was experienced as much brighter and more alive, and that they could obviously see more subtle distinctions among colors than they ordinarily could. I certainly had had that experience. Was this a purely subjective impression, or did psychedelics like Psilocybin actually enhance the ability to discriminate different shades of color?

To test this, a color discrimination test was used. I do not recall its technical name, but it was labeled the "bottlecap test" in my mind because it consisted of more than one hundred identical size bottlecaps. The top of each bottlecap was a different color. Altogether they ranged through the whole color spectrum. They were presented shuffled in random order, and my job was to arrange them in a line from blue through red, with each adjacent color being the smallest change from the previous color. The shades of color were close enough that ordinary people generally made a fair number of mistakes.

I took this test while near the peak of a Psilocybin experience one day. This was scientific research, so I had made a strong commitment before taking the drug to do my best, as I firmly believed it was important to test this question. As I began the test, though, my perspective in that altered state of consciousness was quite different. The test was so shallow, it could not begin to tap the profundity of what I was experiencing! Yet I understood that my earlier self, a distant thing but one I knew I would come back to some day, had made a commitment to do this test as accurately as possible. So, I worked away at it.

When the test was analyzed later, the results were very odd. Overall, my color discrimination accuracy was about the same as it ordinarily was. If you looked at individual parts of the test, though, there were long runs of perfect scores, implying better than ordinary color discrimination, mixed in with much larger errors than I ordinarily made, indicating worsened color discrimination. Had the Psilocybin made me better or worse at perceiving color? The question could not really be answered on the basis of the test results. The question, as framed and worked on by ordinary consciousness methods, did not have a clear answer.

Fortunately, we had a second perspective, an altered state of consciousness perspective because of my "inside" observations on what had happened during the test. I had been doing my best by ordinary consciousness standards, but by the altered state of consciousness standards of the Psilocybin-induced state, I was also quite impatient. If the slightly changed color bottlecap that I needed was nearby, I saw it quickly and put it in the right place. When I couldn't find it right away, though, my rapidly changing mind, without my full recognition, picked almost any nearby bottlecap and hallucinated in the right shade of color on it, so I actually perceived just the shade I needed and could put the bottlecap in place, finish the silly test, and get on to more interesting experiences! In my altered state of consciousness this was an intelligent thing to do, given the inherent values of the altered state. Thus, at times my color discrimination was superb, but when I became impatient, the machinery of my mind put more value on finishing than on being consistent with another set of standards, ordinary consciousness standards, that was foreign to my current state of consciousness; thus, the massive mistakes by ordinary consciousness standards.

In this example we have the advantage that I returned to my ordinary state of consciousness with some memory of the altered state of consciousness and could report on why my functioning looked strange by ordinary state standards. Insofar as someone who survives death may be in one or more altered states of consciousness, they may make similar "mistakes" by ordinary consciousness standards, and they may not be able to return to an ordinary state to explain their mistake.

How many of our tests for survival look meaningless, shallow, or silly to someone in some altered state of consciousness in an after-death state? How many of the "mistakes" made by ostensibly surviving people in trying to prove their survival seem like obviously intelligent actions from their altered state of consciousness point of view? If someone had called me long distance while I was in the Psilocybin-induced state and asked me to prove that I was me, beyond any shadow of a reasonable doubt, I would have found their request very odd, given my state of mind and the "sensible" (to me in that state) answers I would have given might have seemed very strange to them. An obvious research project for survival research, then, is to investigate how people's sense of identity changes and how they communicate in a variety of altered states of consciousness while they are still living.

More Appropriate Tests For Survival

We can summarize the implications for improving the quality of survival research around the question of "Who might survive death?"

The ordinary personality, ordinary "I", does not seem a likely candidate for more than temporary survival. It has little enough unity itself, being made of many "I"s itself, each of which often fails to "survive" the shocks of ordinary life for very long. The shock of dying might destroy many of these aspects of ordinary "I" either temporarily or permanently. Further, ordinary "I", ordinary consciousness is heavily dependent on a number of body-based processes for its stabilization, processes like exteroceptive and interoceptive input. Without these processes consciousness can change drastically, as in ordinary dreaming. Unless something very analogous to an external world and a body is provided in the after-death state, much of ordinary "I" would seem unlikely to survive.

If we want to ask "Does John Smith survive death?", we had better get to know the full range of possible manifestations of "John Smith" before he dies. Aside from knowing factual and personality details about the ordinary "John Smith" what is the drunken "John Smith" like? How about the "John Smith" when he has lost his body temporarily through sensory deprivation or Ketamine administration? Or the "John Smith" in a disoriented state in unfamiliar surroundings? Or the "John Smith" after a profound meditative experience? Or the "John Smith" in a state of sexual arousal, or when carried away with anger, or in a state of depression? Or the "entity" that may appear in some altered state of consciousness that tells us the "John Smith" is a small and not very important manifestation of something much greater?

When we can identify all of these "John Smiths", we will be in a much better position to ascertain if any of them survive.

I end this chapter with a Sufi teaching story that adds a needed vital flavor to this discussion.

The Tale Of The Sands

A stream, from its source in far-off mountains, passing through every kind and description of countryside, at last reached the sands of the desert. Just as it had crossed every other barrier, the stream tried to cross this one, but it found that as fast as it ran into the sand, its water disappeared.

It was convinced, however, that its destiny was to cross this desert, and yet there was no way. Now a hidden voice, coming from the desert itself, whispered: "The wind crosses the desert, and so can the stream."

The stream objected that it was dashing itself against the sand and only getting absorbed; that the wind could fly and this was why it could cross a desert.

"By hurtling in your own accustomed way you cannot get across. You will either disappear or become a marsh. You must allow the wind to carry you over to your destination."

"But how could this happen?"

"By allowing yourself to be absorbed in the wind."
This idea was not acceptable to the stream. After all, it had never been absorbed before. It did not want to lose its individuality. And, once having lost it, how was one to know that it could ever be regained?

"The wind," said the sand, "performs this function. It takes up water, carries it over the desert, and then lets it fall again. Falling as rain, the water again becomes a river."

"How can I know this is true?"

"It is so, and if you do not believe it, you cannot become more than a quagmire, and even that could take many, many years; and it certainly is not the same as a stream."

"But can I not remain the same stream that I am today?"

"You cannot in either case remain so," the whisper said. "Your essential part is carried away and forms a stream again. You are called what you are even today because you do not know which part of you is the essential one."

When he heard this, certain echoes began to arise in the thoughts of the stream. Dimly, he remembered a state in which he—or some part of him, was it?—had been held in the arms of a wind. He also remembered—or did he?—that this was the real thing, not necessarily the obvious thing to do.

And the stream raised his vapour into the welcoming arms of the wind, which gently and easily bore it upwards and along, letting it fall softly as soon as they reached the roof of a mountain many, many miles away. And because he had had his doubts, the stream was able to remember and record more strongly in his mind the details of the experience. He reflected, "Yes, now I have learned my true identity."

The stream was learning. But the sands whispered, "We know, because we see it happen day after day; and because we, the sands, extend from the riverside all the way to the mountain."

And that is why it is said that the way in which the Stream of Life is to continue on its journey is written in the Sands.[9]

Footnotes

1. Symposium on Consciousness and Survival, entitled "Transpersonal Qualities of Mind and Being"; also Tart, *Waking Up* (Boston: Shambhala, 1986).

2. The interested reader will find more information in my *States of Consciousness* (El Cerrito, CA: Psychological Processes, Inc., 1983). (Originally published in New York: Dutton, 1975).

3. P. Stafford, *Psychedelics Encyclopedia* (Los Angeles: J. P. Tarcher, 1977).

4. See also Tart, "The Controversy About PSI: Two Psychological Theories", *Journal of Parapsychology*, 46:1-20, 198; "Who's Afraid of Psychic Powers? Me?", Part 1, *The Open Mind*, 1, No. 3, 1-5, 1984; Part 2, *The Open Mind*, 1, No. 5, 1-5, 1984; "Acknowledging and Dealing with the Fear of PSI", *Journal of the American Society for Psychical Research*, 78:133-43, 1984. With respect to the unacknowledged fear of psychic abilities and in a more general way, see Tart, "Defense Mechanisms: Obstacles to Compassion", *The Open Mind*, 3, No. 2, 1-9, 1985.

5. Tart, *States of Consciousness*.

6. Ibid.

7. "Laboratory PK: Frequency of Manifestation and Resemblance to Precognition", *Research in Parapsychology* (Metuchen, NJ: Scarecrow Press, 1982), pp. 101-2.

8. Tart, "A Survey of Expert Opinion on Potentially Negative Uses of PSI, United States Government Interest in PSI, and the Level of Research Funding of the Field". In W. Roll (Ed.), *Research in Parapsychology* (Metuchen, NJ: Scarecrow Press, 1979), pp. 54-5.

9. I. Shah, *Tales of the Dervishes*, 1967, pp. 2-4.

IV

THE SURVIVAL OF CONSCIOUSNESS: A TIBETAN BUDDHIST PERSPECTIVE

Sogyal Rinpoche

This chapter is the culmination of five years teaching and research. I will synthesize my experience of contemporary Western approaches and the insight of ancient Buddhist knowledge of death and dying.

The traditional mandala of the Wheel of Life is a map of our state of mind and its projections which arise from ignorance, habitual patterns, and negative emotions. As we struggle to achieve the goals of life and satisfy desires, we sink deeper and deeper into the swamp of *samsara*, the vicious circle of life and death. The meditative approach of the wisdom of Buddha has given us a clear insight into how to free ourselves from this chain and how to transform this very confusion into self-nourishment so as to enrich our lives.

If we familiarize ourselves with the true nature of mind revealed in the moment of change, and gain some confidence in its recognition, then we become more sensitive to this gap or transition and more prepared when it happens in a more powerful way at death. That which dies at death is the grasping which dilutes the pure energy of our mind and clouds its natural space. At the moment of death, when that grasping habit dies, if we let go, the chance of awakening, or breaking our karmic shell, presents itself most prominently. Death offers mind the chance to change its view of grasping; it opens the way to personal change and growth. Death is the greatest purifier.

When clouds evaporate, the clear sky is naturally there. After the fire, only the pure gold remains. So also, what survives after change is what is true. In this truth enlightenment takes place. This is the Buddhist sense of eternity, the space where even discontinuity is part of a fundamental continuity. Death itself is the open space of emptiness.

Until we reach a deeper perspective on the nature of death, and a new respect for its life-enhancing qualities, we will never be able either to properly care for the dying or personally understand and experience the meaning of life. Yet, recent years have seen a great change in medical, scientific, and religious attitudes toward care of the dying, the experience of bereavement, and death itself.

What I would like to share with you is based on Tibetan Buddhist teachings, particularly *The Tibetan Book of the Dead*. This is knowledge of how to deal with death and dying. I hope it will help in preparing for our own deaths, helping dying persons, and also aiding people who are already dead, but who are not beyond reach of help. But at the same time I would like to say that to really equip oneself fully in this way requires a lifetime of dedication and training in the Buddhist point of view. One must have a certain understanding of one's own mind so that when a person is dying, the true nature of the mind is manifested in its fullest force. For one to prepare for death or to help someone else who is dying, that person generally needs seven years or more of training in the understanding of the mind. Even so, I present briefly the fundamental attitude that is necessary in order to help the dying.

First, I would like to comment on the research and work that is being done in this country on death and dying. From my point of view there is something lacking, even in the marvelous work of Elisabeth Kubler-Ross and others like her. They rely only on the reports of people who have died and come back. I think it would be very helpful if there were more research into the wisdom of other cultures which are more deeply rooted and more ancient. The experiences of these people who have died clinically for a few minutes are only the first experiences that occur at death. These initial experiences cannot reveal the nature of the many other experiences that follow. So, one cannot jump to conclusions and assume that the entire death process is revealed in the few minutes these people have lived through. The wonderful benefit of this research is to make death less horrible and therefore easier to face. At the same time, however, there is a danger of relating to death too romantically. We even use these findings as a way to escape the total process of death and thus fail to prepare properly for dying.

The most crucial attitude toward death is acceptance. When death is not accepted, there is fear and panic. That is why Buddhist teachings stress the development of mindfulness and recognition of impermanence and death. Everything that is seen in life is constantly changing or dying. If one can understand the aspect of change and flow with it, then there is less pain and suffering. On the other hand, if one tries to freeze this process by wanting things to be solid and to be always as they are now, when they break or separate there is tremendous pain, disappointment, and shock. The first thing one is taught in Buddhism is to see that the nature of life is change.

The great Tibetan yogi Milarepa said that because he feared death and impermanence, he retreated into the mountains. There he meditated upon impermanence and death. Upon learning to accept them, he was able to come back into the world and start living again.

Death cannot be prepared for as if it were a moment that is somehow separate from the rest of life. Rather, it is prepared for from now onward by accepting the change that constantly occurs. If one can flow with change now, then at the big moment of change called death, one can let go naturally. It is very simple because the Truth is simple, and change *is* the Truth, or true nature of this world.

However, if the changing nature of life is not understood, then one pretends that everything will be all right and will remain the same. That cover-up thinking, which is done again and again, creates an insensitivity to change and even to death. This is one of the reasons that this generation has institutionalized death in hospitals. So many deaths are seen happening on television that one is no longer moved by it. It seems that death only happens to other people. In fact, this is like the logic with which people hope to win lotteries! You think that *you* are the lucky one. But when death comes, you are unprepared. There is no way to know with certainty how or when death will occur. For this reason the holy places in Tibet contain prayers that say, "May my death be peaceful. May my death not be traumatic. May my death be clear to me so that it becomes an opportunity for liberation."

In order for death to be clear in that way, it must be understood that the mind has two levels. First, there is the inherent Mind, the awareness when our mind is truly clear—the deep Mind, which is like the sun, brilliant and shining. That is the Buddha-Mind. On that level our individual mind and the Buddha-Mind are one. Then, on the surface, there is the cloudy mind, the thinking mind, which is flickering, jumping, and confused. It is because this confused mind covers the sun of our original Buddha-Mind that we are stuck and not free. In order to recognize the inherent wisdom of the Buddha-Mind, the clouds of confusion and thinking must be removed. All the teachings are aimed at trying to remove the cloud of confusion that covers the sun of our inherent Buddha-Nature. Once these clouds are removed through spiritual practice, our true Mind can spontaneously manifest. The way of making this cloud disappear is by letting our grasping and confusion go.

Each of us has surely experienced a moment of life when we are able to let go a little bit, when we are calmer and in touch with a sense of a kind of spaciousness or tranquility. In that state the mind becomes clear, sharp, and direct. It is as though there is a crack in the cloudy sky, and the sun of our inherent Buddha-Mind comes out. In that moment there is a feeling of oneness and knowingness. There is also a vision of tremendous light.

That kind of mystical or spiritual experience comes very directly and vividly at the moment of death. Sometimes it comes so strongly that this light or sun of true Mind almost blinds us. We may faint or go unconscious at that moment, and as a result we withdraw. We don't let ourselves go and recognize the inherent Buddha-Nature of our own minds. We do not gain liberation.

You see, when you are dying, you are leaving your gross body and your world behind, but most importantly you have to leave behind your assumptions about the world that are in your head. But letting go is not easy. You must have a bit of this experience beforehand in order to pass through your own death or to tell confidently someone else to let go in the moment of death. If that dying person has had no experience of the inherent Mind or has not done spiritual practice in life, then you must have had certain experience of it yourself in order to guide them at that moment. It is a very real moment, and if you cannot speak with great feeling for the Truth, the person will feel the hollowness of your words.

When I was a child, traveling with my teacher, Jamyang Khyentse, we visited all the main monasteries in Tibet. With us was an old monk who had a fantastic family background because of his brother's very spectacular, miraculous death. This old monk began to sense that he would die soon and he did not want to continue to the next monastery, preferring to die in the open spaces. So, we camped with thirty tents near a lake. Because this old man had been a great practitioner, he was still very aware and alert while dying.

One morning he suddenly called my aunt, who was attending him. I went with her to his bedside. At that moment he breathed out, and his eyes suddenly looked up into the sky. He became very calm, and his pulse stopped. My aunt rushed out and called my teacher. He came running in, and when he saw the dying monk, he started laughing. He said, "Oh, old man, don't stay in that meditation." This particular meditation that the monk was apparently doing was one in which the individual consciousness is dissolved into the consciousness of the universe. My teacher said, "Don't stay in that meditation because sometimes there are distractions that can deter you from liberation and the experience of luminosity. Come out, come out from that." To our surprise, he came back. Then my teacher said, "Look, I'll help you. We'll go out together." Then he sat down and performed a meditation called *powa*. In this practice a high lama or teacher can help the dying person push beyond the grasping nature of the confused mind. He helps to cut away the ego.

In the moment of death we sometimes need to do something to shoot us out of the body. In the Tibetan tradition, either one learns to do it for oneself or a teacher helps the dying person. There are many stories of such struggles in Tibet. When someone is dying, the lama utters the sound "ah" very suddenly, and that gives the push. So, at this moment in the story of the old monk, my teacher said "ah" one time. Then he said it with the monk. The second time they said it together the old man went slightly faint, and with the third time he went completely silent and died.

The transference of mind, or consciousness, into the luminosity is the same as sending your own mind, stuck in the clouds, back into the sun. If this is understood on an absolute level, the need for transference from the teacher in the form of the *powa* ejection is unnecessary.

My teacher summed up this wisdom in one line: "At the moment of death, leave behind both your attachment and your aversion." The most important thing is to keep your mind pure without any grasping and to direct the mind into its inherent luminosity. This luminosity or light is our experience of the emptiness of the Buddha-Mind. When that luminosity appears, you can relate to that light directly with your inherent intelligence; then there is freedom. If that does not happen, you become lost in confusion. Then after the luminosity experience you wake up from the light and begin to relive the past experiences that were strongest in life. This return to the past creates rebirth, which is simply a continuation of our habits and tendencies. If you can cut away the force of these habits at the moment of seeing the luminosity and let go, you are free. But if you do not let go and rather dwell in your past, you will be reborn.

From the accounts of many Tibetans who have died and come back, we have learned how this process continues. After the experience of luminosity, if you fail to recognize it as your own true Mind, you faint or lose consciousness. Then when you wake up, you begin to feel like you are being blown everywhere. You cannot stay in one place. You are blown by the wind to all of the places you have been in life. It is said that you go to a place even if you only spit there once.

At this time your consciousness is so clear that you can read other people's minds. You become clairvoyant. This is a stage where the deceased's relatives as well as friends can help or harm a lot because the dead person can know their minds. If the relatives are fighting over the goods left behind, that can make the deceased one lose faith in them and turn vengeful. This can result in the dead remaining associated with the gross realm as a ghost. It is also possible that if a priest or someone else doing a service for the deceased is not sincere, then that person may lose faith in the teaching.

If you wish to be helpful to those who are dying or have recently died, the most important thing is to tell the truth. The person must be told that he or she is dying. If you don't tell them, there is much confusion. After dying, the person may not know that he or she has in fact died. Also, you must refrain from pleading for them not to go. This would make the person more and more attached. If you are a friend, you should be there in a strong and clear way. The person dying is feeling very insecure because their whole world is falling apart. The absence of strength in the face of another's death is a reflection of our own personal anxiety. To beg the dying person to stay in life is not in their best interest at all. At the moment of death, friends and relatives must release a dying person. When loved ones communicate deeply, there is a feeling of oneness—there is no separation. The dying person feels that he or she can go. A person can hold on and not die for many days if you do not give permission for them to go. This can be very traumatic. For the dying person the most important thing is to keep the mind clear and pure and not to think of those left behind.

In Sikkim in the early sixties, there was an old nun who had been practicing spirituality all her life. She became ill and could tell that she would die soon. She started packing her things up and simplifying her life. Then one morning my aunt, who is also a very great teacher, checked the old nun's pulse and saw the signs of the elements dissolving. She immediately called an old man in our family, who was also a great teacher.

It was about nine o'clock in the morning. He came into the room and told the nun, "I think it is time for you to go. You must see what your teachers have taught you to see. This is the time to put your visualizations into practice. Whichever wisdom of the Buddha you can relate to, unite your mind with that and don't think about us here behind. It is OK. I am going shopping; when I come back, perhaps I won't see you, so goodbye."

He did this with a smile and the nun also laughed. That kind of confident humor is important. Also, in that moment we cannot give the dying person new teaching. Whatever one believes in most is what should be affirmed. If a person believes in a particular form or image of God, that is the form that will comfort them after death.

If you are there with the dying person, you can call all the power of all the Masters and the Buddhas and help the person. They should also ask the Buddhas to help them go freely and well. It is very simple. Buddhas are not biased. They come more easily to lamas than to ordinary people, but they come equally, like the way the sun shines equally on everybody. If you ask their help with confidence, their blessing will be there.

In *The Tibetan Book of the Dead*, one hears of many visions that come to a dying person. These visions are not accorded by different figures of Buddhas. Rather, they are the different energies in the mind that is leaving. In a sense, the true Mind is beginning to shine. As it does so, one is slightly awestruck by visions. Some of these rays are peaceful; some are powerful; some are quite wrathful. Because you are not used to these visions, you may react or recoil from them. But if you can realize that these visions are the display of energies of your own mind, then there is liberation and freedom.

I mentioned earlier spiritual practice is a way to prepare for death. It is important if you have been practicing for a while that you learn to "essentialize". In other words, you must know what your practice is so that at the moment of death you must be able to do it very spontaneously. You can't just say, "Wait a minute; I have to do my practice." That does not work. It is a matter of whether you've got it or not. You must be involved in real meditation, that is, meditation that reveals the Buddha-Mind.

Many people have asked me what to do when someone dies suddenly. When someone is murdered or killed in an accident or commits suicide, the spirit may become trapped in the body. There may be no experiences of visions and such. Rather, the person remains attached to the body until someone wakes him up.

Once there was a Tibetan family whose son was killed by robbers. The family came to know of this, but they didn't know where the body was. So they asked a great yogi to try to see where the spirit of their son had gone. This lama went everywhere. He looked in all the heavens and hells, but he could not find him. Then it occurred to him that maybe the spirit was still in the body. The lama then performed the powa ceremony that cuts away the ego. When he did this, the spirit was freed, and the lama was able to guide it through the bardo.

If anyone has killed himself or has been killed, it is important to inform a teacher. You should also ask the help of all the Buddhas and all the great Masters. The best form of bereavement is to do spiritual practice. Meditate and pray and try to reassure the dead person. Tell the dead to look into the nature of Mind. Tell him or her that all the experiences they may go through are only their own mental projections. They have more of an opportunity than us to recognize the true Nature because the mind is more receptive after death. So, if you tell the deceased these things, you will aid the release from this gross world. In fact, if you are really meditating when someone has died, you directly show the true Nature of Mind to that person. You don't have to say anything. If you know what your meditation is and can remain in that with great simplicity and strength, the deceased catches that clarity.

Therefore, if you are with someone who is dying, you must both let go. If you do this, it will be a tremendous learning process for you as well because death is a powerful situation. It is really the moment of truth. It can change your way of life! If it is possible, the best thing you could do would be to go on a retreat after the death. Then really do as much practice as you can. Come face to face with the truth of impermanence. Even the greatest teaching of a Buddha's life is his death. This is one of the reasons many of the great teachers are ill at this time. They show us how suffering is a reality. In fact, in Buddhism facing the Truth is the most important thing.

Dying is itself the best way of living now. I'll give you an example. There was a great teacher who before he would go to bed every night would put away everything and leave nothing pending. He even put the cups upside down. Then the next day, if he had life, he was grateful and began again. That kind of preparation is not being futuristic; it is being very present. Even so, taking care of the present should also prepare us for death. Otherwise there is a problem being in the here and now. You can get stuck here if you forget about the inevitability of death. It is even worse to be stuck in the present than to be stuck in the past. So, you should be here now, but don't get stuck.

V

CAN OUR MEMORIES
SURVIVE
THE DEATH OF OUR BRAINS?

Rupert Sheldrake

Memory And Survival

Most people in the Western world take for granted the assumption that memories are somehow stored inside the brain. The idea that experiences have traces or imprints or "engrams" in brain tissue has a long ancestry. Aristotle expressed this idea by comparing memories with the impressions left by seals in wax. From time to time the analogies have been updated, the latest being in terms of holograms.

Clearly, if our memories are stored inside our brains, when our brains decay after death our memories must decay with them. Therefore they cannot survive bodily death. This means that conscious survival of bodily death is impossible in principle, unless we can imagine some kind of conscious survival without memory. I find such a possibility inconceivable; stripped of all my memories, conscious and unconscious, I would not be me, and I cannot imagine how I would retain any kind of conscious identity.

Theories of survival of bodily death presuppose, at least implicitly, that some sort of memory remains after the decay of the brain. Even theories of reincarnation which do not require conscious memories of previous lives to be recalled in subsequent incarnations suppose that habits, interests, and dispositions are carried over from one life to another, which means that there must be some transfer of memory.

The conventional theory of memory traces is in fact an *assumption* which follows from the currently orthodox theory of life, the mechanistic theory, according to which all aspects of life and mind are ultimately explicable in terms of the known laws of physics and chemistry. If the mind is nothing but an aspect or an epiphenomenon of physical processes going on in the brain, then memories *must* be located in the nervous tissue. But how well is this assumption supported by scientific evidence?

The Elusiveness Of Memory Traces

A vast amount of effort has been expended in an attempt to localize and identify the hypothetical memory traces, and tens of thousands of experimental animals have been expended in this process. Nevertheless, the traces have so far eluded detection.

The classical investigations were made by Karl Lashley, using rats, monkeys, and chimpanzees. For over thirty years he tried to trace conditioned reflex paths through the brain and to find the locus of specific memory traces, or "engrams". To do this, he trained the animals in a variety of tasks, ranging from simple conditioned reflexes to the solution of difficult problems. Either before or after the training, nerve tracts within the brain were surgically cut or portions of the brain were removed, and the effects on initial learning or post-operative retention were measured.

He first became skeptical of the supposed path of conditioned reflex arcs through the motor cortex when he found that rats trained to respond in particular ways to light showed no reduction in accuracy of performance when almost the entire motor cortex was cut out. Likewise, most of the motor cortex of monkeys was removed after they had been trained to open various latch boxes. This operation resulted in a temporary paralysis, but after eight to twelve weeks they recovered sufficiently to be able to make the movements required to open the latches. They were then exposed to the puzzle boxes and opened them promptly without random exploratory movements.

He then showed that learned habits were retained if the associative areas of the brain were destroyed. Habits also survived a series of deep incisions into the cerebral cortex which destroyed cross-connections within it. Moreover, if the cerebral cortex was intact, removal of subcortical structures such as the cerebellum did not destroy the memory either.

With more complex types of learning which involved remembering the way through the maze, rats lost the ability if more than half their cerebral cortex was removed. The amount of loss, measured in terms of the practice required for relearning, was on average proportional to the amount of cortex destroyed. It did not seem to matter which parts of the cortex were destroyed; what mattered was the quantity.

Lashley started out as an enthusiastic supporter of the idea of localized memory traces, but at the end of his career was forced to abandon this idea:

> It is not possible to demonstrate the isolated localization of a memory trace anywhere within the nervous system. Limited regions may be essential for learning or retention of a particular activity, but within such regions the parts are functionally equivalent.[1]

In reviewing the types of human memory loss that follow brain damage, he came to a similar conclusion:

> I believe that the evidence strongly favors the view that amnesia from brain injury rarely, if ever, is due to the destruction of specific memory traces. Rather, the amnesias represent a lowered level of vigilance, a greater difficulty in activating the organized pattern of traces, or a disturbance of some broader system of organized functions.

Lashley did not consider the possibility that memories might not be stored inside the brain at all. He interpreted the evidence against localized traces in terms of a multiple representation of traces throughout an entire functional area. He thought this indicated that

> The characteristics of the nervous network are such that when it is subject to any pattern of excitation, it may develop a pattern of activity, reduplicated through an entire functional area by spread of excitations, such as the surface of a liquid develops an interference pattern of spreading waves when it is disturbed at several points.

He suggested that recall involved "some sort of resonance among a very large number of neurons". These ideas have been carried further by his former student Karl Pribram in his proposal that memories are stored in a distributed manner analogous to the interference patterns in a hologram.[2]

Analogous experiments have shown that even in invertebrates such as the octopus, specific memory traces cannot be localized. Observations on the survival of learned habits after destruction of various parts of the brain have led to the seemingly paradoxical conclusion that "memory is both everywhere and nowhere in particular".[3]

Not only have the hypothetical memory traces proved to be spatially elusive, but their physical nature has also remained obscure. The idea of specific RNA "memory molecules" was fashionable in the 1960s, but has now been more or less abandoned. The theory of reverberating circuits of electrical activity, giving a kind of echo, may help to account for short-term memory over periods of seconds or minutes, but cannot plausibly explain long-term memory. The most popular hypothesis remains the old favorite that memory depends on modifications of the synaptic connections between nerve cells in a manner still unknown.

If memories are somehow stored in synapses, then the synapses themselves must remain stable over long periods of time: Indeed the nervous system as a whole must be stable if it is to act as a memory store. Until recently this was generally assumed to be the case, even though it has long been known that there is a continuous process of cell death within the brain. But recent evidence suggests that the nervous system may be more dynamic than previously supposed.

Studies on the brains of canaries, and in particular those parts involved in the learning of song, have shown that not only do many new connections between nerve cells continue to develop, but many new nerve cells appear. In males the number of neurons increases as the birds mature in the spring, but then decreases by about 40% by the autumn. As the new mating season approaches, the number of nerve cells increases again, and so on. Such changes have also been found in other parts of the brains of canaries and there is now evidence that in adults of other species, there also is a turnover of neurons in the forebrain, the "seat" of complex behavior and learning, with new cells being formed while others die.[4]

Brains also appear to be more functionally dynamic than previously thought. Recent studies on monkeys have shown in sensory areas of the brain that "map" different parts of the body are not "hard wired" or anatomically frozen, but are unexpectedly fluid. In one series of experiments the regions of the sensory cortex connected with touch sensations from the monkeys' hands were localized. The "map" in the brain was found to be subdivided into regions for each of the five fingers and for other surfaces of the hand. After one or more of the fingers was amputated, it was found that sensory inputs from the remaining adjacent fingers gradually shifted over a period of weeks into the missing finger's hitherto exclusive brain region. The increased areas of brain connected to the adjacent fingers were associated with an increase in the acuity of sensation in these fingers.[5]

The dynamism of the nervous system is also shown when the brain is damaged. For example, if a portion of the sensory cortex is injured, the appropriate sensory "map" which was in the injured region can shift to the region surrounding it, although with some loss in acuity. This movement of the "map" probably does not depend on a growth or movement of nerve cells, but rather on a spatial shift of nerve cell activity.[5]

This dynamism in the structure and functioning of the nervous system presents the concept of memory traces with great difficulties; and at the molecular level there is also a dynamism which makes long-term storage problematic, as Francis Crick has recently shown. The time span of human memory is often years or tens of years:

Yet it is believed that almost all the molecules in our bodies, with the exception of DNA, turn over in a matter of days, weeks, or at the most a few months. How then is memory stored in the brain so that its trace is relatively immune to molecular turnover?

Crick has suggested a mechanism whereby "molecules in the synapse interact in such a way that they can be replaced by new material, one at a time, without altering the overall state of the structure." His ingenious hypothetical scheme involves protein molecules which he endows with a number of unusual properties.[6] There is as yet no evidence that such molecules exist.

Thus the trace theory of memory is very far from being well-established; it is still essentially speculative. A number of contemporary philosophers have drawn attention to a further serious difficulty of a logical nature. If memories are somehow encoded and stored as traces within the brain, then there must be some way in which they are *retrieved* from the memory store. But for a retrieval system to function, it must somehow be able to recognize the appropriate memories. And to do so, it must itself have some sort of memory for what is to be retrieved: Hence the very notion of a memory retrieval system begs the question for it presupposes what it seeks to explain.[7]

The Hypothesis Of Formative Causation

An alternative approach to the problem of memory is provided by the hypothesis of formative causation, described in detail in my book *A New Science of Life.*[8] This hypothesis starts not from the phenomenon of memory itself but with a consideration of the coming into being of form in plants and animals.

The mechanistic approach to biology, in spite of its successes at the molecular level, has failed to shed much light on the way in which embryos develop from relatively simple egg cells into organisms containing tissues and organs of great structural complexity. During this process, more complex structures come into being from less complex ones. What are the causes of the forms they take up? Biologists wedded to the reductionist or mechanistic approach assume that these must somehow be entirely explicable in terms of complex physio-chemical interactions between the parts. But others (including myself) are convinced that this mechanistic approach is too limited. There is, to say the least, an open possibility that the phenomena of life depend on laws or factors as yet unrecognized by the physical sciences. The problem is to say what sort of things these factors are and how they work.

The most influential alternative to the mechanistic paradigm is provided by the holistic or organismic philosophy. Biologists working within this framework of thought have developed a new kind of field concept to help account for the development and maintenance of form and order in living organisms. These fields, called *morphogenetic fields*, from the Greek morphe (form) and genesis (coming-into-being), can be thought of by analogy with magnetic fields, which have a shape, even though they are invisible. (In the case of a magnet, this shape can be revealed by the patterns taken up by iron filings scattered around it.) Morphogenetic fields through their own structure mold developing cells, tissues, and organisms. Thus for example in a human embryo a developing ear is molded by an ear-shaped morphogenetic field, and a developing leg by a leg-shaped field.

But what are these fields, and where do they come from? For over fifty years their nature and even their existence has remained obscure. However, I believe that these fields are just as real as the electromagnetic and gravitational fields of physics, but that they are a new kind of field with very remarkable properties. Like the known fields of physics, they connect similar things across space with seemingly nothing in between, but in addition they connect things across *time.*

The idea is that the morphogenetic fields which shape a growing animal or plant are derived from the forms of previous organisms of the same species. The embryo as it were "tunes in" to the forms of past members of the species. The process by which this happens is called *morphic resonance*. Similarly, the fields which organize the activities of an animal's nervous system are derived from past animals of the same kind. In their instinctive behavior, animals draw on a sort of species "memory bank" or "pooled memory".

This new hypothesis leads to a range of surprising predictions which provide ways of testing it experimentally. It is in the chemical realm that the most unambiguous tests should be possible. The hypothesis of formative causation applies not only to living organisms but also to chemical systems such as crystals. It predicts that the patterns in which molecules arrange themselves when they crystalize should be influenced by the patterns taken up in previous crystals of the same substance. This influence should act directly through both space and time with the result that substances should crystalize more readily all over the world the more often they have been crystalized before.

New chemicals synthesized for the first time are indeed usually difficult to crystalize and do in fact tend to form crystals more readily as time passes. The conventional explanation is that tiny fragments of previous crystals get carried from laboratory to laboratory on the clothing or beards of migrant scientists and "infect" solutions of the substance in question. When no such carrier can be identified, crystal "seeds" are assumed to have traveled around the world as microscopic dust particles in the air. But according to the hypothesis of formative causation, crystalization should occur more readily with the prior frequency of crystalization, even if migrant scientists are kept well away and dust particles are filtered out of the air. This prediction could fairly easily be tested experimentally.

Another kind of experimental test is possible in the realm of animal behavior. If a number of animals, rats for example, learn a new trick which rats have never before performed, then other rats of the same breed all over the world should be able to learn the same trick more easily, even in the absence of any known kind of connection or communication. The larger the number of rats that learn it, the easier it should become for subsequent rats everywhere else.

Remarkably enough, there is already evidence from a long series of experiments carried out with rats in America, Scotland, and Australia that this effect actually occurs. The rate of learning of the ability to escape from a water maze increased in successive batches of rats, whether or not they were descended from trained parents. This increased rate of learning was found in the different laboratories separated by thousands of miles.[8]

In relation to human beings, this hypothesis suggests that on average it should be getting easier and easier for people to learn to ride bicycles, to type, swim, or program computers just because more and more people have already learned to do these things. Such improvements do in fact seem to have occurred. However, it is not possible to separate any possible effects of morphic resonance from various cultural and environmental factors which have also changed with time. Specially designed experiments are necessary to test for the effects of morphic resonance. Some preliminary experiments have already been performed with encouraging results.

Tuning In To The Past

According to the hypothesis of formative causation, organisms tune in to similar organisms in the past, and the more similar they are, the more specific is the tuning. Now in general an organism resembles *itself* in the past more closely then it resembles any other organism, and it will accordingly be strongly influenced by morphic resonance from its own past states. In the realm of form, this means that its form will tend to be stabilized and remain fairly constant in spite of changes in its chemical constituents and material components. When we come to consider the influence of past patterns of behavior, this self-resonance[1] has even more interesting consequences. Both habit memories and memories of particular past events may be given directly by morphic resonance from the organism's own past. *These memories need not be stored inside the brain.*

In order to see more clearly the difference between the morphic resonance and the trace theories of memory, consider the analogy of a transistor radio. The music coming out of the loudspeaker depends on the energy supplied by the battery, on the components of the set and the way they are wired together, *and* on the transmissions to which the set is tuned. Slight damage to the set may lead to distortions in the sound, while more severe damage leads to a loss of the ability to receive the transmissions altogether. But of course these facts do not mean that the music is actually produced or stored within the set. And brain damage resulting in memory loss does not prove that lost memories were stored inside the brain: The damage might simply prevent the brain from tuning in to its own past states.

The loss of memory associated with brain damage is of course usually taken to prove that memories are inside the brain. Another piece of evidence which is commonly assumed to support the trace theory of memory is the discovery of Wilder Penfield that the electrical stimulation of the temporal lobes of the brains of epileptic patients can result in the evocation of vivid memories which are experienced consciously by the patients. But here again this need not mean that the memories are actually stored inside the nervous tissue. If one stimulates the tuning circuit of a radio or a TV set, the tuning may be changed such that transmissions from a different station are picked up; but this would not of course mean that these new programs are stored inside the components of the tuning circuits that were stimulated. Interestingly, Penfield himself on further reflection abandoned his original conclusions:

> In 1951 I had proposed that certain parts of the temporal cortex should be called 'memory cortex', and suggested that the neuronal record was located there in the cortex near points at which the stimulating electrode may call forth an experiential response. This was a mistake. . . . The record is not in the cortex. [9]

If we pick up our own memories by tuning into our own past states, and these memories are not stored inside our brains, then why don't we tune into other people's memories? Perhaps we do. If we tune into the memories of large numbers of people in the past, we would not be aware of all the specific memories of particular events in their lives, but rather a kind of composite or pooled memory which would contain the basic forms or patterns of their experience and thought. This idea closely corresponds with C. G. Jung's theory of the archetypes in the collective unconscious; and Jung's approach to psychology harmonizes well with the notion of morphic resonance.

It might also be possible to pick up particular people's memories which are very recent—only a few seconds old. In this case there might be a transference of thoughts, or in other words, a process which is equivalent to telepathy. In this way the hypothesis of formative causation might provide a bridge between science and at least some of the phenomena of parapsychology.

It might also be possible to tune into the experience of particular people in the past who are now dead. If so, then it might be possible to gain access to "memories of past lives", a phenomenon for which there seems to be persuasive evidence.[10]

Implications For Survival

If this new approach to the phenomena of memory is supported by experimental evidence, it will lead to a major change in the scientific context for the question of the conscious survival of bodily death. If memories are not stored inside the brain, there is no reason why they should decay when the brain decays. They may remain potentially present, and it may still be possible to tune into them.

However, this hypothesis does not automatically lead to the conclusion that such survival occurs. From a theoretical point of view, this depends on the way we think about the relation of the mind to the body. On the one hand, this hypothesis can be interpreted within the framework of a sophisticated and updated philosophy of materialism. If the conscious self is nothing but an aspect of the functioning of the brain and its associated fields, then the brain would still be essential for the process of tuning into memories, even if they are not stored inside the brain but rather given directly by morphic resonance with a person's own past. In this case the decay of the brain would still result in the extinction of consciousness. The memories would not exactly be destroyed, but they would be lost because there would no longer be a way of recovering them: The decay of the brain would involve the dissolution of the tuning system.

On the other hand, if the conscious self is not identical with the functioning of the brain, but rather *interacts* with the brain through the morphic fields, then it is possible that the conscious self could continue to be associated with these fields even after the death of the brain, and retain the ability to tune into its own past states. Both the self and its memories could survive the death of the body. Precisely *how* the conscious self could interact with the morphic fields associated with mental activity is of course obscure. But it does not seem inconceivable that a field theory of the mind may be developed which is compatible both with a new scientific understanding of memory and with the possibility of a conscious survival of bodily death.

Footnotes

1. K. S. Lashley, "In Search of the Engram", *Symposia of the Society for Experimental Biology*, 4:454-482, 1950.

2. K. H. Pribram, *Languages of the Brain* (Monterey, CA: Brooks, 1977).

3. B. B. Boycott, "Learning in the Octopus", *Scientific American*, 212 (3):42-50, 1965.

4. G. Kolata, "New Neurons Form in Adulthood", *Science*, 224:1325-1326, 1984.

5. J. L. Fox, "The Brain's Dynamic Way of Keeping in Touch", *Science*, 225:820-821, 1984.

6. F. Crick, "Memory and Molecular Turnover", *Nature*, 312:101, 1984.

7. H. A. Bursen, *Dismantling the Memory Machine* (Reidel: Dordrecht, 1978).

8. R. Sheldrake, *A New Science of Life: The Hypothesis of Formative Causation* (Los Angeles: J. P. Tarcher, 1982).

9. W. Penfield, *The Mystery of the Mind* (Princeton: Princeton University Press, 1975).

10. I. Stevenson, *Twenty Cases Suggestive of Reincarnation* (Charlottesville: University of Virginia Press, 1974).

VI

NEUROPEPTIDES, THE EMOTIONS, AND BODYMIND

Candace Pert

In this talk, I am going to describe an array of fascinating, mostly new findings about the chemical substances in the body called neuropeptides. Based on these findings, I am going to suggest that neuropeptides and their receptors form an information network within the body. Perhaps this suggestion sounds fairly innocuous, but its implications are far reaching.

I believe that neuropeptides and their receptors are a key to understanding how mind and body are interconnected and how emotions can be manifested throughout the body. Indeed, the more we know about neuropeptides, the harder it is to think in the traditional terms of a mind and a body. It makes more and more sense to speak of a single integrated entity, a "body-mind".

Most of what I will describe are laboratory findings, hard science. But it is important to remember that the scientific study of psychology traditionally focuses on animal learning and cognition. This means that if you look in the index of recent textbooks on psychology, you are not likely to find a listing for "consciousness", "mind", or even "emotions". These subjects are basically not in the realm of traditional experimental psychology, which primarily studies *behavior* because it can be seen and measured.

The Specificity Of Receptor Sites

There is one field in psychology where mind—at least consciousness—has been objectively studied for perhaps twenty years. This is the field of psychopharmacology wherein researchers have developed highly rigorous ways to measure the effects of drugs and altered states of consciousness.

Research in this field evolved from an assumption that no drug acts unless it is "fixed"—that is, somehow gets attached to the brain. And so researchers initially imagined hypothetical tissue constituents to which a drug might bind—much the way a key fits a lock—and they called these "receptors". In this way, the notion of specific brain receptors for drugs became a central theory in pharmacology. It is a very old idea.

In the past several years, a critical development has been the invention of new technologies for actually binding drugs to these receptor molecules and for studying both their distribution in the brain and body and their actual molecular structure.

My initial work in this area was in the laboratory of Solomon Snyder at Johns Hopkins University, where we focused our attention on opium, a drug that obviously alters consciousness and that also is used medicinally, to alleviate pain. I worked long and hard, over many months of initial failure, to develop a technical system for measuring the material in the brain with which opium interacts to produce its effects. To make a long (and technical) story short, we used radioactive drug molecules, and with this technology were actually able to identify the receptor element for opium in the brain. You can imagine, therefore, a molecule of opium attaching itself to a receptor—and then from this small connection, large changes follow.

It next turned out that the whole class of drugs to which opium belongs—they are called opiates and they include morphine, codeine, and heroin, as well as opium—attach to the *same* receptors. Further, we discovered that the receptors were scattered throughout not only the brain but also the body.

After finding the receptor for the external opiates, our thinking took another step. If the brain and the other parts of the body have a receptor for something taken from *outside* the body it makes sense to suppose that something produced *inside* the body also fits the receptor. Otherwise, why would the receptor be there?

This perspective ultimately led to the identification of one of the brain's own form of opiates, a chemical substance called beta endorphin. Beta endorphin is created in the brain's own nerve cells and consists of peptides—thus it is a neuropeptide. Furthermore peptides grow directly off the DNA which stores the information to make our brains and bodies.

If you picture an ordinary nerve cell, you can visualize the general mechanism. In the center (as in any cell) is the DNA, and a direct printout of the DNA leads to the production of a neuropeptide, which then traverses down the axons of the nerve cell to be stored in little balls at the end waiting for the right electro-physical events that will release it. The DNA also leads to the production of receptors, which are made out of the same peptide material but are much bigger. What has to be added to this picture is the fact that 50 to 60 neuropeptides have been identified, each of them as specific as the beta endorphin neuropeptide. We have here an enormously complex system.

Until quite recently, it had been thought that the information of the nervous system was distributed across the gap between two nerve cells, called the synapse. This meant that the proximity of the nerve cells determined what could be communicated.

But now we know that the largest portion of information coming from the brain is kept straight not by the close physical juxtaposition of the nerve cells, but by the specificity of the receptors. What was thought of as a highly rigid linear system appears to be one with far more complex patterns of distribution.

Thus when a nerve cell squirts out opiate peptides, the peptides can act "miles" away at other nerve cells. The same is true of all neuropeptides. At any given moment, many neuropeptides may be floating along within the body, and what enables them to attach to the correct receptor molecules is, to repeat, the specificity of the receptors. *Thus, the receptors serve as the mechanism that sorts out the information exchange in the body.*

The Biochemistry Of The Emotions

What is this leading up to? To something very intriguing—the notion that the receptors for the neuropeptides are in fact the keys to the biochemistry of emotion. In the last two years, the workers in my lab have formalized this idea in a number of theoretical papers[1], and I am going to review briefly the evidence to support it.

I should say that some scientists might describe this idea as outrageous. It is not, in other words, part of the established wisdom. Indeed, coming from a tradition where the textbooks do not even contain the word "emotions" in the index, it was not without a little trepidation that we dared to start talking about the biochemical substrate of emotions.

I will begin by noting a fact that neuroscientists have agreed on for a long time: that emotions are mediated by the limbic system of the brain. The limbic system refers to a section of neuroanatomical parts of the brain which include the hypothalamus (which controls the homeostatic mechanism of the body and is sometimes called the "brain" of the brain), the pituitary gland (which regulates the hormones in the body), and the amygdala. We will be talking mostly about the hypothalamus and the amygdala.

The experiments showing the connection between emotions and the limbic system were first done by Wilder Penfield and other neurologists who worked with conscious, awake individuals. The neurologists found that when they used electrodes to stimulate the cortex over the amygdala they could evoke a whole gamut of emotional displays—powerful reactions of grief, of pain, of pleasure associated with profound memories, and also the total somatic accompaniment of emotional states. The limbic system was first identified, then, by psychological experiments.

Now when we began to map the location of opiate receptors in the brain we found that the limbic system was highly enriched with opiate receptors (and with other receptors too, we eventually learned). The amygdala and the hypothalamus, both classically considered to be the main components of the limbic system, are in fact blazing with opiate receptors—40-fold higher than in other areas of the brain.

These "hot spots" correspond to very specific nuclei or cellular groups that physiological psychologists have identified as mediating such processes as sexual behavior, appetite, and water balance in the body. The main point is that our receptor-mapping confirmed and expanded in important ways the psychological experiments that defined the limbic system.

Now let me bring in some other neuropeptides. I have already noted that 50 to 60 substances are now considered to be neuropeptides. Where do they come from? Many of them are the natural analogs of psychoactive drugs. But another major source—very unexpected—is hormones. Hormones historically have been conceived of as being produced by glands—in other words, not by nerve cells. A hormone presumably was stored in one place in the body, then traveled over to its receptors in other parts of the body. The prime hormone is insulin, which is secreted in the pancreas. But, now, it turns out that insulin is not just a hormone. In fact, insulin is a neuropeptide, made and stored in the brain, and there are insulin receptors in the brain. When we map insulin, we again find hot spots in the amygdala and hypothalamus. *In short, it has become increasingly clear that the limbic system, the seat of emotions in the brain, is also the focal point of receptors for neuropeptides.*

Another critical point. As we have studied the distribution of these receptors, we have found that the limbic system is not just in the forebrain, in the classical locations of the amygdala and the hypothalamus. It appears that the body has other places in which many different neuropeptide receptors are located—places where there is a lot of chemical action. We call these spots *nodal points,* and they are anatomically located at places that receive a lot of emotional modulation.

One nodal point is the dorsal (back) horn of the spinal cord, which is the spot that sensory information comes in. This is the first synapse within the brain where touch-sensory information is processed. We have found that for virtually all the senses for which we know the entry area, the spot is always a nodal point for neuropeptide receptors.

I believe these findings have amazing implications for understanding and appreciating what emotions do and what they are about. Consider the chemical substance angiotensin, another classical hormone which is also a peptide and now shown to be a neuropeptide. When we map for angiotensin receptors in the brain, we again find little hot spots in the amygdala. It has long been known that angiotensin mediates thirst, so if one implants a tube in the area of a rat's brain that is rich with angiotensin receptors and drops a little angiotensin down the tube, within 10 seconds the rat will start to drink water, even if it is totally sated with water. So, chemically speaking, angiotensin translates as an altered state of consciousness, a state that makes animals (and humans) say, "I want water." In other words, neuropeptides bring us to a state of consciousness and to alterations in those states.

Equally important is the fact that neuropeptide receptors are not just in the brain, they are also in the body. We have mapped and shown biochemically that there are angiotensin receptors in the kidney identical to those in the brain, and in a way that is not yet quite understood, the kidney-located receptors conserve water. The point is that the release of the neuropeptide angiotensin leads both to the behavior of drinking and to the internal conservation of water. Here is an example of how a neuropeptide—which perhaps corresponds to a mood state—can integrate what happens in the body with what happens in the brain. A further important point that I only mention here is that overall integration of behavior seems designed to be consistent with survival.

My basic speculation here is that neuropeptides provide the physiological basis for the emotions. As my colleagues and I argued in a recent paper in the *Journal of Immunology*[2]: The striking pattern of neuropeptide receptor distribution in mood-regulating areas of the brain, as well as their role in mediating communication through the whole organism, makes neuropeptides the obvious candidates for the biochemical mediation of emotion. It may be too that each neuropeptide biases information processing uniquely when occupying receptors at nodal points with the brain and body. If so, then each neuropeptide may evoke a unique "tone" that is equivalent to a mood state.

In the beginning of my work, I matter-of-factly presumed that emotions were in the head or the brain. Now I would say they are really in the body as well. They are expressed in the body and are part of the body. I can no longer make a strong distinction between the brain and the body.

Communicating With The Immune System

I now want to bring the immune system into this picture. I have already explained that the hormone system, which historically has been studied as being separate from the brain, is conceptually the same thing as the nervous system. Packets of juices are released and diffuse very far away, acting via the specificity of receptors at sites far from where the juices are stored. So, endocrinology and neuroscience are two aspects of the same process. Now I am going to maintain that immunology is also part of this conceptual system and should not be considered a separate discipline.

A key property of the immune system is that its cells move. They are otherwise identical to the stable brain cells, with their nuclei, cell membranes and all of the receptors. Monocytes, for example, which ingest foreign organisms, start life in your bone marrow, and they then diffuse out and travel through your veins and arteries, and decide where to go by following chemical cues. A monocyte travels along in the blood and at some point comes within "scenting" distance of a neuropeptide, and because the monocyte has receptors for the neuropeptide on its cell surface, it begins literally to chemotax, or crawl, toward that chemical. This is very well documented, and there are excellent ways of studying it in the laboratory.

Now, monocytes are responsible not just for recognizing and digesting foreign bodies but also for wound healing and tissue-repair mechanisms. What we are talking about, then, are cells with vital, health-sustaining functions.

The new discovery I want to emphasize here is that *every* neuropeptide receptor that we have looked for (using an elegant and precise system developed by my colleague, Michael Ruff) is also on human monocytes. Human monocytes have receptors for opiates, for PCP, for another peptide called bombasin, and so on. *These emotion-affecting biochemicals actually appear to control the routing and migration of monocytes, which are so pivotal in the immune system.* They communicate with B-cells and T-cells, interact in the whole system to fight disease and to distinguish between self and non-self, deciding, say, which part of the body is a tumor cell to be killed by natural killer cells, and which parts need to be restored. I hope this picture is clear to you.

A monocyte is circulating—this health-sustaining element of the immune system is traveling in the blood—and then the presence of an opiate pulls it over, and it can connect with the neuropeptide because it has the receptor to do so. It has, in fact, many different receptors for different neuropeptides.

It turns out, moreover, that the cells of the immune system not only have receptors for these various neuropeptides; as is becoming clear, they also make the neuropeptides themselves. There are subsets of immune cells that make beta endorphins, for example, and the other opiate peptides. In other words, these immune cells are making the same chemicals that we conceive of as controlling mood in the brain. They control the tissue integrity of the body, and they also make chemicals that control mood. Once again, brain and body.

Mind As Information

What do these kinds of connections between brain and body mean? Ordinarily they are referred to as "the power of the mind over the body". As far as I am concerned, that phrase does not describe what we are talking about here. I would go further. We are all aware of the bias built into the Western idea that consciousness is totally in the head. I believe the research findings I have described indicate that we need to start thinking about how consciousness can be projected into various parts of the body. When we document the key role that the emotions, expressed through neuropeptide molecules, play in affecting the body, it will become clear how emotions can be a key to the understanding of disease. Unfortunately, people who think about these things do not usually work in a government laboratory.

My argument is that the three classic areas of neuroscience, endocrinology, and immunology, with their various organs—the brain (which is the key organ that the neuroscientists study), the glands, and the immune system (consisting of the spleen, the bone marrow, the lymph nodes, and of course the cells circulating through the body)—that these three areas are actually joined to each other in a bi-directional network of communication and that the information "carriers" are the neuropeptides. There are well-studied physiological substrates showing that communication exists in both directions for every single one of these areas and their organs. Some of the research is old, some of it is new.

The word I would stress in regard to this integrated system is network, which comes from information theory. For what we have been talking about all along is information. In thinking about these matters, then, it might make more sense to emphasize the perspective of psychology—literally the study of the mind—rather than of neuroscience. A mind is composed of information, and it has a physical substrate, which is the body and the brain; and it also has another immaterial substrate that has to do with information flowing around: Perhaps, then, mind is the information flowing among all of these bodily parts. Maybe mind is what holds the network together.

The Unity Of The Variety

The last point I am going to make about the neuropeptides is an astounding one, I think.

As we have seen, neuropeptides are signaling molecules. They send messages all over the body (including the brain). Of course, to have such a communications network, you need components that can talk to each other and listen to each other. In the situation we are discussing here, the components that "talk" are the neuropeptides, and the components that "hear" are the neuropeptide receptors. How can this be? How can 50 to 60 neuropeptides be produced, float around, and talk to 50 or 60 types of listening receptors which are on a variety of cells? Why does order rather than chaos reign?

The finding I am going to discuss is not totally accepted, but our experiments show that it is true. I have not published it yet, but I think that it is only a matter of time before everybody can confirm these observations.

There are thousands of scientists studying the opiate receptors and the opiate peptides, and they see great heterogeneity in the receptors. They have given a series of Greek names to the apparent heterogeneity. However, all the evidence from our lab suggests that in fact *there is actually only one type of molecule in the opiate receptors, one long polypeptide chain whose formula you can write.* This molecule is quite capable of changing its conformation within its membrane so that it can assume a number of shapes.

I note in passing that this interconversion can occur at a very rapid pace—so rapid that it is hard to tell whether it is one state or another at a given moment in time. In other words, receptors have both a wave-like and a particulate character, and it is important to note that information can be stored in the form of time spent in different states.

As I said, the molecular unity of the receptors is quite amazing. Consider the tetrahymena, a protozoa that is one of the simplest organisms. Despite its simplicity, the tetrahymena can do almost everything we can do—it can eat, have sex, and of course it makes the same neuropeptide components that I have been talking about. The tetrahymena makes insulin. It makes beta endorphins. We have taken tetrahymena membranes and in particular studied the opiate receptor molecules on them; and we have studied the opiate receptor in rat brains and on human monocytes.

We believe that we have shown that the molecular substance of *all* opiate receptors is the same. The actual molecule of the human-brain opiate receptor is identical to the opiate receptor components in that simplest of animals, the tetrahymena. I hope the force of this clear. The opiate receptor in my brain and in your brain is, at root, made of the same molecular substance as the tetrahymena.

This finding gets to the simplicity and the unity of life. It is comparable to the four DNA-based pairs that code for the production of all the proteins, which are the physical substrates of life. We now know that in this physical substrate there are only 60 or so signal molecules, the neuropeptides, that account for the physiological manifestation of emotions—for enlivening emotions, if you will, or perhaps better yet, for flowing energy. The protozoa form of the tetrahymena indicates that the receptor molecules do not become more complex as an organism becomes more complex: *The identical molecular components for information flow are conserved throughout evolution. The whole system is simple, elegant, and it may very well be complete.*

Is The Mind In The Brain?

We have been talking about mind, and the question arises: Where is it? In our own work, consciousness has come up in the context of studying pain and the role of opiate receptors and endorphins in modulating pain. A lot of labs are measuring pain, and we would all agree that the area called periaqueductal gray, located around the third ventricle of the brain, is filled with opiate receptors, making it a kind of control area for pain. We have found that the periaqueductal gray is also loaded with receptors for virtually all the neuropeptides that have been studied.

Now, everyone knows that there are yogis who can train themselves so that they do or do not perceive pain, depending on how they structure their experience. Women in labor do the same thing. What seems to be going on is that these sort of people are able to plug into their periaqueductal gray. Somehow they gain access to it—with their consciousness, I believe—and set pain thresholds. Note what is going on here. In these situations, a person has an experience that brings with it pain, but a part of the person consciously does something so that the pain is not felt. Where is this consciousness coming from— this conscious I—that somehow plugs into the periaqueductal gray so that he or she does not feel a thing?

I want to go back to the idea of a network. A network is different from a hierarchical structure which has one top place. You theoretically can plug into a network at any point and get to any other point. A concept like this seems to me valuable in thinking about the processes by which a consciousness can manage to reach the periaqueductal gray and use it to control pain.

The yogi and the laboring woman both use a similar technique to control pain—breathing. Athletes use it, too. Breathing is extremely powerful. I suggest that there is a physical substrate for these phenomena, the brain stem nuclei. I would say that we now must include the brain stem nuclei in the limbic system because they are nodal points, thickly encrusted with neuropeptide receptors and neuropeptides.

The idea, then, goes like this: breathing has a physical substrate which is also a nodal point, this nodal point is part of an information network in which each part leads to all the other parts, and so, from the nodal point of the brain stem nuclei, the consciousness can, among other things, plug into the periaqueductal gray.

I think it is possible now to conceive of mind and consciousness as an emanation of emotional information processing, and as such, mind and consciousness would appear to be independent of brain and body.

Can Mind Survive Physical Death?

One last speculation, an outrageous one perhaps, but on the theme I was asked to consider for this symposium on "Survival and Consciousness". Can the mind survive the death of the physical brain? Perhaps here we have to to recall how mathematics suggests that physical entities can suddenly collapse or infinitely expand. I think it is important to realize that information is stored in the brain, and it is conceivable to me that this information could transform itself into some other realm. The DNA molecules surely have the information that makes the brain and body, and the bodymind seems to share the information molecules that enliven the organism. Where does the information go after the destruction of the molecules (the mass) that compose it? Matter can neither be created nor destroyed, and perhaps biological information flow cannot just disappear at death and must be transformed into another realm. Who can rationally say "impossible"? No one has yet mathematically unified gravitation field theory with matter and energy. The mathematics of consciousness has not even been approached. The nature of the hypothetical "other realm" is currently in the religious or mystical dimension, where Western science is clearly forbidden to tread.

Footnotes

1. C. B. Pert, M. R. Ruff, R. J. Weber, M. Herkenham, "Neuropeptides and their receptors: A psychosomatic network", *J. Immunol.* 1985:35.2. See also: C. B. Pert, *Cybernetics* 1985;1:1; F. O. Schmitt, "Molecular regulation of brain function: A new view", *Neuroscience* 1984; 13:991.

2. C. B. Pert, M. R. Ruff, R. J. Weber, M. Herkenham, op. cit.

Harris Dienstfrey first adapted this talk for an article in Advances *(Volume 3, Number 3, Summer 1986), a quarterly journal of the Institute for the Advancement of Health. It was further revised for the Spring 1987* Noetic Sciences Review.

VII

A POSSIBLE CONCEPTION OF
LIFE AFTER DEATH

John Hick

It has very often been assumed that the notion of human survival of bodily death poses a straightforward question: Do we live on after bodily death?, which rightly expects a straightforward yes or no answer. Few indeed have thought that the true answer is easy to come by; but many have thought that the question itself is easy enough to ask. Much of the empirical evidence, in the form of "spirit communications" through mediums, seems at first to support that assumption. A deeper analysis, however, has opened up more complex possibilities. To a great extent this deeper analysis was achieved in the classic period of parapsychological research towards the end of the nineteenth and early in the present century. The observations, analyses and theorizings of some of the workers then were of the highest order and have seldom been equalled. Modern parapsychologists have of course at their command greatly superior technology, more sophisticated mathematical techniques, and a more impressive line of jargon, but not often a better or even an equal theoretical power and intellectual penetration.

In praising those classic contributions I am not referring to work on physical phenomena—spirit materializations, direct voice mediumship, poltergeists, and so on, which often seem to have fallen far short of the rigorous standards of control, aided by such devices as infra-red photography that we rightly require today. I am referring to work in the field of trance mediumship, including automatic writing, and in particular to the investigations of the small group of outstanding mediums, such as Mrs. Piper, Mrs. Verrall, Mrs. Leonard, and Mrs. Willett (whom we now know to have been Mrs. Coombe-Tennant). It is true that such researchers as Richard Hodgson, Mrs. Sidgwick, William James, and others would have been aided by tape recorders if these had then been invented, but not, I think, to an extent that would have made any significant difference to their conclusions. Their reports are now buried in the back numbers of the *Proceedings of the Society for Psychical Research*, and a subsidiary reason for my referring to them here is to draw attention to a very rich store of what is today largely neglected material.

When we read the transcripts of the trance communications, and the texts of the automatic writings of Piper and Leonard, our first impression is one of the presence of still-living personalities who have passed through bodily death. We find the "spirits" (I shall use invisible quotation marks around the word from now on) talking very much as though they were living people communicating from a distance by telephone or letter. Sometimes of course the person on the phone (speaking through the entranced medium), or writing the letters (producing automatic scripts through the medium's hand), is a "control" (again, invisible quotation marks henceforth), who is relaying messages from some other deceased individual, who is thus communicating indirectly through both control and medium. But whether operating through a control or directly through the medium, these spirits, and also the spirit controls, seem essentially like living people who have moved to a distant part of the world, or better, if we may anticipate the likely technology of the future, who have emigrated by rocket to live on the surface—or perhaps beneath the surface—of another planet. They seem to be the same conscious individuals with memories connecting them continuously with the time when they were here on Earth. They speak the same language, and apparently operate in terms of the same system of concepts and framework of presupposition. They are, so to speak, still on the same mental wavelength as we and still very much interested in our goings-on in this world.

There is, however, one puzzling feature of most of the well-known published trance material. This is that the spirits say very little about their own world and their own lives in it. We gain no impression of their activities apart from the brief periods when they are communicating with us on Earth. I know that there are exceptions to this, but the prevailing general impression is that expressed, back in the classic period of trance communications, by Professor J. H. Hyslop when he said in his long discussion of the Piper mediumship that "there is not one sentence in my record from which I could even pretend to deduce a conception of what the life beyond the grave is".[1]

It is almost as though the spirits' whole life took place in the seances with only blank periods in between! And this is precisely what some very experienced and thoughtful early students of the phenomena concluded might well be the case. William James, for example, in his study of the Piper material, favored the idea of the communicators

> ... all being dream creations of Mrs. Piper, probably having no existence except when she is in a trance, but consolidated by repetition into personalities consistent enough to play their several roles.[2]

For example, Mrs. Piper's spirit control Phinuit claimed to be a French doctor, Jean Phinuit Scliville, who had practiced in London as well as in France and Belgium in the first half of the nineteenth century. However, Richard Hodgson established by ordinary detective methods that he was not what he claimed to be. Phinuit could not speak French; he displayed no special medical knowledge; and there was no record of his having attended the medical schools at which he claimed to have studied. In order to understand what he was, Mrs. Sidgwick drew upon the phenomenon of hypnosis. Mrs. Sidgwick, who was Principal of Newnham College, Cambridge, was one of the most powerful intellects of her generation, and what looks in the bibliographies like a modest article in the *Proceedings of the SPR* called "A Contribution to the Study of the Psychology of Mrs. Piper's Trance Phenomena"[3] is in fact a book-length study (of 657 pages) which constitutes one of the most important contributions that we have to parapsychological literature.

Under hypnosis, as many have today witnessed in the performance of stage hypnotists, people may exhibit considerable powers of impersonation. If the hypnotist suggests to them that they are, say, visitors from outer space, they will play out this role, mobilizing their relevant knowledge and a latent dramatic ability and inventiveness to sustain it and will, at least on one level of their consciousness, actually believe that they are the persons being impersonated. Sometimes another level of consciousness monitors all that is going on without however, being able to intervene, whilst at other times the whole person is completely immersed in the hypnotic role and on return to normal life has no memory of what took place under hypnosis. Mrs. Sidgwick suggested that Phinuit, as also Mrs. Piper's other controls, were Mrs. Piper herself in an auto-hypnotic state impersonating spirits who had been suggested to her jointly by the spiritualist subculture of her time and by her circle of sitters. Phinuit accordingly existed only in this intermittent context; but in it he elaborated and solidified his own character, developing his identity from seance to seance.

Thus far, then, we have the hypothesis that the medium goes into a self-induced hypnotic state in a context which suggests to her the role of a spirit control relaying messages between the spirit world and Earth. If we add the further feature, for which there is independent evidence, that genuine (that is, not fraudulent) mediums tend to be excellent ESP subjects, we have a possible explanation of how it is that to a much greater extent than could be accounted for purely by chance, the spirit messages are appropriate to the deceased individuals from whom they purport to come. For it could be that information in the sitters' minds about a deceased person, including fairly complete character impressions, affects the medium's mind in its highly suggestible hypnotic state and is built into the drama of spirits presenting themselves to the control, who then relays their messages to the sitters.

However, both Mrs. Sidgwick and Richard Hodgson, who spent so much time investigating the Piper mediumship, thought that her controls may well sometimes have displayed information going beyond what might have been derived telepathically from her sitters. And they point out that if human personality survives bodily death, there may be ESP between living persons and disembodied survivors, as well as between the living. And so one possibility is that deceased persons sometimes try to use a medium's personation of them by impressing her mind with the information which they want to have conveyed, in this indirect and hard-to-control way, to the sitters on Earth. This might account for the very uneven quality of the material. However, yet another possibility to be considered is that the medium receives telepathic impressions of the deceased Mr. X without Mr. X himself being consciously involved. For telepathy does not normally require the conscious intent of the sender. In this scenario it would not be correct to say that Mr. X is, from his own point of view, communicating through the medium with relatives and friends on Earth. The situation would be more like someone else writing letters in his name and without his knowledge. Yet a further possibility to be noted is that Mr. X no longer exists as a conscious person, but that when we die there remains something like what C. D. Broad called a psychic factor,[4] consisting in a more or less coherent nexus of ideas, character traits, and memories which persists for a longer or shorter period until it gradually disintegrates, and that it is this that a medium is able to tap for impressions that feed her hypnotic impersonations. This latter hypothesis could perhaps even be stretched to cover those cases, such as the famous Chaffin will case, in which information which was not at the time known to any living person is presented through a medium.

This range of possibilities, reflecting our ignorance rather than our knowledge, shows how difficult it is with our present evidence to establish the straightforward survival hypothesis. That hypothesis is fully compatible with the facts, but represents by no means the only possible way of accounting for them. Many who have personally conversed through a medium with what professes to be a deceased relative or friend have been unable to doubt that this was indeed the person whom they had known on Earth, still intellectually alive and with the same distinctive character, emotional pattern, and personal mannerisms. But those who have not had that experience may well feel that it is possible in such a situation to be mistaken, misled by a natural desire for contact with loved ones who have died and for assurance that they have not finally perished.

Where then does the empirical research leave us? It leaves us at present in uncertainty. One of the most recent attempts to weigh up the parapsychological evidence is that of the veteran psychologist and former President of the Society for Psychical Research, who died recently, Dr. Robert H. Thouless, in a lengthy discussion in the Society's 1984 *Proceedings* of the question "Do We Survive Bodily Death?" He concluded:

> There seem to be many converging lines of evidence which suggest that [death] is the passage to another life, but we cannot yet be certain that this is the case. It is a future task of parapsychology to reduce to a minimum this uncertainty and to find out all we can about the nature of this future life. This task is very far from being yet completed.[5]

This would seem to be a fair if not very startling or newsworthy conclusion at this time.

Needless to say, the fact that we cannot establish life after death by empirical evidence does not mean that there is no life after death. We must not mistake absence of knowledge for knowledge of absence! We should therefore keep in mind the other possible ground for expecting such a continuation, namely that offered by the world's religious traditions. I am not going to attempt here to justify religious belief, although I have tried to do that elsewhere. The subject is much too large to be treated within the limits of this text. Accordingly, what now follows is addressed primarily to those who are convinced that the religious experience of humanity does not consist purely of human projection, although it does undoubtedly involve a considerable human element, varying from culture to culture, but is at the same time a cognitive response to a divine reality transcending physical nature and human consciousness. Each of the great historical ways of experiencing and conceiving that reality has found that it must include within its understanding of the universe a belief in a larger human existence that transcends our present life. But this belief takes a number of very different forms. I propose to treat these different religious conceptions of life after death as providing our range of options, and then try to see if there are any considerations that can reasonably guide us in an attempt to choose among them.

One major difference between the traditions concerns the time scale of the formation of perfected or fully-developed human creatures. Each of the great religions holds that the ultimate human state, whether it is to be attained by all or only by some, is one of union or communion with the divine reality. From our present earthly standpoint, the difference between union and communion seems considerable, but in that final state it may perhaps be transcended, somewhat as in the Christian conception of the Trinity as three in one and one in three. The traditions all point in their different ways to an eschaton which lies beyond our present conceptuality. But when we turn from that ultimate state to possible penultimate states, and thus from eschatology to pareschatology, we meet more clearly defined options. The big distinction is between the Western doctrine of a single temporal life and the Eastern doctrine of many such lives.

The dominant Christian (and also Jewish and Moslem) view is that our temporal existence, during which moral and spiritual change and growth are possible, is limited to this present life; and after this comes a divine judgment followed by eternal heaven or hell, or heaven via a purgatorial phase which is not, however, thought of as a further period of active living and growing. Our existence, according to this view, consists of two very unequal phases, an eternal state, preceded by this brief earthly life in which we exercise a fateful freedom and responsibility. Thus, it is assumed that the function of our present life is to become, through our own free responses and choices, persons to whom either eternal heaven or eternal hell is appropriate.

But is this picture morally realistic? Consider the facts that: (a) A large proportion of the human babies who have been born during the last hundred thousand years or so, a proportion probably approaching and quite possibly exceeding 50% have died at birth or in infancy, so that for them it would seem that the purpose of life has remained unfulfilled. (b) The circumstances into which people are born and in which they have to live vary so greatly in their propitiousness for moral and spiritual growth that it is hard to see how we could be assessed on our performance in this one brief and chancy life. c) Very few people can be said to be morally fitted, by the time of their death, for either eternal bliss or eternal torment. To some extent this last point is met by the fact that, in traditional Christian theology, the divine judgment is not so much ethical as theological. The saved are those who believe in Jesus Christ as their Lord and Savior and who put their trust in the efficacy of his atoning death. However, in our pluralistically conscious age, this seems arbitrary and implausible, and much Christian thought has moved decisively away from it.

Such a move may well lead Christians to consider again the alternative view of the Hindu, Buddhist, Jain, and Sikh traditions, or some further variation of its central theme. The basic thought here is that one life-span is not enough for the transformation of human beings from the self-centeredness of our natural state to the unity or community with the divine reality which is the ultimate aim of human existence. I think we must admit that this is a morally realistic view. But another important insight accompanies it. This is implicit rather than explicit in most Hindu and Buddhist discussions, but can be made explicit as follows. It is the very finitude of our earthly life, its haunting brevity, that gives it shape and value by making time precious and choice urgent. If we had before us an endless temporal vista, devoid of the pressure of an approaching end, our life would lose its present character as offering a continuum of choices, small and large, through which we participate in our own gradual creating. There is thus much to be said for the view that the formation of persons through their own freedom requires the boundaries of birth and death. But if one such natural span is not sufficient for our growth to a total unitive or communitive centeredness in the divine reality, then our present life would seem likely to be followed by further such finite phases rather than by a single limitless existence continuing without end. And so perhaps we should consider seriously the basic Eastern option of a series of finite lives, the series ending only when we have attained to a final self-transcendence, when the discipline of temporal life is no longer needed.

Eastern thought has always assumed that any such further lives will be lived on this Earth. The Hindu and Buddhist traditions do indeed speak of a great range of other spheres of existence, heavens and hells, in addition to this Earth. But they also hold that it is only as human beings in this world that we can make substantive progress towards final liberation from the self-centered ego. I see in this belief an implicit recognition of the need for the boundary pressures of birth and death to make possible any profound development of the self. Hindus and Buddhists accordingly see it as a rare privilege to have been born into this world. For here and here alone do we have the opportunity of spiritual growth.

However, when we turn to the empirical evidence for reincarnation or rebirth, we find, in my opinion, the same kind of ambiguity and uncertainty that we discovered in the empirical evidence for survival. There are innumerable claimed memories of former lives, both the spontaneous memories of children, and sometimes of adults, and also memories systematically induced under hypnosis. A large collection of spontaneous memories has been made by Professor Ian Stevenson of the University of Virginia in his four-volume work *Cases of the Reincarnation Type* from India, Sri Lanka, Lebanon, Turkey, Thailand, and Burma.[6] And many further instances of apparent memories of previous lives have been garnered through hypnotic regression, some of the best known being the Bridey Murphy case[7] and the cases reported by Alexander Cannon.[8] But although the best examples in both categories are impressive and satisfy some people, they are not objectively convincing to every rational person who studies them. The majority who dismiss this range of evidence as insufficient have never in fact made a serious detailed study, and are therefore expressing a prejudice rather than a responsible judgment. But nevertheless, there are some who have looked rather carefully at the detailed reports, and I would include myself among them, who still do not consider that they constitute conclusive or even nearly conclusive evidence.

Almost invariably the reported spontaneous childhood memories of a previous life come from societies in which reincarnation is a matter of general belief. The believer in reincarnation will say that it is in these societies that children with such memories are allowed to express them rather than being treated as over-imaginative or untruthful. The skeptic, on the other hand, will say that in those societies the idea is suggested to children by their surrounding culture and sallies of the imagination can be too readily accepted as previous-life memories and encouraged by the family. Further, the interest of investigators, particularly visiting foreign investigators, may enhance the family's local importance and may in general be something for the village to encourage rather than discourage. Again, it was inevitable that Stevenson's well-recorded cases were not investigated as soon as the child had begun to speak of a previous life but after a longer or shorter lapse of time during which the story had time to develop, to become consolidated, and to attract supporting testimony that was later hard to test in any rigorous way.

It is also regrettable, from an ideal point of view, that in almost all cases the investigation had to be conducted through an interpreter, with the consequent difficulty of totally discounting all possibility of bias or misunderstanding. Yet another difficulty, of a different kind, is suggested by the range of options which we noted concerning human survival. Could it be that those who have "memories" of a previous life are good ESP subjects, receiving genuine impressions of persons who have died derived either from those persons, still existing in a spirit world, or from a "psychic factor" or set of mental traces left behind by them? Once again, it is impossible to banish the specter of ambiguity. And there is also ambiguity in the hypnotic regression cases, witnessed to by the controversy which has always surrounded them.

However, these ambiguities and uncertainties are only ambiguities and uncertainties. They do not authorize us to dismiss the idea of reincarnation. Nor should we necessarily treat it as a simple all-or-nothing issue. Conceivably, some people reincarnate and others do not. There is a further possibility which deserves to be identified and considered. This is that we do indeed go through a series of lives, each having its own beginning and end and being a sphere for the exercise of freedom and responsibility, but that these are not all in the same world, but on the contrary in different worlds. Perhaps Hindu and Buddhist teaching is right in holding that there are many spheres of existence but wrong in holding that none of them, other than this Earth, is such as to provide opportunity for further moral and spiritual growth. But if we are going seriously to consider the idea of other worlds why should we exclude the possibility that they may be at least as appropriate to a person-making process as is this world?

If there should be such other worlds in which continued person-making can take place, where are they? Contemporary physics and scientific cosmology are in such a state of flux that they intensify the general ambiguity. But nevertheless they do seem to speak today of the possibility of plural spaces within a single super-space. Thus, Paul Davies, Professor of Theoretical Physics at the University of Newcastle, England, says that

What is usually regarded as 'the universe' might in fact be only a disconnected fragment of space-time. There could be many, even an infinite number of other universes, but all physically inaccessible to the others.[9]

A plurality of spaces might include a plurality of worlds, some of them sustaining intelligent life, and each such world having its own unique history, its own proper concerns and excitements, achievements and dangers, and each constituting a possible environment for moral and spiritual growth through practical challenge and response.

Let us then tentatively entertain the thought that having died in this world we are either immediately or after an interval born in another physical world in another space. This thought also of course carries with it the possibility that we have already lived before in another such world.

Major questions now arise. One concerns the nature of the "we" who are to be thus re-embodied. What precisely is it that reincarnates?

We have noted the effect of temporal boundaries in giving shape, character, and meaning to our present life. This insight has a further implication which can be expressed by saying that we human creatures, living between birth and death, are essentially historical beings, constituents of a certain particular segment of the human story. And as historical beings we are largely formed by the culture into which we were born. There are no such things as human beings in general, but only beings who are human in this or that particular cultural pattern and as part of this or that stage of history. Thus, you and I are not incidentally but essentially twentieth century Western persons. We cannot be abstracted from our cultural and historical setting. This, at least, is true of what we may call the empirical self, created by heredity and environment within a particular historical and cultural setting.

But this is not a complete account of us. In addition to this empirical or public self, formed in interaction with others within a common historico-cultural matrix, there is a basic moral and spiritual nature, or dispositional structure, for which I propose to use the traditional name "soul". I said that this exists in addition to our empirical self. But that may be a misleading way of putting it. For our empirical self and our basic nature are not two distinct entities. The terms refer rather to two continuously interacting levels on which the stream of self-consciousness which I call "me" operates. One is the level of moral and spiritual response and choice. Here our fundamental nature is expressing itself. Such basic dispositional attitudes as a tendency to be compassionate, generous, and forgiving, or to be unloving, grasping, and resentful, and again, to be open or closed to the divine mystery, can express themselves through a variety of different empirical selves enmeshed in different historico-cultural contexts. They could be lived out, or incarnated, in the lives of, let us say, a male Tibetan peasant of the fifth century BCE and a female American lawyer of the twentieth century CE. In these extremely different circumstances the same basic dispositional structure would result in very different empirical lives. However, we must not think of the soul as our more basic nature, as fixed and unchanging. On the contrary, like the empirical self, it is changing in some degree all the time as we respond to life's tasks and experiences. The main distinction, for our present purpose, is that whereas our empirical self can only be described in terms of a particular historico-cultural context, our basic nature or soul can be described independently of the concrete ways in which its basic traits express themselves in particular circumstances.

You will appreciate that I am not here propounding a dogma but constructing a thought-model to stimulate reflection. This thought-model suggests that what is going on in human life is the growth of a multitude of souls—individual moral and spiritual natures—towards union or communion with the divine life. It may be that in this long process souls are embodied a number of times as different empirical selves. What reincarnates in this view—which is fairly close to both Hindu and Buddhist teaching—is not the empirical self but the basic moral and spiritual dispositional structure, the soul. At bodily death the empirical self, with its culture-bound personality and time-bound memories, begins gradually to fade away, our consciousness becoming centered in the moral/spiritual attitudes which constitute the soul; and that soul, or dispositional structure, is then able to be embodied again to engage once more in the creative process.

A further question that arises for this hypothesis concerns its relation to time. Do all these supposed worlds exist within the same time-frame, so that our life in world two is subsequent in the same time-sequence to our life in world one? If we are relating the plurality-of-worlds conception to the physicists' talk of a plurality of spaces, we must be prepared to follow them in what they say about time. They seem to have abandoned the Newtonian notion of a single absolute time within which each event occurs either before or after or simultaneously with each other event. Time is conceived of as relative to the observer, and spaces that are not spatially related to one another will not be related within a single time-frame. It would thus not be appropriate to say that life two comes *after* life one; and neither would it be appropriate to say that it occurs before it or simultaneously with it!

On the other hand, the idea of re-embodiment in many worlds does seem to require a causal relationship between these worlds such that the basic character of my empirical self in world two depends upon the basic character that I had when I died in world one. The distinction that we have already drawn between the basic moral/spiritual character, or soul, and the psychophysical self, is relevant at this point. For the causation involved between worlds one and two will not be physical but more like the kind of mental resonance that occurs in ESP. It will involve the transmission of information, but information whose content is a basic character, or system of moral/spiritual traits. This body of information is called in some Hindu systems the linga sharira, sometimes translated as "spiritual body", and in some Buddhist systems is called a karmic system, and is regarded in each as constituting the continuant from life to life. However, whereas Hinduism and Buddhism hold that the karmic system or linga sharira influences the development of a new empirical self within the evolution of life on this Earth, I am suggesting the possibility that it may influence the formation of a new individual within the process of life in another world which is part of another space.

Understood from a religious point of view, such a series of lives constitutes a long creative process leading to unity with or community within the divine life. The formation of new empirical selves will go on as long as they are needed as vehicles for the development of the deeper self or soul. Then, eventually, temporal life will be subsumed into eternal life, samsara into nirvana, history into the Kingdom of Heaven.

Let me return in conclusion to the parapsychological evidence for survival. I suggested that this evidence remains inconclusive. But nevertheless, it may be of interest to relate it to a plurality-of-worlds hypothesis such as I have very sketchily outlined.

If after death our basic nature is embodied again as another empirical self, it is of course theoretically possible that this happens immediately. The Theravada tradition within Buddhism teaches precisely that. On the other hand, the Hindu tradition and much of the Mahayana tradition speak of an intermediate period between embodied lives, and if we want to keep open the possibility of incorporating the spiritualist evidence, we shall opt for this possibility.

Let us entertain the hypothesis, then, that after bodily death consciousness continues in a now disembodied state as a center both of moral and spiritual freedom and of memories and personality traits formed in relation to this world. In this next phase, as it is described in the classic Buddhist *Bardo Thodol*, there is no new sensory input, and the environment of which we are aware is a mind-dependent projection of our own memories, desires, fears, and beliefs. Such a dream-like phase would seem to correspond with what in Western Spiritualist literature has been called Illusion-land or Summer-land. The *Bardo Thodol* describes the experiences that a devout medieval Tibetan Buddhist may be expected to have in this state. But a modern Western and largely secular mind might well project the kind of banal continuation of the present life that we find in, for example, the Raymond communications through Mrs. Leonard, recorded by Lodge, this being one of the notable exceptions to the generalization that the spirits tell us practically nothing about their own world.

But this *Bardo* (meaning between two) phase only lasts for a certain time, during which the memories and characteristics of the empirical self gradually fade and the deeper nature, now at the center of consciousness, moves on to a new phase which is evidently beyond the possibility of communication with persons in this world. In the Spiritualist scenario this next phase is roughly equivalent to the deva worlds of Buddhist and Hindu cosmology. I have however been suggesting the possibility that the phase after the bardo period may be (as the *Bardo Thodol* itself teaches) a new embodiment, and that this may be in another world which is part of another sub-space within this unimaginably vast and complex universe. In Christian terms, of course, such a re-embodiment is the resurrection of the dead, and the novelty, from a Christian point of view, of this idea is that it includes a series of resurrections instead of only one.

I need hardly say that this thought-model is highly speculative. It is offered as an attempt—a feeble attempt whose only merit might be to provoke others to make their own attempts—to discriminate among the options offered by the great religious traditions and by such ambiguous empirical evidence as we have.[10]

Footnotes

1. J. H. Hyslop, "A Further Record of Observations of Certain Trance Phenomena", *Proceedings of the Society for Psychical Research*, Vol. 16, Part 41, 1901, p.291.

2. William James, "Report on Mrs. Piper's Hodgson-Control", *Proc. SPR*, Vol. 23, Part 58, 1909, p.3

3. *Proc. SPR*, Vol. 28, Part 71, 1915.

4. C. D. Broad, *The Mind and Its Place in Nature* (New York: Harcourt, Brace, 1925).

5. *Proc. SPR*, Vol. 57, No. 213, 1984, p.50.

6. Ian Stevenson, *Cases of the Reincarnation Type* (Charlottesville: University of Virginia Press, 1975-83), 4 Vols.

7. M. Bernstein, *The Search for Bridey Murphy* (New York: Doubleday, 1956).

8. Alexander Cannon, *The Power Within* (New York: Dutton, 1953).

9. Paul Davies, *Other Worlds: Space, Superspace, and the Quantum Universe* (London: J. M. Dent, 1980).

10. For a further development of these and related ideas see my *Death and Eternal Life* (New York: Harper and Row, 1976).

VIII

THE MIND-BODY PROBLEM
AND QUANTUM REALITY

P. C. W. Davies

It may seem surprising that a physicist should concern himself with the problem of consciousness, still less the possibility of the survival of that consciousness. Physics is normally associated with the material universe, whereas consciousness traditionally belongs to philosophy and religion, or more recently psychology.

Yet in the past physics has frequently encompassed subjects that began as branches of philosophy or religion; the nature of space and time is an obvious example. In recent years physicists have given increasing attention to the concept of mind, or the observer, and indeed in one branch of physics at least, the issue cannot be avoided. David Deutsch, a follower of John Wheeler, recently wrote:

Epistemology is now being incorporated into physics, just as the scope of physics has historically been successively extended to take over other sciences such as astronomy, chemistry, geometry and most recently computer science.[1]

For many people the existence of mind and its possible survival is assumed to be inescapably supernatural and hence beyond the scope of science altogether. There is, however, no logical reason why mind cannot exist and even survive bodily death in a universe without a God, just as God's existence does not logically require other minds and their survival. And of course we could also imagine that there is a God, but that he does not need to interfere directly in the process of perpetuating a person's mind after bodily death, being content to allow this to occur through natural physical mechanisms, as with birth.

The question that I shall address here then is whether physics has room for or even requires consciousness and whether the survival of consciousness after bodily death has any place at all within the framework of current physical theory. (Even if the answer were negative that would not rule out the possibility of survival. It would merely demand that our present conception of the physical universe would have to be modified or extended if such a possibility were to be entertained.)

"Observers" In Physical Theory

By tradition, the existence of conscious observers has been regarded by physicists as an incidental rather than a fundamental feature of the universe. More recently, however, two contexts have arisen in which observers are taken to be fundamental to our understanding of physical reality. The first of these goes under the title of the Anthropic Principle, and consists of a loose collection of arguments along the following lines: One can readily imagine hypothetical universes in which the laws of physics and/or the initial conditions at the origin of the universe are such as to preclude the existence of life, at least in the form that we know it. Mathematical analysis suggests, in fact, that most of the important complex structures in the universe, and especially biological organisms, are remarkably sensitive to the precise form of these laws and conditions, and to the values that nature has assigned to the so-called "fundamental constants" such as Newton's gravitational constant G or the mass of the electron—numbers which appear to be otherwise arbitrary. If we were to imagine the Deity "twiddling the knobs" a little, the merest touch would apparently cause the universe to fall apart. For full details I cite my book *The Accidental Universe*[2] and the monumental work by John Barrow and Frank Tipler, *The Cosmological Anthropic Principle*.[3]

The upshot of these studies is that the range of cognizable universes within the set of all possible universes is probably exceedingly small, so that our very existence already places very strong constraints on the possible structure of the laws of physics and the possible initial conditions. The complication is that consciousness is indeed a *fundamental* rather than an incidental feature of the universe. Our existence is written into the laws of physics. (Note that this need not imply a pre-existing design.)[4]

The second area of physical theory in which observers are apparently indispensible is quantum mechanics.[5] This subject normally treats the behavior of microscopic systems such as atoms, nuclei and subatomic particles, but is also crucial to understanding the laser, the microchip and other practical devices. Quantum mechanics is a supremely successful theory of matter, and has never been seriously questioned in its routine application.

Where quantum theory does run into puzzle and paradox concerns its interpretation.[6] Boiled down to its essentials, the problem is this. A quantum particle (e.g. an electron) is described by a mathematical object called a *wave function* denoted ψ. (Later we shall see that ψ often behaves like a wave.) The theory provides an evolution equation that ψ must satisfy, and the equation can be solved to determine how ψ will change with time. This in turn enables the physicist to find out how the electron will move about with time. The difference between quantum mechanics and the old Newtonian classical mechanics is that the description of the electron furnished by ψ is only *probabilistic*. It enables one to predict only how likely it is that the electron will move to such-and-such a place. It does not generally give a precise prediction. This vagueness or indeterminism of quantum mechanics is a key feature, and is inescapable.

The oddity at issue here concerns not the breakdown of determinism and exact predictability as such but rather the very peculiar thing that happens to the wave function when a measurement or observation is made. So long as the electron is left unobserved, its behavior will, within the limitations of the probabilistic nature of quantum mechanics, be described by a ψ changing in accord with the above-mentioned evolution equation. But when an observation is made ψ suddenly jumps, or "collapses", into a new form. This abrupt change is in complete violation of the evolution equation, and is simply postulated ad hoc.

Let me give a concrete example of the collapse of the wave function. Suppose an electron is placed in an impenetrable box. According to the theory, ψ settles down to a form where its value is essentially constant throughout the box, signifying that the electron is equally likely to be found at any point within. Now suppose that the box is divided into two by an impenetrable screen, and the two halves A and B are separated and transported apart (light years if need be). So long as nobody looks to see, ψ will remain of equal magnitude in both A and B. But at the instant someone investigates whether the electron is in one half-box, say A (and suppose it is), ψ collapses so that its value is boosted in A and vanishes in B.

The abrupt change which occurs here signifies that the system has made a transition from the merely possible to the actual. That is, ψ describes the probability of where the electron will be found. Prior to the observation this has the value 1/2 for each half-box. But after the observation the electron is known to be in A with certainty, hence ψ must change to take this into account. If ψ *didn't* collapse, we could not know where the electron was and the world would be in a ghostly hybrid state with the particle somehow in both half-boxes at once!

This hybrid state is technically known as a *superposition*. A general state ψ will be a superposition of many possible actual states. In fact, the situation is even more enigmatic than in the example given because the wave functions in a superposition usually interpenetrate each other (unlike those restricted to A and B) and combine to produce an observable effect called interference. When an observation is made, one of these wave functions is "projected out" and describes the actual state of the world determined by the observations. When this happens the interference effects disappear.

Now it can rightly be objected that it is not surprising if the electron behaves differently when isolated than it does when it is being observed because in order to observe an electron you must interact with it and inevitably disturb its motion. This fact led to a number of investigations of the physics involved in the act of measurement, most notably by the mathematician John von Neumann.[7] You can describe the measurement apparatus by quantum mechanics too, leading to a grand wave function for the combined system of electron plus measurement apparatus. Analysis shows that the effect of coupling the apparatus to the electron does indeed cause the part of the wave function that describes the latter to jump (if regarded in isolation) but the total wave function does not jump. It continues to satisfy the total evolution equation, and continues to manifest the interference effects of superposition. In other words, no real observation actually occurs.

The involvement of the measuring apparatus thus merely shifts the problem of what happens to a quantum system when it is observed back one stage. To get the more embracing wave function to collapse, the system electron plus measuring apparatus must *itself* be measured by some other external device, and so on. This is the measurement paradox.

Resolutions Of The Paradox Of Quantum Measurement

The source of the difficulty about quantum measurement and the collapse of the wave function is that ψ has a unique status in physical science. Unlike all other mathematical quantities in physics, which describe how a system *is*, ψ describes our *knowledge* of the system. When an observation is made our knowledge inevitably abruptly changes, and this is reflected in the collapse of ψ. So we already see how mind seems to be entering the picture in an absolutely central way. On the one hand the wave function evolves with time and is associated with the activity of the electron; on the other hand its form and hence this very activity seems to depend on the experimenter's state of mind.

Again, an example is helpful. The inherent vagueness of quantum mechanics is encapsulated in the famous uncertainty principle of Werner Heisenberg. This states that you cannot determine at the same moment both where a quantum particle is and what it is doing. Greater accuracy in one attribute is traded for uncertainty about the other. However, the experimenter can *choose* which sort of observation to make. If she decides to measure the position of the electron, she detects an electron-at-a-place. If she decides instead to measure the speed, she gets an electron-with-a-speed. Either measured quantity is well-defined on measurement, but the act of measurement inevitably means that the other quantity is not well defined. An electron simply *does not have* a well-defined position and motion at all times. Which property it shall have *depends on the choice of the experimenter*.

Needless to say this almost mystical quality of quantum mechanics has led to decades of controversy about its meaning. Einstein flatly refused to accept it. The "conventional view" was articulated most forcefully by Niels Bohr. Bohr maintained that it is meaningless to ascribe physical qualities such as position or speed to a quantum particle in the absence of a specified experimental measurement strategy. This strongly positivistic position places the nature of reality squarely at the feet of the observer and suggests that, in the absence of observation, the external world is less than real, hung in a ghostly superposition of contending realities. (Einstein once remarked, dumbfounded, that this implied the moon did not exist when you didn't look at it.)

The trouble with Bohr's position is that it is vague about exactly what constitutes an observation. Some bold physicists (for example, Eugene Wigner) have gone so far as to state explicitly that only when a conscious observer becomes aware of the result of a quantum measurement does the wave function collapse. Thus they introduce a genuine dualist mind-matter interaction that works in both directions.[8]

Other physicists have tried to resolve the measurement paradox differently. In the so-called statistical interpretation, for example, we are asked to relinquish all attempts to describe individual quantum processes and deal instead with ensembles.[6] The so-called many-universes interpretation avoids the collapse of the wave function by postulating that when a wave function is in a superposition of states, each state corresponds to an actually existing universe. Thus there is not just one physical reality, but an infinity of "worlds" co-existing in parallel, each representing a quantum alternative. According to this interpretation, our own minds are likewise split (and being continually further divided) into near-duplicates, each perceiving a slightly different "reality". The many-universes interpretation is very popular with cosmologists, who like to apply quantum physics to the universe as a whole.[9]

A few die-hards have tried to avoid the measurement paradox by following in the tradition of Einstein, and searching for a deeper level of description of nature than quantum mechanics. These approaches have assumed that behind the paradoxical world of the quantum lies a more familiar classical world of common-sense reality, in which the external world has a well-defined, concrete existence independent of the observer. In these so-called "hidden variables" theories the uncertainty and indeterminism of quantum mechanics are no longer inherent, but are attributed to a substratum of chaotic influences that, crudely speaking, jiggle electrons and other particles about randomly, to make them *appear* to show unpredictable behavior. The most articulate champion of such theories is David Bohm.[10]

Recently, hidden variable theories received a major blow with the results of an experiment by Alain Aspect and his co-workers in France.[11] The object of the experiment was to test something known as Bell's theorem.[12] This is a mathematical restriction on the degree to which spatially separated simultaneous events can be correlated. Bell's theorem makes only two assumptions, which are, very roughly: 1) physical systems possess well-defined physical attributes independent of measurements made on them; 2) no physical influences can exceed the speed of light. The first assumption we may call common-sense reality and is typified by hidden variable theories. The second is a consequence of the theory of relativity, and few physicists would be prepared to abandon it. Condition 2 is often referred to as "locality" because it restricts the influences that can instantaneously affect a system to those at the same spatial point. Recall from the box example given before the strongly nonlocal flavor of quantum mechanics as demonstrated by the instantaneous collapse of ψ in the distant half-box.

Aspect's experiment clearly demonstrated a violation of Bell's theorem in an actual quantum system, consisting of pairs of correlated photons traveling in opposite directions several metres apart, where simultaneous measurements were made on each. We are thus forced to abandon either the assumption of common-sense reality or locality. Bohm, in an attempt to retain the former, abandons the latter, but to avoid conflict with the huge body of experimental evidence in favor of no faster-than-light propagation, his theory has become rather contrived and complicated. The great majority of physicists defend locality, and (with Bohr) relinquish instead the common-sense view of reality, the view that the world "out there" possesses a complete and independent set of well-defined physical attributes in the absence of observation.

Software-Hardware Duality And The Mind

I have already remarked that the quantum wave function has a unique status in physics in that it represents *knowledge* rather than a material object (or field). Yet its form is inextricably mixed up with material objects, indeed, in many instances ψ behaves as though it represents a real wave similar to any other. Thus a beam of electrons can display diffraction phenomena identical to, say, sound waves. This is the famous "wave-particle" duality of quantum physics. An electron, which we are tempted to think of as a particle, often behaves more like a wave. Conversely light, which by tradition is regarded as an electromagnetic wave, takes on corpuscular properties in, for example, the photoelectric effect. This wave-particle duality is strange enough, but even stranger when we realize that the wave is really a wave of information or knowledge *about* the electron and not a wave *of* electron-substance.

There is a helpful analogy here with computer science. Information in computing is related to software, which employs concepts such as program, input-output, calculation, answer, and so on. This contrasts the hardware of the machine itself, about which one uses words like wiring, electronic impulse, microchip, etc. In quantum mechanics the particle is the hardware whereas the wave is the software.

Now when a computer is executing some operation there are two distinct levels of description about what is going on. The first is the hardware level. An engineer could give you a detailed account of which circuits are firing and how the electronic impulses are propagating around the machine in accordance with the laws of electric circuit theory. The other description is at the software level used by the programmer. He will refer to the same sequence of events in terms like: "It's calculating the number π to a million decimal places". Both descriptions are correct at their own level. They are not contradictory but *complementary.*

A similar situation holds in quantum mechanics. The wave and particle aspects of, say, an electron are complementary to each other. You can set up an experiment to observe the wave-like behavior or an entirely different experiment to see the particle-like behavior. Similarly the position-motion dichotomy of Heisenberg's uncertainty relation represents complementary qualities of a particle.

During the process of quantum measurement something very strange happens. At the bottom level of description we have, say, an electron moving about. This is the hardware. The electron is coupled to some complicated measuring device which in turn is coupled to an even more complicated system—the experimenter. Somehow, somewhere in this complicated chain hardware gets converted into software: The experimenter becomes aware of the state of the electron. The result is that ψ jumps abruptly and the subsequent career of the electron is drastically altered.

It will by now be clear that the duality (or complementarity) of quantum mechanics parallels the mind-body duality of philosophy. Indeed I would go so far as to claim that they are one and the same. After all, the last link in the chain of coupling between electron and consciousness is production of awareness in the electrochemical activity inside the brain.

I do not think we have yet solved the mind-body problem, just as we have not solved the quantum measurement problem. I have a hunch that the way forward is to introduce explicit "software laws" into physics, that is, to entertain the possibility of organizing principles complementary to the analytical dynamical laws of traditional physics. However, I am convinced that mind is not substance, as in the old-fashioned ideas of dualism. Mind belongs to a higher descriptive level than brain. Somehow software and hardware are becoming entangled in what Douglas Hofstadter has called a "strange loop".[13]

Wheeler seems to have drawn similar conclusions.[14] He refers to existence as "the closed circuit of meaning" (c.f. Hofstadter's strange loop). The point here is that the subatomic world is ultimately built out of waves ψ but waves which relate to knowledge or, as Wheeler prefers it, meaning. But the conscious beings who possess that knowledge are themselves made up from the quantum particles and fields being described here. Wheeler expresses it thus:

> Circuit closed how? Physics supplies the machinery for constructing meaning, and meaning supplies the machinery for constructing

physics. The first half of the 'meaning circuit' is familiar in the main. Physics gives sight and sound and all the other agencies of communication. It also gives the biology to make the communicators! And out of communication comes meaning.

The other half, the 'return portion' of the 'meaning circuit' is stranger. The demand for meaning we are to understand as the origin of probability amplitude and phase, and phase we are to learn to consider as the definer of all fields, of all geometry, of all space-time—and in the end, therefore, of all particles and all physics. Physics, in this view, is the child of meaning even as meaning is the child of physics.

Can Mind Survive?

If mind is analogous to computer software (more accurately, the running of a computer program), then the question naturally arises as to whether it has any independent existence. The situation is rather like that of a symphony. Does Beethoven's Fifth still exist when it is not being played? In a sense yes; in a sense no. I am reminded of a rather delightful story in Dennett and Hofstadter's The Mind's I [15] in which the tortoise tells Achilles that his faculties are so developed he can enjoy music merely by hanging a record on the wall and appreciating the pattern of the groove!

The Christian computer scientist Donald McKay writes:

If a computer operating a given program were to catch fire and be destroyed, we would certainly say that that was the end of that particular embodiment of the program. But if we wanted that same program to run in a fresh embodiment, it would be quite unnecessary to salvage the original computer parts or even to replicate the original mechanism. Any active medium (even operations with paper and pencil) which gave expression to the same structure and sequence of relationships could in principle embody the very same program. [16]

I do not want to get too involved in the issue of disembodied minds, or the possibility of reincarnation. Clearly, if mind is *pattern* rather than *substance*, then it is capable of many different representations. The conclusion I should like to draw instead is more modest, yet nevertheless important. We are all agreed that, at least insofar as human beings are concerned, mind is a product of matter, or put more accurately, mind finds expression through matter (specifically our brains). The lesson of the quantum is that the link works the other way too: Matter can only achieve concrete, well-defined existence in conjunction with mind.

Footnotes

1. D. Deutsch, "On Wheeler's Notion of 'Law Without Law in Physics'", to appear in *Foundations of Physics*.

2. P. C. W. Davies, *The Accidental Universe* (Cambridge University Press, 1982).

3. J. D. Barrow and F. J. Tipler, *The Cosmological Anthropic Principle* (Oxford University Press, 1985).

4. See Davies, *God and the New Physics* (Dent/Simon & Schuster, 1983).

5. For an introductory review see, for example, Davies, *Other Worlds* (Dent/ Simon & Schuster, 1980), or H. Pagels, *The Cosmic Code* (Michael Joseph/ Simon & Schuster, 1982).

6. See, for example, Davies and J. Brown, *The Ghost in the Atom* (Cambridge University Press, in the press) based on a BBC Radio documentary, or at a more advanced level, B. d'Espagnat, *In Search of Reality* (Springer-Verlag, 1983).

7. J. von Neumann, *Mathematical Foundations of Quantum Mechanics* (Princeton University Press, 1955).

8. E. Wigner, "Remarks on the Mind-Body Question", *The Scientist Speculates*, I. J. Good, editor (Heinemann, 1962).

9. See, for example, B. S. DeWitt and N. Graham, *The Many-Worlds Interpretation of Quantum Mechanics* (Princeton University Press, 1975).

10. D. Bohm, *Wholeness and the Implicate Order* (Routledge & Kegan Paul, 1980).

11. A. Aspect, P. Grangier and G. Roger, *Phys. Rev. Letters 49*, 91, 1982; A. Aspect, J. Dalibard and G. Roger, *Phys. Rev. Letters 49*, 1804, 1982.

12. J. Bell, *Physics 1*, 195, 1964.

13. D. Hofstadter, *Godel, Escher, Bach: An Eternal Golden Braid* (Basic Books, 1979).

14. J. A. Wheeler in *Proceedings of the NATO Advanced Study Institute Workshop on Frontiers of Nonequilibrium Physics* (Plenum, 1984).

15. D. Hofstadter and D. C. Dennett, editors, *The Mind's I* (Harvester/Basic Books, 1981).

16. D. MacKay, *The Clockwork Image* (Inter-Varsity Press, 1974).

IX

THE INNER SELF-HELPER: TRANSCENDENT LIFE WITHIN LIFE?

Jacqueline A. Damgaard

The issue of the survival of consciousness after physical death is a question which has been crucial for every human society. For today's societies that is especially so. Willis Harman, President of the Institute of Noetic Sciences, suggests that there are three types of metaphysics upon which our culture and our own individual lifestyles might be viewed: Materialistic monism (M-1) views the universe as composed of matter-energy which gives rise to mind and requires the probing of reality and consciousness through study of the measurable, physical world. Dualism (M-2) allows for the existence of both matter-energy and mind-spirit with their appropriate processes of study. Transcendental monism (M-3) asserts that the universe is mind-spirit, which gives rise to matter, the study of which must be undertaken through subjective exploration.

Sandra L. Vaughan contributed to this paper.

It is logically impossible to "prove" any scientific assertions about possible experiences after the death of our physical matterbound bodies, since any such investigation, regardless of approach (materialistic or subjective), can only be conducted while we are still based in our physical bodies, in a three-dimensional world. What *is* possible is a vigorous exploration of our predeath predicament in order to expose untapped possibilities of our predeath condition.[1] It is quite possible that the "inner self-helper" (ISH), a remarkable, higher level state of consciousness discovered by Ralph Allison[2] during the treatment of a patient diagnosed with multiple personality, is fertile ground for just such exploration of consciousness and ergo the phenomenology of consciousness itself.

In this chapter I will discuss multiple personality as a psychiatric category, providing explanations of its known phenomenology, diagnostic signs, types of alter elements (states of consciousness), and treatment. I will then focus on the characteristics of the ISH in particular, its similarity with the Jungian "self" archetype, and the use of ISH states in psychotherapy. Finally, I will explore the possible implications of the ISH phenomenon for survival of consciousness (ergo the human species at large) and as a guide in choosing a preferred metaphysic from which to view the world.

Multiple Personality Disorder

The phenomenon of Multiple Personality Disorder (MPD) was first reported by P. Janet at the end of the nineteenth century.[3] Shortly thereafter Morton Prince's famous case, Christine Beauchamp, appeared in the literature.[4] However, it was not until the last three decades that MPD has been receiving increased attention, first through the popular media with *The Three Faces of Eve*[5] and *Sybil,*[6] and then through increased interest and legitimizing professionally by the current publication of numerous scholarly articles and even recently the devotion of entire issues of psychological journals to the topic.[7]

The current *Diagnostic and Statistical Manual of Mental Disorders, Third Edition,*[7a] lists five dissociative disorders, among them Multiple Personality Disorder.[6] The three diagnostic criteria for MPD are 1) the existence within an individual of two (or more) distinct personalities, each of which is in control of the body at different times; 2) the personality that is dominant determines ongoing behavior; and 3) each personality is complex and has its own unique history, behavior patterns, and social relationships.

Phenomenology

The experience of people with MPD is bewildering and anguishing. They may "wake up" in some unknown place, amnestic as to how they arrived there and in the company of people they may not know. They may be confused about the date or even the year. Projects that were begun earlier may have been neglected, stopped, or forgotten, making it difficult to accomplish goals or to experience any sense of continuity. They may be called by a name that is unfamiliar, find strange objects in their possession, or be accused of some inconsistent or even criminal behavior. They may be plagued with headaches, nightmares, mental fogginess, amnesia, and many seemingly intractable, confusing, physical problems. The simplest tasks may seem impossible to accomplish and their consciousness may be assaulted with commanding voices controlling their life, or telling them to self-mutilate or even to commit suicide. By definition, such a life has few solid personal relationships and is very lonely. The multiple has often consulted numerous doctors who hypothesize a wide array of physical and psychological diagnoses, including pejorative ones, but who have been of no significant help. The multiple continues to look for help, a friend, an explanation. All in all, life usually seems overwhelming.

Diagnostic Traits

Combining suggestions by Cornelia Wilbur[8], George Greaves[9] and Ralph Allison[10], Greaves, Bradsma, Burns and Damgaard[11] have formulated a list of common diagnostic clues. First, there is a distortion regarding time, including time losses such as blackouts, blank times, seizures, and fits. Second, there are reports that the patient has done something which involves highly uncharacteristic behavior. Third, the patient recalls being addressed by an unfamiliar name or finding objects or writings/drawings in their possession for which there is no knowledge, or hearing voices although inside the head experienced as separate from the patient. Fourth, the use of the pronoun "we" in the patient's speech, when it is used self-reflectively. Finally, there are spontaneous emergings of other personality states during hypnosis. Combined with several of the above symptoms, there is frequently found to be a history of severe headaches, child abuse, neglect, or abandonment.

Etiology

Several ideas have been presented concerning the important contributory factors in the development of MPD. Braun and Sachs[12] have emphasized two major predisposing factors: 1) a natural, inborn capacity to dissociate; and 2) exposure to severe, overwhelming trauma (often physical or sexual abuse). In a detailed study of 100 MPD cases, Putnam et al.[13] found an 83 percent incidence of sexual abuse and a 75 percent incidence of physical abuse during childhood. Frequent, unpredictable, and inconsistently alternating abuse and love can also be significant trauma, and the psychic and environmental atmosphere of extreme ambivalence thereby generated is noted by Greaves[9]. Boor[15] summarized the environmental conditions of children who develop MPD:

> Multiple personality patients often are described as high-minded and idealistic, which are characteristics likely to be fostered by the pronounced religious, authoritarian, or perfectionistic environments that often characterize their childhoods. Arduous standards of conduct required by restrictive environments, coupled with severe family discord, parental psychopathology, physical abuse, sexual trauma, and parental absence or rejection, which in various combinations also usually characterize their childhoods, are likely to foster guilt and ambivalence, especially regarding the expression of anger or sex.

Kluft[14] has suggested a four-factor theory of MPD: 1) the capacity to dissociate; 2) life experiences that traumatically overwhelm the non-dissociative adaptive capacities of the child's ego, such that dissociation is enlisted as a drastic defense; 3) the presence of certain shaping influences and substrates which determine the form taken by the dissociative defenses; and 4) inadequate provision of stimulus barriers, soothing, and restorative experiences by significant others.

Personality Structures

The personality system of an MPD victim is composed of various attitude and behavior complexes termed "ego states". Greaves has distinguished two types of functions around which these ego states form: One, buffer-elements are those ego states which arise in the face of trauma, often during some sadistic, sexual, or an otherwise terrifying act on the part of a significant adult, where the child splits off an ego state to serve as a buffer between the trauma and the original self. In certain traumas a number of serial buffering splits may occur during the incident in order to diffuse psychic energy and prevent a psychotic break. Two, operative ego states arise out of a state of helplessness and are formed to execute specific, necessary tasks (like grocery shopping, caring for children). In some patients there may be elements of these two that have blended.

Several authors have found ways to categorize the ego states within a higher order description. For example, R. B. Allison worked with the three categories—persecutors, rescuers, and inner self-helpers (ISHs).[16] J. D. Beahrs[17] further differentiated persecutors into three types—the demon with disowned rage turned inward, the tyrant with a compulsive and vicious critical parent energy which is aimed at torturing the child ego states, and following Watkins[18] the avenger who first creates an imaginary playmate upon whom all rage is projected, and then forms a subsequent amnesic barrier between the two. S. B. Walters[19] identifies nine prototype elements including: 1) the one who takes the pain; 2) the angry one; 3) the joyful one or the happy hedonist; 4) the intellectual; 5) the nurturer/wise one; 6) the warrior; 7) the task-specific one with Rip Van Winkle effect (may not appear for years if not needed); 8) the inner self-helper; and 9) the presenting personality.[12] G. B. Greaves et al.[11] proposed five category types: 1) the original self; 2) the co-conscious self; 3) inner self-helpers; 4) gatekeeper elements; and 5) persecutor elements, which all seem to be organized around higher level functions for the overall system. In an attempt to synthesize and utilize the key characteristics of the above analysis, I have developed the following categories for a working conceptualization. I have indicated where there may be more than one of a given type of ego states present in the person's system.

The original self is that core structure out of which the entire multiple system develops, sometimes called the "host personality" or "core personality" by others. Frequently the original self ego state is not the dominant ego state or even the ego state which comes for therapy. Originally it was thought that treatment required the abreaction (expressive release of emotions) of traumatic feelings from the other ego states and then a "loading" into this original personality for the integration. Currently, ideas are more flexible and each case is evaluated separately concerning the best ego state to receive the integrations.

The presenting personality is the ego state which brings the person for treatment and is often unaware of the underlying multiplicity. This state is usually quite depressed, confused, and depleted from trying to live an effective and meaningful life without awareness of the individual's fragmented personality structure. It is also the one more likely to be in charge of the day-to-day responsibilities.

The persecutor ego state has encapsulated different parts and amounts of the individual's anger and rage. This state is quite menacing to the body of the patient and is initially dangerous to the patient and therapist, until this energy is rechanneled for constructive purposes. It is expedient to do this redirecting very early in treatment to prevent later crises.

The nurturing/caretaker/wise ego state is able to balance caring and wisdom. It is extremely helpful in nurturing the infant and child states, who need holding and protection in various forms throughout the process of therapy.

The protector ego state can be somewhat like S. B. Walters'[19] warrior, in that its job is protection of the person and it will resort to physical harshness and drastic means if necessary to protect the other states and the integrity of the whole person.

The intellectual ego state is accomplished at clear, facile thinking, undistracted by feelings, and very effective with problem solving and other intellectual tasks. It often has a major cooperative role in insuring the person's survival.

The infant, child, adolescent ego state usually has a specific name, age, and physical appearance (seen internally), and has developed as needed throughout the traumatic childhood of the patient. They vary in number, with the older ones often engaged in a kind of parenting of the younger ones, until relieved by a therapist who understands how to help. Much of the abreactive work is done with these ego states, as they are so frequently created to buffer and absorb emotional pain.

The gatekeeper is an operative ego state formed by the ISH to provide a "gatekeeping" function for the system. The gatekeeper determines which ego state should be active in the body or have consciousness at any given time, thus facilitating a sense of internal balance or control in the whole psychic system. The therapist can shortcut costly clinical time by asking the gatekeeper ego state to make internal contact with the ISH to receive information or guidance and to report that response to the therapist.

The inner self-helper is an ego state which seems to have an executive function over the system. The job of the ISH is to help the person survive until the goal of wholeness can be accomplished. The ISH knows the complete chronological and emotional history of the patient's life and is aware of the multiplicity. It has an awareness of the needs of the person and many creative, grounded ideas regarding the most productive directions to take in therapy (the best co-therapist I've ever had!). Additional characteristics of the ISH will be elaborated upon later.

Ego state A is said to be co-conscious with ego state B if it has memory of the events occurring when B is active. It is possible for A to be co-conscious with B, while B is totally unaware of A's existence, ergo the one-way amnestic barrier so often found in clinical descriptions. A and

B may also be mutually co-conscious. It is helpful to plot diagramatically any multiple's system to keep track of just how the inner consciousness is structured. The only type of ego state found to be consistently co-conscious with all others is the ISH.

Treatment

During the early work with MPD, therapists attempted through hypnosis to bring about integration by simply facilitating shared co-consciousness among the existing or known ego states. This usually resulted in a resplitting on the patient's part when out of hypnosis and experiencing some sort of stress in the real world. Possibly these types of integrations failed to "hold" because of the large amount of highly charged emotional affect bound within a particular ego state. Most therapists currently treating multiple personalities have found that this bound negative affect must be expressed and released in order for one ego state to integrate with another in a permanent manner.

Thigpen and Cleckley thought their widely known patient Eve was "cured" when she was able to create a new and healthier personality which was to be the new ego and leader of the system.[5] However, Eve's autobiography clearly describes the lack of success with that approach, as she later split many more times and required a different mode of treatment for a final successful integration.[20]

Currently a number of prominent clinicians have developed from clinical experience their own individual, overall systems of treatment. Although diverse, each appears to be experiencing success.[21-25] The conceptual model worked out by Greaves and Burns most closely applies to the clinical approach that I employ in my treatment with multiples.[26] Although exhaustive and intensive, this approach, I have found, reduces therapy time considerably and the resulting integration is complete and not a fragile facsimile.

This treatment model rests upon the assumption that "there is an identifiable personality structure in multiple personality that is unique to the disorder, and that psychic energy is distributed at various places in this structure in finite amounts. Furthermore, through psychotherapeutic intervention, the psychic energy can be moved around . . . the structure itself can be made to change".[26] This restructuring is thought to occur through the following eight phases.

Phase One: Transference. The therapist needs to project several qualities to offset the patient's caution or disorientation. These include power sufficient to protect the patient against feared experiences; scrupulous honesty to overrule the amount of previously experienced lying by the patient; patience in the face of the patient's anger; and firmness regarding the overall direction of treatment to help the patient with their resistance. When these have been established, the patient will begin to experience trust and even relief.

Phase Two: Education. During this period of treatment the patient must come to an emotional understanding of multiplicity (often by watching videotape), which can be quite overwhelming and frightening. As these feelings recede the patient is able to learn their system, including the ego states present and their descriptive and functional attributes, needs, and interrelationships.

Phase Three: Alliance. Once the awareness of multiplicity surfaces throughout the system, different ego states form alliances to accomplish certain goals. It is helpful at this step to form a therapeutic alliance with the ISH or gatekeeper ego state immediately, to use its input for shaping and facilitating the therapy process. (Some therapists only consult the ISH ego state when stuck or puzzled.) During the alliance phase the entire history of the multiple's life, including amnestic traumas, can be given in unbelievable detail by the ISH.

Phase Four: Abreaction. This is the most difficult part of the therapy, during which all of the emotionally encapsulated affect and memory are identified and worked through in detail. Any particular traumatic event may take several sessions to release completely. During this phase of therapy the patient will present the most resistance and avoidance due to the intensity of the pain and the issues of trust involved.

Phase Five: Integration. During this phase ego states which have been completely discharged of emotion come together in a permanent blend. Sometimes this occurs spontaneously and at other times hypnotically guided fantasies involving metaphors of coming together which are meaningful to the patient may be helpful. At the end of integration there is still quite a bit of amnesia in the primary personality and resplitting remains a possibility under stress. This is a very abbreviated description of a quite complicated and delicate process.

Phase Six: Post-Integration. The patient at this stage often reports feeling strange. Rather than being compartmentalized they report having the experience of many feelings at once for the first time, and may feel overwhelmed and confused as to how to make decisions and how to operate in the world. Colors may seem vivid, time may seem distorted, as the patient experiences life without splitting for the very first time. Skills may seem temporarily lost and it may be difficult to arrange attitudes and desires in hierarchies for effective decision making. Nightmares occur during this phase as a part of the spontaneous recovery of memory.

Phase Seven: Fusion. Fusion is "that phase which follows the post-integrative phase in which there is dramatic restoration of memory, the patient becomes very stable, and *abandons the capacity for further splitting*".[26] The ISH may be integrated fully or may remain as a voice heard internally. The patient, however, is able to handle emotionally stressful experience without splitting. Often guilt or self-reproach over past behaviors must be worked through.

Phase Eight: Post-Fusion. Time must now be spent with the patient helping to form a new way of living in an integrated consciousness. It is possible that additional therapists may facilitate this process as the new self is learning new ways to be in the world.

Just as the process within one phase may be going on somewhat simultaneously with the process in another, so the movement forward is not as linear as is here laid out. Regardless, the phase definitions are a helpful tool for tracking and mapping the therapy process.

The Inner Self-Helper (ISH)

In 1974 Ralph Allison[2] described the discovery of the inner-self-helping (ISH) ego state in his first multiple patient. A phone call had been made to Dr. Allison the previous weekend that this patient could not remember. She then "found" herself in her car, sitting beside two dirty hitchhikers that she did not remember letting into the car. At this point she had to accept emotionally the fact that she really did have several "personalities" (ego states) with amnestic barriers. She decided to take hold of her therapy and get to the bottom of this confusion. She cleared her house of people, set up a tape recorder, and began to call out and dialogue with Betsy (her raucous element). Betsy consistently and beratingly denied having made the phone call. After 20 or 30 minutes of fighting, a new voice appeared, calm and reasonable, and said:

"I hear you. I'm trying to help you, but I'm warning you, listen clear . . . I've got so much information, if you'll just listen . . . I made the phone call . . . I know everything that's happened. . . . I'm your only hope . . . I'm strong but I have to have your confidence and I have to have your belief in me . . . you and I can become one solid person . . . I'm not going to press myself . . . but I will be there to help you."

Thus spoke the first ISH to be identified, later called Beth by Dr. Allison. This was also the first instance of what is now a commonly used technique called Internal Dialogue Therapy, where communication is facilitated between ego states through tape recordings, hypnotic fantasy meeting,[27] and group therapy,[23] where different ego states have different chairs and move back and forth like a group discussion, drawing on one ego state while another is "in the body", and so on.

Since that time Allison[10] has worked with many MPD patients and has discovered a number of characteristics of the ISH states which seem different from the other ego states. These seem consistent with my experiences with the ISH. There is no date of origin or information ("I have always been with her"). The ISH is not created to handle a patient's unexpressed anger or other feelings from a violent trauma. The ISH is present from birth as a separate ego state. There is no capacity for hate. The ISH feels only love or good will. The ISH expresses both awareness and belief in God and may also believe in the Devil. The ISH serves as a conduit for God's healing power and love. The ISH may be the part which creates the other ego states as needed. The ISH sometimes calls on a higher power for help. It never expresses a desire to lead a separate life—rather it wants to become one with the others. The ISH knows that the condition of multiplicity exists, and understands the patient's entire past history, which is available for easy recall. The ISH can usually predict future actions with great accuracy. The ISH has no conception of gender, referring to the self equally as male or female. Other than love and good will, the ISH lacks emotions, seeming to be pure intellect. The ISH answers questions and communicates in the manner of a computer repeating programmed information, and expects to be a working partner with the therapist and can see the therapist's errors and help correct them. Often the ISH believes in reincarnation and often speaks of being next to God and consequently difficult to summon directly. The ISH is usually not known by the presenting personality. It can often be suppressed by the other ego states, and comes through usually by request of the therapist, unless an emergency is occurring—then the ISH will influence another ego state to call the therapist. Finally the ISH is able to bring memories through to the different ego states, as those are ready to process them.

The ISH is known to have powerful abilities and to be a strong ally. However, there is often active resistance from the presenting personality to working with the ISH once its presence has been established, because the presenting personality may feel inferior, controlled, or overly parented. Allison has gone so far as to state: "Only when all personalities decide to subordinate themselves to the direction and authority of the Beth-personality (ISH), can order come out of chaos, and healing proceed."[2]

Allison calls out the ISH early in therapy to use as co-therapist to the process. This is a procedure similar to the one described during the

Alliance Phase outlined above. In ten patients that I have worked with to date with a reliable MPD diagnosis, eight have one or more ISH states. Another was my first MPD patient when I was unaware of the ISH phenomenon and never requested it. The final patient has some indication of an ISH ego state, but says it is too soon in the process for the ISH to come forward.

Other therapists approach the ISH in a variety of ways. For example, Greaves elicits an ISH only if the therapy seems confused or in need of one.[27] Kluft reports only about 50% of his some 150 MPD patients showing evidence of the ISH ego state, but it is unclear whether he purposely attempts to elicit this state or whether it is occurring spontaneously during the therapy process.[24]

With regard to the spiritual quality of the ISH, Allison[10] mentions three different types of self definitions that he has witnessed: 1) I am God; 2) I am not God; I can make mistakes, but I seldom do; and 3) I am the creation of God's man-made knowledge of God, a teacher on the path of the WAY, leading to real inner truth. This final definition is reminiscent of the Jungian Self archetype.

In his early theory Jung saw the Self as equivalent to the total personality or psyche; however, when he began to explore the racial history of homo sapiens and discovered the presence of archetypes, he found one that represented the human striving for unity.[28] This archetype expresses itself through various symbols, the most familiar being the mandala or magic circle.[29] Hall and Lindsey, prominent personality theorists state:

> The Self is the mid-point of the personality, around which all of the other systems are constellated. It holds these systems together and provides the personality with unity, equilibrium, and stability. . . . The Self is the life's goal, a goal people constantly strive for but rarely reach. Like all archetypes, it motivates man's behavior and causes him to search for wholeness, especially through the avenues provided by religion.[30]

Jung writes about the locus of the self archetype as being poised midway between the conscious and unconscious:

> If we picture the conscious mind with the ego at its centre, as being opposed to the unconscious, and if we now add to our mental picture the process of assimilating the unconscious, we can think of this assimilation as a kind of approximation of conscious and unconscious, where the centre of the total personality no longer coincides with

the ego, but with a point midway between the conscious and the unconscious. This would be the point of a new equilibrium, a new centering of the total personality, a virtual centre which, on account of its focal position between conscious and unconscious, ensures for the personality a new and more solid foundation.[31]

This description could aptly be substituted for what integration might be like for MPD patients, or anyone, for that matter. Jung describes access to a part of our being that has the highest goals of wholeness and balance in the foreground, some kind of contact with the God-energy, and information about our individual systems which might facilitate growth towards a more self-centered existence. This coincides well with our description of the ISH.

Implications For Survival Of Consciousness And Metaphysics
Here I will allow myself total speculative license! Willis Harman lists a number of phenomena which might have suggestive weight for the possibility that consciousness exists apart from the soma; these include near-death experiences, out-of-body experiences, mediumship and past life memories. At a minimum the phenomenon of the ISH could be added to this list as a possible state of consciousness which appears closest to pure spirit or omniscience, and may most closely resemble that aspect of ourselves which could continue beyond physical death.

One of the hallmark research findings in MPD ego state experiments is the discovery that different states vary in regard to internal self perception (physical appearance, age, voice quality, etc.) as well as external physical characteristics, such as visual acuity, EEG patterns, allergies, drug sensitivities, skills, habits, vocabulary, taste discrimination, and performance on IQ and projective tests.[9] In the same physical body an adult ego state who smokes, wears glasses, is right-handed, good at math, allergic to sulfur, with a normal IQ can exist alongside a child ego state who has never smoked, has 20/20 vision, is left-handed, paints, has no medication allergies, and scores in the 130s on the same IQ test. This is suggestive of the tenets of the M-3 (Transcendental Monism) metaphysic, inasmuch as we watch the mind of the ISH create many manifestations of matter (soma) quickly and at will, as different ego states surface and change. Perhaps this is one glimpse of spirit creating and commanding matter again and again.

Rather than being a demonstration of some obtuse form of pathology with particularly entertaining pathonomonic symptoms, MPD is in my estimate one of the most visible demonstrations of the manifest creativity of consciousness. The study of MPD provides a kaleidoscope of glimpses of the human mind, as it goes into action to protect itself from becoming psychotic. The multiple stumbles across the powers of consciousness by accident of heritage. What if we were to explore the arenas of consciousness entered by the multiple by volition? It is incumbent upon the student of the mind, the hopeful for the species, and the believers in a Higher Order to seek the ISH within oneself and to push the edges of their consciousness in search of the potential of other selves within. Long-term behavioral and vocal characteristics are mere puppets to the strings of the complicated consciousness of the multiple. If an individual who is amnestically coping with severe psychic trauma, confusion in their affairs, loneliness, and fear of prosecution for crimes never committed (by memory) can speak several languages (having never remembered learning them), paint professionally in one ego state, and practice medicine while in another, what is the human mind and consciousness capable of under the best conditions? The Bible says that man was created in the image of God. Perhaps, for the sake of the survival of our species and the planet, we will know more of what this means before it is too late.

Thoughts On The Internalization Of God And Reality

Willis Harman reminds us that "ultimately, each one of us bets his life on some picture of reality, recognizing (perhaps), in the scientific sense at least, we can never know."[1] In 15 years of clinical practice I have observed the manner in which most people seem to come to their view. My experience coincides with a model suggested by Clarence Borshure and Barbara Findeisen[32]: 1) I am *unconscious about* a particular subject and it is not even in my awareness. 2) Having heard the topic mentioned, I am *in mystery about* gathering information and have some vague sense of it. 3) I decide to *do something about* gathering information from authority sources in order to evaluate and discover more about this topic. 4) I formulate a *belief system* about it, where I have taken a position and made up my mind regarding it, perhaps even in terms of right or wrong. 5) If my belief system isn't too rigid, I may have an *experience* with feeling, body, mind, and spirit, which seems inconsistent with my belief system. 6) I move to *knowing* about it through trusting my own experience and inner authority. 7) I may then move to *unknowing,* where I let go of limiting beliefs and rely more on trusting without needing to know—"I know I do not know". 8) Ultimately I may move to *natural knowing,* which is the love and wisdom of being in the present without fear, accepting what is with joy and spontaneity, and with ultimately no awareness of differences and separations. *Could this be final integration for all of us?*

Some people seem to establish their personal metaphysic on steps 1-4 and have erected belief systems internalized from other "authorities" by which they live, although usually not without a certain uneasiness that often may surface at the time of death, when "real knowing" seems so important.

Other people emphasize more the knowing from personal experience and while they may recognize limitations here in that we can only experience certain events in any lifetime, still they often seem more at peace with their convictions.

It would be interesting to study the lifestyle, health, emotional happiness, and spiritual definition experienced by groups of people living from the three different metaphysics Harman outlined. Although we would still not know the "true" one, if there be such a thing, we could learn something about the quality of the pre-death experience resulting from each.

Some people take the approach, "Since I can't be certain, why not err in the most useful direction." For instance, a 12-year old boy I once saw in therapy told me: "I don't know if there is a God or not, so I'm going to act all the time as if there is. If there is no God, I haven't lost much, but if there is and I deny it, think of the trouble I will be in!"

My own bias is M-3, which asserts that the "ultimate stuff" of the universe is consciousness. As one of those people who strongly value my own personal inner experience, meditation has allowed me to experience a state of consciousness that feels like M-3 must feel, like the voice of Spirit saying:

> To you who read, I speak. To you, who through long years and much running to and fro, have been eagerly seeking, in books and teaching, in philosophy and religion, for you know not what—Truth, Happiness, Freedom, God; To you whose Soul is weary and discouraged and almost destitute of hope; To you, who many times has obtained a glimpse of that 'Truth' only to find, when you followed and tried to reach it, that it disappeared in the beyond, and was but the mirage of the desert. . . . Who am I? I who speak with such seeming knowledge and authority? Listen! I am you, that part of you who is and knows; who knows all things, and always knew, and always was Yes, I am you, Your Self; that part of you who says I am and is I am; That transcendent, innermost part of you which quickens within as you read, which responds to this. My Word, which perceives its Truth, which recognizes all Truth, and discards all error wherever found. Not that part which has been feeding on error all these years. For I am your real Teacher, the

only real one you will ever know, and the only master. I, your Divine Self.[33]

As I was finishing this paper I happened upon a paper written by Dennis Stillings, one paragraph of which caught my eye:

How would God prove His existence or deliver a message of incontestable authority in the face of modern scientific skepticism? What could the extraordinary proof be for such an extraordinary event? We have built scientific walls a mile high and a hundred feet thick to keep out, a priori, any contact with matters of the spirit. Signs in the physical world are called 'anomalous phenomena', and—if their actual occurrence isn't denied—it is assumed that a 'natural' explanation for such things will be found, which is merely begging the question. If God were to prove His existence, or even give us a short message, what means would He have for doing it? *How could He get our attention?*[34]

Of course, in his paper Stillings was looking at the possibility of the nuclear bomb. I would hope the attempt to address the issues posed by this book would be another alternative.

Footnotes

1. W. H. Harman, "Survival of Consciousness After Death: A Perennial Issue Revisited". Paper prepared for Consciousness and Survival: A Symposium. Washington, DC, October 1985.

2. R. B. Allison, "A New Treatment Approach for Multiple Personalities", *Am.J. Clin. Hypn.* 17:15-32, 1974.

3. P. Janet, *L'Automatisme Psychologique* (Paris: Felix Alcan, 1889).

4. M. Prince, *The Dissociation of a Personality* (New York: Longmans Green, 1906).

5. C. Thigpen, H. Cleckley, *The Three Faces of Eve* (New York: McGraw-Hill, 1957).

6. F. R. Schreiber, *Sybil* (New York: Henry Regenry, 1973).

7. *American Journal of Clinical Hypnosis,* 26: 2, 1983; *Psychiatric Annals,* 14:1, 1984; Psychiatric Clinics of North America, 7:1, 1984; and *International Journal of Clinical and Experimental Hypnosis,* 32: 2, 1984.

7a.   American Psychiatric Association, *Diagnostic and Statistical Manual of Mental Disorders*, Third Edition (Washington, DC: American Psychiatric Association, 1980).

8.   J. M. Brandsma, A. M. Ludwig, "A Case of Multiple Personality Diagnosis and Therapy", *Int. J. Clin. Exp. Hypn.* 22:216-233, 1974.

9.   G. B. Greaves, "Multiple Personality: 165 Years After Mary Reynolds", *J. Nerv. Ment. Dis* .168:577-596, 1980.

10.   R. B. Allison, *Minds in Many Pieces* (New York: Rawson, Wade, 1980).

11.   G. B. Greaves, J. M. Brandsma, J. M. Burns, J. A. Damgaard, "The Phenomenology, Morphology, Dynamics, and Etiology of Complex Multiple Personality and Their Implications for Treatment", unpublished monograph (Atlanta, September 1983).

12.   B. G. Braun, R. G. Sachs, *The Development of Multiple Personality Disorder: Predisposing, Precipitating, and Perpetuating Factors, in Childhood Antecedents of Multiple Personality.* Edited by R. P. Kluft. (Washington, DC, American Psychiatric Press, 1985).

13.   F. W. Putnam, R. M. Post, J. J. Guroff, et al., "100 Cases of Multiple Personality Disorder". Paper presented at the Annual Meeting of the American Psychiatric Association as New Research Abstract #77, New York, 1983.

14.   R. P. Kluft, "Treatment of Multiple Personality Disorder: A Study of 33 Cases", *Psychiat. Clin. North. Am.* 7:9-29, 1984.

15.   M. Boor, "The Multiple Personality Epidemic: Additional Cases and Inferences Regarding Diagnosis, Etiology, Dynamics, and Treatment", *J. Nerv. Ment. Dis.* 170:302-304, 1982.

16.   R. B. Allison, "Psychotherapy of Multiple Personality", unpublished monograph, 1977.

17.   J. O. Beahrs, *Unity and Multiplicity: Multilevel Consciousness of Self in Hypnosis, Psychiatric Disorder and Mental Health* (New York: Brunner/Mazel, 1982).

18.   J. G. Watkins, H. H. Watkins, personal communication, 1980.

19.   S. B. Walters, "A Delineation and Study of the Nature of the Multiple Personality Toward Earlier Diagnosis of the Multiple Personality Syndrome", *Dis. Abst. Int.* 42:10, 1982.

20.   E. Lancaster, *The Final Face of Eve* (New York: McGraw-Hill, 1958).

21.   B. G. Braun, "Age Progression as a Diagnostic, Prognostic, and Therapy Tool", paper presented at the American Society for Clinical Hypnosis, Boston, November, 1981.

22. B. G. Braun, "Hypnosis in the Diagnosis and Treatment of Multiple Personality", paper presented at the Society for Clinical and Experimental Hypnosis, Denver, 1979.

23. David Caul, "Group and Videotape Techniques for Multiple Personality Disorder", *Psychiat. Annal.* 4:43-50, 1985.

24. R. P. Kluft, "An Overview of Treatment", paper presented at the American Psychiatric Association, New Orleans, 1981.

25. M. Bowers, S. Brecher-Marer, B. Newton, et al., "Therapy of Multiple Personality", *Int. J. Clin. Exp. Hypn.* 19:57-65, 1971.

26. G. B. Greaves, S. M. Burns, "Notes on Our Treatment of Multiple Personality", unpublished monograph, Atlanta, 1983.

27. G. B. Greaves, personal communication, 1985.

28. R. Wilhelm, C. G. Jung, *The Secret of the Golden Flower* (New York: Harcourt, Brace, and World, 1931).

29. C. G. Jung, "Mandalas", in *Collected Works, Vol. 9*, Part 1 (Princeton University Press, 1959).

30. C. S. Hall, G. Lindzey, *Theories of Personality* (New York: Wiley, 1970).

31. C. G. Jung, "The Relations Between the Ego and the Unconscious", in *Collected Works, Vol. 7* (Princeton University Press, 1953).

32. C. Borshure, B. Findeisen, personal communication, 1984.

33. Anonymous, *The Impersonal Life* (Marina del Rey: DeVorss, 1941).

34. D. Stillings, "Meditations on the Atom and Time: An Attempt to Define the Imagery of War and Death in the Late Twentieth Century", unpublished monograph, 1985.

X

SURVIVAL OF CONSCIOUSNESS AFTER DEATH: MYTH AND SCIENCE

Stanislav Grof

I have spent all my professional life in a very controversial field, studying the clinical and heuristic potential of non-ordinary states of consciousness induced by psychedelics and various non-drug means. I learnt very early in this process that it was not wise to share indiscriminately the observations of this work with my colleagues. It has been my experience that when scientific observations show a radical departure from the leading paradigms, most professional colleagues tend to question the ability, if not sanity, of the researchers, before they start questioning the validity of their beliefs. During my work in Europe, I found only a handful of professionals who were sufficiently open-minded to look seriously at the new data. This situation started to change when I moved to the United States. As I was traveling and lecturing in this country, I met many like-minded researchers from various disciplines whose findings were as incompatible with traditional thinking in science as my own. They contacted me, because I did not hesitate to talk publicly about certain areas considered taboo in Western science.

I met many anthropologists, parapsychologists, psychologists, psychiatrists, and professionals from other disciplines who had papers and even entire manuscripts stored in drawers, because they did not dare to present the data from their research to their Newtonian-Cartesian colleagues. I am deeply interested in the information in such papers and appreciate very much opportunities that this volume provides to create a more open atmosphere in which h onest exchange is possible.

I would like to say a few words about my background, so that you understand the context from which I have drawn the material I will be discussing. The observations and data to which I will be referring came from two major sources—approximately two decades of psychedelic research with LSD and other psychoactive substances and ten years of work with various experiential non-drug techniques. Since the issues related to psychedelic drugs are associated with many misconceptions, I would like to emphasize that the work in Europe and in the United States that I am referring to was in both instances government sponsored and medically supervised research, conducted in the Psychiatric Research Institute in Prague, Czechoslovakia, and in the Maryland Psychiatric Research Center in Baltimore, Maryland. Its various aspects have been described in several books.[15,16,18]

Participants in these two psychedelic research programs covered a very wide range from "normal volunteers" through various categories of psychiatric patients to individuals dying of cancer. The non-patient population consisted of clinical psychiatrists and psychologists, scientists, artists, philosophers, theologians, students, and psychiatric nurses. The patients with emotional disorders belonged to various diagnostic categories; they included psychoneurotics, alcoholics, narcotic drug addicts, sexual deviants, persons with psychosomatic disorders, borderline cases, and schizophrenics. In the cancer study that included over 150 patients with advanced forms of malignancy, the objective was not treatment of cancer, but relief from emotional and physical pain and change of the attitude toward death through deep mystical experiences induced by psychedelics.[20]

I have conducted personally more than 3,000 psychedelic sessions and have had access to records from over 2,000 additional sessions run by my colleagues in Czechoslovakia, Great Britain, and the USA. The two different approaches that were used in this work are called the *psycholytic* and the *psychedelic* therapeutic technique. They differ in the dosages used, in their treatment strategies, and in the underlying therapeutic philosophies and have been described in detail in another context.[16]

The original motive for the use of LSD and other psychedelic drugs was to explore their potential to intensify, deepen, and accelerate the therapeutic process in Freudian analysis. However, when I started using LSD as a therapeutic tool, it became obvious that the traditional model used in psychoanalysis was superficial and inadequate to account for the broad spectrum of experiences that became available in psychedelic sessions. It was necessary to create a new model of the psyche, much more extensive and encompassing than the one generally accepted in academic psychiatry. In addition to the traditional biographical-recollective level and the Freudian individual unconscious, the new cartography includes the perinatal realm of the psyche, focusing on the phenomena of birth and death, and the transpersonal domain.[15]

Since this research involved a powerful "mind-altering" drug, it is quite natural to question to what extent it is legitimate to use it as a source of data for a psychological theory. There has been a tendency among professionals to see the LSD state as a "toxic psychosis" and the experiences induced by the drug as a chemical phantasmagoria that has very little to do with how the mind functions under more ordinary circumstances. However, systematic clinical research with LSD and related psychedelics has shown that these drugs can best be understood as unspecific amplifiers of mental processes. They do not create the experiences they induce, but activate the deep unconscious and make its contents available for conscious processing. The observations from psychedelic sessions have, therefore, general validity for the understanding of the human psyche.

I have been able to confirm this during the last decade when my wife Christina and I have developed a non-drug experiential technique that we call holotropic therapy. It combines controlled breathing, evocative music, and focused body work. In our workshops where we use this approach, we have been seeing the entire spectrum of experiences characteristic of psychedelic sessions. When the phenomena described in this presentation can be triggered by something as physiological as hyperventilation, there can be no doubt that they reflect genuine properties of the human psyche.

The experiences of all the categories of the new cartography— biographical, perinatal and transpersonal—are quite readily available to most people. They can be observed in sessions with psychedelic drugs, various forms of experiential psychotherapy using breathing, music, dance, and body work, and quite regularly in dreams. Laboratory mind-altering techniques, such as biofeedback, sleep deprivation, sensory isolation or sensory overload, and various kinesthetic devices (the "witches' cradle" or the rotating couch) can also induce many of these phenomena.[17]

There exists a wide spectrum of ancient and Oriental spiritual practices that are specifically designed to facilitate access to the perinatal and transpersonal domains. For this reason, it is not accidental that the new model of the psyche shows great similarity to those developed over the centuries, or even millennia, by various great mystical traditions. It is of special interest to me that this cartography includes also the experiences that are of importance in eschatalogical mythologies, the ancient books of the dead, and other frameworks in which the phenomenon of death (and rebirth) play a significant role.

The entire experiential spectrum has been described by historians, anthropologists and students of comparative religion in the context of various shamanic procedures, aboriginal rites of passage and healing ceremonies, death-rebirth mysteries, and trance dancing in ecstatic religions. Recent consciousness research has thus made it possible for the first time to review seriously ancient and non-Western knowledge about consciousness and aim for a genuine synthesis of age-old wisdom and modern science.

The discussion of the problem of survival of consciousness after death begins with a brief excursion into history and anthropology, taking a crosscultural look at the concepts of death and attitudes toward it. This issue is at the core of the conflict between the mystical worldview of "perennial philosophy", as Aldous Huxley called it,[21] and the understanding of the universe and human nature developed by Western mechanistic science.

In all the ancient and non-Western cultures, we find religious and philosophical systems, cosmologies, ritual practices, and various elements of social organization which are based on the belief that consciousness or existence in some form continues beyond the point of biological demise. Whatever specific concepts of afterlife prevail in the various cultures, in all of them death is seen as a transition or transfiguration and not as the final annihilation of the individual. In some eschatological systems, individual consciousness undergoes a complex posthumous journey with specific stages, ordeals, and abodes; in others it reincarnates and continues to exist on Earth in a new body. An important alternative concept sees death as an opportunity for final liberation and merging with the Absolute.

In all ages and in many different countries, we find more or less elaborate maps guiding the deceased through the eschatological experiential territories. The best known examples of this kind are *The Tibetan Book of the Dead (Bardo Thotrol)* and its Egyptian counterpart, *Pert Em Hru*. However, comparable texts or body of knowledge can be found in the Hindu and the Moslem tradition, in the ancient Mayan culture, and in many other contexts. The medieval European counterpart of these is the *Ars Moriendi* or *Art of Dying*.[31]

In addition, ancient and non-Western cultures have developed a variety of powerful ritual events that can be seen as experiential training for death. In a supportive, socially sanctioned context, these gave the initiate an opportunity to experience a profound encounter with death and transcendence. Rituals of this kind combine two important functions: On the one hand, they mediate a deep process of transformation in the neophyte, who discovers an entirely new way of being in the world. On the other, they help overcome the fear of death and serve as a preview of and preparation for actual dying. The rites of passage of different cultures[13] and the ancient mysteries of death and rebirth based on the myths of Tammuz and Ishtar, Isis and Osiris, Pluto and Persephone, Attis, Adonis, and Wotan can be mentioned here as important examples. Many of the experiences that were instrumental in such training for dying belong to the standard repertoire of psychedelic states and of sessions with the new experiential psychotherapies.

The situation in Western cultures in regard to death and dying is radically different from the attitudes and practices described above. An educated Westerner subscribes to the assumption of mechanistic science that consciousness is a product of the physiological processes in the brain and ceases to exist at the time of biological death. He or she sees the belief in any form of afterlife and the concept of the "posthumous journey of the soul" as expressions of primitive fears, magical thinking, and superstition. Modern society has isolated aging, sick, and dying individuals in nursing homes and hospitals. Medicine exhibits its technological wizardry in mechanical prolongation of life and treats the dying in isolation from meaningful human support. Until recently, the massive denial of death characteristic of Western civilization extended into psychology and psychiatry that showed little interest in the death experience and offered no psychological support for the dying.

The attitude of Western culture toward the possibility of survival of consciousness after death is closely related to its attitude toward spirituality. If the mechanistic paradigm were actually a true and complete description of reality, an enlightened understanding of the universe based on science would involve acceptance of one's own insignificance as one of four billions of inhabitants of one of the countless celestial bodies in an immense universe that has millions of galaxies. It would also require the recognition that humans are nothing but highly developed animals and biological machines composed of cells, tissues, and organs. In this context, our consciousness is a physiological product of the brain and our psyche is governed by unconscious forces of a biological and instinctual nature. Biological death that involves material destruction of the body and brain then clearly means final and irreversible cessation of consciousness in any form.

When deep spiritual convictions are found in non-Western cultures, with inadequate educational systems, this is usually attributed to ignorance, childlike gullibility, and superstition. In our own culture, such an interpretation obviously will not do, particularly if it occurs in well-educated persons with superior intelligence. Here mainstream psychiatry resorts to the findings of psychoanalysis suggesting that the roots of religious beliefs can be found in unresolved conflicts from infancy and early childhood. It interprets the concept of deities as infantile images of parental figures, the religious attitudes of the believers as signs of emotional immaturity and childlike dependency, and ritual activities as results of a struggle against early psychosexual impulses, comparable to the mechanisms found in obsessive-compulsive neuroses.[12]

Direct spiritual experiences, such as feelings of cosmic unity, death-rebirth sequences, encounters with archetypal entities, visions of light of supernatural beauty, or past incarnation memories are then seen as gross distortions of "objective reality" indicative of a serious mental disease. Anthropologists have discussed shamanism usually in the context of schizophrenia, hysteria, or epilepsy and psychopathological labels have been put on all the great prophets and sages. Even meditation has been discussed in a psychopathological context.[1] With a few exceptions, such as the work of Carl Gustav Jung, Roberto Assagioli, and Abraham Maslow, there has been no recognition of spirituality in Western psychiatry and no notion that there might be some difference between mysticism and psychosis.

I have tried to demonstrate in another context[8] the errors involved in this approach to spirituality. To confuse the Newtonian-Cartesian model of reality with reality itself means to ignore modern philosophy of science with its understanding of the nature of scientific theories and the dynamics of paradigms. In addition, it constitutes a serious logical error; by confusing the map with the territory in Korzybski's sense,[26] it violates the principle of logical typing, which used to be a favorite topic of Gregory Bateson.[2,3]

However, above all, this approach extrapolates the findings from basic sciences into psychology and ignores a vast body of observations from modern consciousness research, particularly those related to trans-personal experiences. Any serious scientific theory has to be an attempt to organize the existing facts, rather than a product of speculative extrapolation. It has to be based on observations of the universe and not on the beliefs of scientists as to what the universe is like or their wishes for what it should be like to fit their theories.

The data accumulated by modern consciousness research throw an entirely new light on the problem of spirituality, in general, and of consciousness after death, in particular. It is absolutely mandatory for the advancement of our understanding of the universe and of human nature to take these data seriously and review drastically the present attitude of most scientists who either are not familiar with this evidence or ignore it. In psychedelic sessions, in experiential psychotherapy, in various forms of meditation, and in spontaneous non-ordinary states of consciousness one can directly experience many of the phenomena described in perennial philosophy and in eschatalogical mythologies.

The content of these experiences is so convincing and self-evident that they typically convey not the sense of "believing", but of "knowing".[23] This naturally is not enough as scientific evidence for the relevance of these insights and could easily be dismissed as psychotic delusions. However, careful study of the phenomenology of these experiences, of the surrounding circumstances, and of the interface between the experiential content and "objective reality" shows that the testimony of the individuals who have experienced non-ordinary states of this kind has to be taken with utmost seriousness.

Fascinating data of this kind have been rapidly accumulating in several modern disciplines. The most important evidence comes from experimental psychiatry and research of non-ordinary states of consciousness induced by psychedelics and various non-drug means, experiential psychotherapies, the new field of thanatology exploring dying and death, parapsychology, study of multiple personalities, field anthropology, and reincarnation studies. Developments in many other disciplines pointing to a radically new image of the universe and human nature, referred to globally as the emerging paradigm, then help to create a context for unbiased study of these new frontiers of science.

I will now focus on the observations from my own research of non-ordinary states of consciousness that are related, indirectly or directly, to the problem of survival. These fall into two different categories. The first of them are perinatal experiences, powerful sequences that involve a profound encounter with death and reliving of birth. They seem to be indistinguishable phenomenologically and experientially from actual dying and result in loss of fear of death and in dramatic changes in one's way of being in the world and hierarchy of values. They represent a real experiential training for death. This statement is based not only on their great similarity to near-death experiences and experiences of clinical death, but also on reports of several cancer patients who had exerienced first the death-rebirth sequences in psychedelic sessions and later actual near-death experiences. I will not discuss the perinatal phenomena in this context and will refer those of you who are interested in this topic to my previous writings.[15,16,19]

Here I will focus on the second category of observations from my research, the transpersonal experiences. I will first discuss the entire group of these experiences, since their existence undermines the mechanistic model of the universe that is the major obstacle in a serious approach to the problem of survival. They suggest that consciousness is not an accidental product of matter, but an equal partner of matter, or even possibly a principle supraordinated to matter. Such a new understanding that sees consciousness as essentially independent of matter naturally provides a context within which the possibility of its surviving physical death appears much more plausible. After a general discussion of transpersonal experiences, I will focus on those types of transpersonal phenomena that are directly related to the problem of consciousness after death. Here belong, particularly, the experiences of communication with discarnate entities, visions of astral realms, out-of-body experiences, and past incarnation memories.

Transpersonal Experiences

Experiential sequences of death and rebirth typically open the gate to a transbiographical domain in the human psyche that can best be referred to as transpersonal. The perinatal level of the unconscious clearly represents an interface between the biographical and the transpersonal realms, or the individual and the collective unconscious. In most instances, transpersonal experiences are preceded by a dramatic encounter with birth and death. However, there exists also an important alternative; occasionally, it is possible to access experientially various transpersonal elements and themes directly, without confronting the perinatal level. The common denominator of this rich and ramified group of transpersonal phenomena is the subject's feeling that his or her consciousness has expanded beyond the usual ego boundaries and has transcended the limitations of time and space.

In ordinary states of consciousness, we experience ourselves as existing within the boundaries of the physical body (the body image) and our perception of the environment is restricted by the physically and physiologically determined range of our sensory organs. Both our

internal perception (interoception) and external perception (exteroception) are confined by the usual spatial and temporal boundaries.
Under ordinary circumstances, we can experience vividly and with all
our senses only the events in the present moment and in our immediate
environment. We can recall the past and anticipate future events or
fantasize about them; however, the past and the future are not available for direct experience.

In transpersonal experiences, as they occur in psychedelic sessions,
self-exploration through non-drug experiential techniques or spontaneously, one or more of the usual limitations appear to be transcended.
Experiences of this kind can be divided into three large categories.
Some of them involve transcendence of linear time and are interpreted
by the subjects as historical regression and exploration of their biological, cultural, and spiritual past, or as historical progression into the future. In the second category, experiences are characterized primarily
by transcendence of the ordinary spatial boundaries rather than temporal barriers. The third group is characterized by experiential exploration of domains that in Western culture are not considered part of objective reality.

In non-ordinary states of consciousness, many people experience
very concrete and realistic episodes which they identify as fetal and
embryonal memories. It is not unusual under these circumstances to experience (on the level of cellular consciousness) full identification with
the sperm and the ovum at the time of conception. Sometimes historical regression goes even further and the experient has a convinced feeling of reliving memories from the lives of his or her ancestors, or even
drawing on the memory banks of the racial or collective unconscious. On
occasion, individuals report experiences in which they identify with
various animal ancestors in the evolutionary pedigree, or have a distinct sense of reliving dramatic episodes from a previous incarnation.

Transpersonal experiences that involve transcendence of spatial
barriers suggest that the boundaries between the individual and the
rest of the universe are not fixed and absolute. Under special circumstances it is possible to identify experientially with anything in the
universe, including the entire cosmos itself. Here belong the experiences of merging with another person into a state of dual unity or assuming
another person's identity, tuning into the consciousness of a specific
group of people, or of expansion of one's consciousness to such an extent
that it seems to encompass all of humanity. In a similar way, one can
transcend the limits of the specifically human experience and identify
with consciousness of animals, plants, or consciousness related to inorganic objects and processes. It is even possible to experience conscious-

ness of the entire biosphere, of our planet, or of the entire material universe.

In a large group of transpersonal experiences, the extension of consciousness seems to go beyond the phenomenal world and the time-space continuum as we perceive it in our everyday life. Here belong numerous visions of archetypal personages and themes, encounters with deities and demons of various cultures, and complex mythological sequences. Additional examples are reports of appearances of spirits of deceased people, suprahuman entities, and inhabitants of other universes.

Visions of abstract archetypal patterns, intuitive understanding of universal symbols (cross, ankh, yin-yang, swastika, pentacle, or six-pointed star), experiences of the meridians and of the flow of chi energy as described in Chinese philosophy and medicine, or the arousal of the Serpent Power (Kundalini) and activation of various centers of psychic energy, or chakras, are additional examples of this category of phenomena. In its furthest reaches, individual consciousness can identify with cosmic consciousness or the Universal Mind. The ultimate of all experiences appears to be identification with the Supracosmic and Metacosmic Void, the mysterious primordial emptiness and nothingness that is conscious of itself and contains all existence in a germinal and potential form.

Transpersonal experiences have many strange characteristics that shatter the most fundamental assumptions of materialistic science and of the mechanistic worldview. Researchers who have seriously studied and/or experienced these fascinating phenomena realize that the attempts of traditional psychiatry to dismiss them as irrelevant products of imagination or as erratic phantasmagoria generated by pathological processes in the brain are superficial and inadequate. Any unbiased study of the transpersonal domain of the psyche has to come to the conclusion that these observations represent a critical challenge for the Newtonian-Cartesian paradigm of Western science.

Although transpersonal experiences occur in the process of deep individual self-exploration, it is not possible to interpret them simply as intrapsychic phenomena in the conventional sense. On the one hand, they form an uninterrupted experiential continuum with biographical-recollective and perinatal experiences. On the other hand, they seem to be tapping directly, without the mediation of the sensory organs, sources of information that are clearly outside of the conventionally defined range of the individual.

The reports of people who have experienced episodes of embryonal existence, the moment of conception, and elements of cellular, tissue and organ consciousness, abound in medically accurate insights into the anatomical, physiological and biochemical aspects of the processes involved. Similarly, ancestral experiences, racial and collective memories in the Jungian sense, and past incarnation memories frequently bring quite specific details about architecture, costumes, weapons, art, social structure and religious practices of the culture and period involved, or even concrete historical events.

Persons who experience phylogenetic sequences or identification with existing life forms not only find them unusually convincing and authentic, but also acquire extraordinary insights concerning animal psychology, ethology, specific habits or unusual reproductive cycles. In some instances, these experiences are accompanied by archaic-muscular innervations not characteristic for humans, or even such complex performances as enactment of a courtship dance.

Those individuals who experience episodes of conscious identification with plants or parts of plants occasionally report remarkable insights into such botanical processes as germination of seeds, photosynthesis in the leaves, the role of auxins in plant growth, exchange of water and minerals in the root system, or pollination. Equally common is a convinced sense of conscious identification with inanimate matter or inorganic processes—the water in the ocean, fire, lightning, volcanic activity, tornado, gold, diamond, granite, and even stars, galaxies, atoms, and molecules.

There exists another interesting group of transpersonal phenomena that can be frequently validated and even researched experimentally. Here belong telepathy, psychic diagnosis, clairvoyance, clairaudience, precognition, psychometry, out-of-the-body experiences, traveling clairvoyance, and other instances of extrasensory perception. This is the only group of transpersonal phenomena that has been occasionally discussed in the past in academic circles, unfortunately with a strong negative bias.

From a broader perspective, there is no reason to sort out the so-called paranormal phenomena as a special category. Since many other types of transpersonal experiences quite typically involve access to new information about the universe through extrasensory channels, the clear boundary between psychology and parapsychology disappears, or becomes rather arbitrary when the existence of the transpersonal domain is recognized and acknowledged.

The philosophical challenge associated with the observations described above—formidable as it may be in itself—is further augmented by the fact that in non-ordinary states of consciousness, transpersonal experiences correctly reflecting the material world appear on the same continuum as—and intimately interwoven with—others whose content according to the Western worldview is not part of objective reality. We can mention in this context the Jungian archetypes—the world of deities, demons, demigods, superheroes and complex mythological, legendary and fairy-tale sequences. Even these experiences can impart accurate new information about religious symbolism, folklore and mythical structures of various cultures about which the person previously had no knowledge.

The ability of transpersonal experiences to convey instant intuitive information about any aspect of the universe in the present, past and future violates some of the most basic assumptions of mechanistic science. They imply such seemingly absurd notions as relativity and arbitrary nature of all physical boundaries, non-local connections in the universe, communication through unknown means and channels, memory without a material substrate, non-linearity of time, or consciousness associated with all living organisms (including lower animals, plants, unicellular organisms and viruses) and even inorganic matter.

Many transpersonal experiences involve events from the microcosm and macrocosm—realms that cannot be directly reached by human senses—or from periods that historically precede the origin of the solar system, formation of planet Earth, appearance of living organisms, development of the central nervous system, and appearance of homo sapiens. This clearly implies that, in a yet unexplained way, each human being contains the information about the entire universe or all of existence, has potential experiential access to all its parts, and in a sense is the whole cosmic network, as much as he or she is just an infinitesimal part of it, a separate and insignificant biological entity.

While the nature of transpersonal experience is clearly fundamentally incompatible with mechanistic science, it can be integrated with the revolutionary developments in various scientific disciplines that have been referred to as the emerging paradigm. Among the disciplines and concepts that have significantly contributed to this drastic change in the scientific worldview are quantum-relativistic physics, astrophysics, cybernetics, information and systems theory, Sheldrake's theory of morphic resonance,[41] Prigogine's study of dissipative structures and order by fluctuation,[36] David Bohm's theory of holomovement,[7] Karl Pribram's holographic model of the brain,[34] and Arthur Young's theory of process.[45]

Experiences Of Discarnate Entities And Astral Realms

Experiences that belong to this category have been the primary focus of interest to the participants in spiritistic seances, to researchers in the area of survival after death, and to writers of occult literature.

They involve encounters and telepathic communication with deceased relatives and friends, contacts with discarnate entities in general, and experiences of the astral realm. In the simplest form of this experience, subjects see apparitions of deceased people and receive from them various messages. The content of these messages can either be addressed to the experiencer, or the recipient can be used as a channel to deliver them to other people. Experiences of this kind have been reported by psychedelic subjects, clients in experiential psychotherapies, and individuals who had near-death experiences.[27,30,31]

Sometimes, the subject does not perceive an individual discarnate entity, but an entire astral realm with various ghostly apparitions. Raymond Moody's description of the "realm of confused spirits" is an example.[30] In a more complex form of this phenomenon, the subject actually enters a trance state and appears to be taken over by an alien entity or energy form. Events of this kind observed in sessions of experiential psychotherapy with or without psychedelic drugs bear a striking resemblance to mediumistic trances occurring in spiritistic seances.[5,6]

In such trances the subject's facial expression is strikingly transformed, the postures and gestures appear bizarre and alien, and the voice is dramatically changed. I have seen individuals in this state talk in languages they did not know, speak in tongues, write automatic texts, produce obscure hieroglyphic designs, and draw intricate unintelligible squiggles. These manifestations are again very reminiscent of those described in spiritistic and occult literature. Most fascinating examples of this phenomenon can be observed in the Spiritist Church in the Philippines and Brazil, inspired by the teachings of Allan Kardec.[24,25]

If the experiences of communication with discarnate entities and spirits of dead friends and relatives involved just visions of these persons and a subjective sense of interaction, the situation would be relatively simple. In that case, these phenomena could be easily discounted as figments of imagination combining elements of memory, human fantasy, and wishful thinking. However, the situation is much more complex than that. Before we discard these phenomena as being absurd and not worth the interest of reputable researchers, let me mention some observations that deserve serious attention.

As the following two examples indicate, experiences of this kind have sometimes certain extraordinary aspects that are not easy to explain. I have personally observed several instances where sequences involving discarnate relatives and friends provided some unusual and verifiable information that the recipients could not have possibly obtained through ordinary means and channels. Similarly, individuals who receive messages from "deceased strangers" find to their great surprise that they have been given an existing address and correct name of the relatives of a person who actually recently died.

Personal survival of physical death is not necessarily the only explanation for these findings and it is certainly possible to conceive of other interpretations than actual communication with objectively existing astral realms of discarnate beings. However, one thing is certain: None of the alternative explanations will be compatible with the traditional Newtonian-Cartesian thinking. In any case, we are dealing here with fascinating phenomena in their own right that should be systematically studied.

To discard the extraordinary features of these experiences and the conceptual challenges associated with them, just because they do not fit the current paradigms in science, certainly is not the best example of a scientific approach. We have to accept the universe as it is, rather than imposing on it what we believe it is or think it should be. Our theories have to deal with the facts in their totality, rather than with a convenient selection of them that fits our worldview and belief system. Until modern Western science is able to offer plausible explanation of all the observations surrounding such phenomena as spiritistic experiences and past incarnation memories, the concepts found in mystical and occult literature have to be seen as superior to the present approach of most Western scientists, who either do not know the facts or ignore them.

The first illustrative example is from psycholytic treatment of a young depressed homosexual patient, whose history was briefly described in my book *Realms of the Human Unconscious* (Ref. 15, pp 57-60) under the name Richard.

In one of his LSD sessions, Richard had a very unusual experience involving a strange and uncanny astral realm. It had an eery luminescence and was filled with discarnate beings that were trying to communicate with him in a very urgent and demanding manner. He could not see or hear them; however, he sensed their almost tangible presence and was receiving telepathic messages from them. I wrote down one of these messages that was very specific and could be subjected to subsequent verification.

It was a request for Richard to connect with a couple in the Moravian city of Kromeriz and let them know that their son Ladislav was doing all right and was well taken care of. The message included the couple's name, street address, and telephone number; all of these data were unknown to me and the patient. This experience was extremely puzzling; it seemed to be an alien enclave in Richard's experience, totally unrelated to his problems and the rest of his treatment.

After some hesitation and with mixed feelings, I finally decided to do what certainly would have made me the target of my colleagues' jokes had they found out. I went to the telephone, dialed the number in Kromeriz, and asked if I could speak with Ladislav. To my astonishment, the woman on the other side of the line started to cry. When she calmed down, she told me with a broken voice: "Our son is not with us anymore; he passed away, we lost him three weeks ago."

The second illustrative example involves a close friend and former colleague of mine, Walter N. Pahnke, who was a member of our psychedelic research team at the Maryland Psychiatric Research Center in Baltimore. He had deep interest in parapsychology, particularly in the problem of consciousness after death, and worked with many famous mediums and psychics, including his friend Eileen Garrett, President of the American Parapsychological Association. In addition, he was also the initiator of the LSD program for patients dying of cancer.

In summer 1971, Walter went with his wife Eva and his children for a vacation in a cabin in Maine, situated right on the ocean. One day, he went scuba-diving all by himself and did not return from the ocean. Extensive and well-organized search failed to find his body or any part of his diving gear. Under these circumstances, Eva found it very difficult to accept and integrate his death. Her last memory of Walter when he was leaving the cabin involved him full of energy and in perfect health. It was hard for her to believe that he was not part of her life anymore and to start a new chapter of her existence without a sense of closure of the preceding one.

Being a psychologist herself, she qualified for an LSD training session for mental health professionals offered through a special program in our institute. She decided to have a psychedelic experience with the hope of getting some more insights and asked me to be her sitter. In the second half of the session, she had a very powerful vision of Walter and carried on a long and meaningful dialogue with him. He gave her specific instructions concerning each of their three children and released her to start a new life of her own, unencumbered and unrestricted by a sense of commitment to his memory. It was a very profound and liberating experience.

Just as Eva was questioning whether the entire episode was just a wishful fabrication of her own mind, Walter appeared once more for a brief period of time with the following request: "By the way, I forgot one thing. Would you please do me a favor and return a book that I borrowed from a friend of mine. It is in my study in the attic." And he proceeded to give her the name of the friend, the name of the book, the shelf, and the sequential order of the book on this shelf. Following the instructions, Eva was actually able to find and return the book, about the existence of which she had had no previous knowledge.

It would certainly have been completely consistent with Walter's lifelong search for a scientific proof of paranormal phenomena to add a concrete and testable piece of information to his interaction with Eva to dispel her doubts. Earlier during his life, he had made an agreement with Eileen Garrett that she would try to give him after her death an unquestionable proof of the existence of the beyond.

Out-of-Body Experiences (OOBE)

The experience of consciousness detaching from one's body, or out-of-body experience (OOBE), has various forms and degrees. It can take the form of isolated episodes, or occur repeatedly as part of psychic opening and other types of transpersonal crises. Among the circumstances that are particularly conducive to OOBEs are vital emergencies, near-death situations, experiences of clinical death, sessions of deep experiential psychotherapy, and ingestion of psychedelic substances, especially the dissociative anesthetic Ketamine (Ketalar). Classical descriptions of OOBEs can be found in spiritual literature and philosophical texts of all ages, particularly in the *Tibetan Book of the Dead (Bardo Thotrol)* and other similar literature. These descriptions were not taken seriously by traditional science until recently when modern research in experimental psychiatry and thanatology confirmed their authenticity.

During less extreme forms of OOBE, one has a sense of leaving the body, detaching from it, and seeing oneself from various distances as an object (heautoscopy). In more advanced forms of OOBE, the individual experiences himself or herself in other rooms of the building, in remote locations (astral projection), flying above the Earth, or moving away from it. A particularly dramatic and moving description of an OOBE in a near-death state can be found in the autobiography of Carl Gustav Jung.[22] In these states the subject can accurately witness events in the areas to which detached consciousness projects. Although this should be in principle impossible according to Cartesian-Newtonian science, the authenticity of this phenomenon has been repeatedly confirmed and is beyond any doubt.

The research of Raymond Moody,[30,31] Kenneth Ring,[38,39] Michael Sabom,[40] Elisabeth Kubler-Ross,[27] my own study,[18] and work of many others have repeatedly confirmed that clinically dead people can have OOBEs during which they accurately witness the resuscitation procedures from a position near the ceiling, or perceive events in remote locations. According to Elisabeth Kubler-Ross, even blind persons have under these circumstances the ability to perceive the environment visually in colors. Modern thanatological research thus confirms the descriptions from the *Tibetan Book of the Dead*, according to which an individual after death assumes the "bardo body" that transcends the limitations of time and space and can freely travel around the Earth.

Observations from psychedelic research, holotropic breathing, and other types of experiential psychotherapy similarly confirmed the possibility of authentic OOBEs during visionary states, as they have been reported in various mystical sources and anthropological literature. Clairvoyance and clairaudience of remote events can occur without a sense of actually being there, in the form of astral travel to the location involved, or as instant astral projection. In rare instances, the subject can actually actively control and direct the astral space travel. The renowned OOBE veteran and researcher Robert Monroe[29], who had struggled for many years with spontaneous and elemental OOBEs, not only learnt how to control them, but also developed specific exercises and electronic technology to facilitate their occurrence. The authenticity of OOBEs has been demonstrated in controlled clinical experiments by the famous psychologist and parapsychologist Charles Tart at the University of California in Davis.[43]

The following example is a remarkable out-of-body experience with accurate perception of a remote location reported by Kimberly Clark who works as a social worker in Seattle. The circumstances of this case were so extraordinary and convincing that the event instigated in her a lasting interest in OOBEs.

My first encounter with a near-death experiencer involved a patient named Maria, a migrant worker who was visiting friends in

Seattle and had a severe heart attack. She was brought into the hospital by rescue squad one night and admitted to the coronary care unit. I got involved in her case as a result of her social and financial problems. A few days after her admission, she had a cardiac arrest. Because she was so closely monitored and was otherwise in good health, she was brought back quickly, intubated for a couple of hours to make sure that her oxygenation was adequate, and then extubated.

Later in the day I went to see her, thinking that she might have some anxiety about the fact that her heart had stopped. In fact, she was anxious, but not for that reason. She was in a state of relative agitation, in contrast to her usual calmness. She wanted to talk to me about something. She said: 'The strangest thing happened when the doctors and nurses were working on me: I found myself looking down from the ceiling at them working on my body.'

I was not impressed at first. I thought that she might know what had been going on in the room, what people were wearing, and who would be there, since she had seen them all prior to her cardiac arrest. Certainly she was familiar with the equipment by that time. Since hearing is the last sense to go, I reasoned that she could hear everything that was going on, and while I did not think she was consciously making this up, I thought it might have been a confabulation.

She then told me that she had been distracted by something over the emergency room driveway and found herself outside, as if she had 'thought herself' over the emergency room driveway and, in just that instant, she was out there. At this point, I was a little more impressed, since she had arrived at night inside an ambulance and would not have known what the emergency room area looked like. However, I reasoned that perhaps at some point in time her bed had been by the window, she had looked outside, and this had been incorporated into the confabulation.

But then Maria proceeded to describe being further distracted by an object on the third floor ledge on the north end of the building. She 'thought her way' up there and found herself 'eyeball to shoelace' with a tennis shoe, which she asked me to try to find for her. She needed someone else to know that the tennis shoe was really there to validate her out-of-body experience.

With mixed emotions, I went outside and looked up at the ledges but could not see much at all. I went up to the third floor and began going in and out of patients' rooms and looking out their windows, which were so narrow that I had to press my face to the screen just to see the ledge at all. Finally, I found a room where I pressed my face to the glass and looked down and saw the tennis shoe!

My vantage point was very different from what Maria's had to have been for her to notice that the little toe had worn a place in the shoe and that the lace was stuck under the heel and other details about the side of the shoe not visible to me. The only way she would have had such a perspective was if she had been floating right outside and at very close range to the tennis shoe. I retrieved the shoe and brought it back to Maria; it was very concrete evidence for me.

Past Incarnation Experiences

This is probably the most fascinating and controversial group of transpersonal phenomena. Past incarnation memories resemble in many ways ancestral, racial, and collective experiences. However, they are usually very dramatic and are associated with an intense emotional charge of a negative or positive quality. Their essential experiential characteristic is a convinced sense of remembering something that happened once before to the same entity, to the same unit of consciousness. The subjects participating in these dramatic sequences maintain a sense of individuality and personal identity, but experience themselves in another form, at another place and time, and in another context.

This sense of reliving something that one has seen before (déja vu) and experienced before (déja vecu) in a previous incarnation is basic and cannot be analyzed any further. It is comparable to the ability to distinguish in everyday life our memories of events that actually happened from our dreams and fantasies. It would be very difficult to convince a person who is relating to us a memory of some-thing that happened last week that the event involved did not really occur and that it is just a figment of his or her imagination. Past incarnation memories have a similar subjective quality of authenticity and reality.

Karmic experiences fall into two distinct categories characterized by the quality of the emotions involved. Some of them reflect highly positive connections with other persons—deep friendship, passionate love, spiritual partnership, teacher-disciple relationship, blood bonds, life and death commitment, extraordinary mutual understanding, or nourishing and supportive exchange. More frequently, they involve dramatic negative emotions. The experiences belonging to this category cast subjects into various internecine past life situations characterized by agonizing physical pain, murderous aggression, inhuman terror, prolonged anguish, bitterness and hatred, insane jealousy, insatiable vengefulness, uncontrollable lust, or morbid greed and avarice.

Many individuals who have experienced negative karmic experiences were able to analyze the nature of the destructive bond between the protagonists of such sequences. They realized that all these seemingly different emotional qualities—such as murderous passion, insatiable desire, consuming jealousy, or mortal anguish—when intensified beyond a certain point, actually begin to resemble each other. There seems to exist a state of high biological and emotional arousal, in which all the extreme affective qualities converge and reach metaphysical dimensions. When two or more individuals reach this universal "melting pot" of passions and instincts, they get imprinted on the situation that caused them, irrespective of the role which they played.

In situations of extreme experiential intensity, the sadistic arousal of the torturer and the inhuman pain of the victim increasingly resemble each other and the rage of the murderer merges at a certain point with the anguish and suffering of the dying victim. According to the insights of the individuals who have had past life experiences, it is this emotional fusion rather than a specific role in the experiential sequence that is instrumental in karmic imprinting. Whenever two individuals get involved in a situation where their emotions reach the state described above, they will have to repeat in subsequent lives in alternating roles the same pattern until they reach the level of awareness which is necessary for the resolution of a karmic bond.

Sophisticated subjects familiar with spiritual literature equated this state of undifferentiated emotional arousal that generates karmic bondage with the Buddhist concept of tanha, the "thirst of flesh and blood", the force that drives the cycle of death and rebirth and is responsible for all human suffering. Others reported their insights into the deep similarity between this state and the strange experiential mixture of emotions and sensations characterizing the final stages of biological delivery. Birth thus seems to represent something like a transformation station, where the intangible "morphogenetic fields" of the karmic record (referred to as the "akashic record" in the spiritual literature) enter the biopsychological life of the individual.

The opening of the realm of past incarnation experiences is sometimes preceded by or associated with complex insights and instructions communicated by non-verbal means. In this way, the individual is introduced to the understanding that the law of karma is an important part of the cosmic order mandatory for all sentient beings. On the basis of this new comprehension, he or she accepts responsibility for the deeds in previous lifetimes that at the time are still covered by amnesia. In addition to this general information, such insights can include details of the mechanisms involved in the cycles of rebirth and the necessary strategies for attaining liberation from karmic bonds.

To reach a sense of complete resolution of a karmic pattern or bond, the individual has to experience fully all the painful emotions and physical sensations involved in a destructive past incarnation scene. In addition, it is necessary to transcend the event emotionally, ethically, philosophically, and spiritually, rise above it entirely, and forgive and be forgiven. Such a full liberation from a karmic pattern and the bondage involved is typically associated with a sense of paramount accomplishment and triumph that is beyond any rational comprehension. When it occurs, it is associated with an overwhelming feeling that one has waited for this moment and worked for the achievement of this goal for centuries. At this point, nothing in the world seems more important than to free oneself from karmic bondage.

This is typically associated with an ecstatic rapture and feelings of overwhelming bliss. In some instances, the individual can see a rapid replay of his or her karmic history and have clear insights as to how this pattern repeated itself in different variations through the ages and has contaminated lifetime after lifetime. Several subjects reported in this context the experience of something like a cleansing "karmic hurricane" or "cyclone" blowing through their past and tearing their karmic bonds in all the situations that involve the pattern which they just resolved.

Past incarnation phenomena are extremely common in deep experiential psychotherapy and have great therapeutic potential. They have also far-reaching theoretical significance, since several of their aspects represent a serious challenge to the mechanistic and materialistic worldview. A therapist who does not allow experiences of this kind to develop in his or her clients or discourages them when they are spontaneously happening is giving up a powerful mechanism of healing and personality transformation. Since the major hindrance in this sense is a philosophical disbelief in reincarnation and karma based on insufficient knowledge of the facts, I would like to explore this issue at some length.

It seems clear that the past incarnation phenomena observed in deep experiential psychotherapy, in meditation, and in spontaneous episodes of non-ordinary states of consciousness are identical with those that are responsible for the fact that the belief in reincarnation is so widespread and universal. The concept of karma and reincarnation represents a cornerstone of Hinduism, Buddhism, Jainism, Sikhism, Zoroastrianism, and the Tibetan Vajrayana Buddhism. Similar ideas can be found in such geographically, historically, and culturally diverse groups as various African tribes, American Indians, pre-Columbian cultures, the Polynesian Kahunas, the Gauls, and the Druids. In ancient Greece, several important schools of thought subscribed to it; among these were the Pythagoreans, the Orphics, and the Platonists. This doctrine was also adopted by the Essenes, the Pharisees, the Karaites, and other Jewish and semi-Jewish groups, and it formed an important part of the kabbalistic theology of medieval Jewry. It was also held by the Neoplatonists and Gnostics and in modern times by the Anthroposophists and certain Spiritualists.

It is not very well known that concepts similar to reincarnation and karma existed also among the early Christians. According to St. Jerome (340-420), reincarnation was given an esoteric interpretation that was communicated to a selected elite. The most famous Christian thinker speculating about the preexistence of souls and world cycles was Origen (186-253), one of the greatest church fathers of all times. In his writings, particularly in the book *On First Principles (De Principiis)* (Origenes Adamantius, 1973), he expressed his opinion that certain scriptural passages could only be explained in the light of reincarnation. His teachings were condemned by the Second Council of Constantinople, convened by the Emperor Justinian in 553, and became a heretical doctrine. The Constantinople Council decreed: "If anyone assert the fabulous pre-existence of souls and shall submit to the monstrous doctrine that follows from it, let him be anathema". However, some scholars believe that they can detect traces of the teachings in the writings of St. Augustine, St. Gregory, and even St. Francis of Assisi.

In addition to the universality of the concept of reincarnation, it is important to emphasize that past life experiences occur in experiential sessions without any programing and often despite the disbelief of the therapist and client. I have observed experiences of this kind long before I myself became open to their existence and started taking them seriously. On many occasions, they emerged in sessions of scientists who had previously considered the belief in reincarnation to be an absurd superstition and cultural delusion of primitive nations, or even manifestation of individual psychopathology.

In several instances, subjects who had not been familiar with this concept had not only dramatic past incarnation memories, but also complex and detailed insights into various specific aspects of this doctrine, as they can be found in various spiritual systems and occult literature. I can mention as an example an uneducated patient who participated in our program of psychedelic therapy for cancer patients in Baltimore. He was almost illiterate and worked at unskilled labor. Despite this, he experienced in his psychedelic session complex insights into reincarnation and the cycles of rebirth and emerged from this session a firm believer in the continuity of lives. The experience helped him greatly to face the grim reality of his terminal cancer with multiple metastases and ultimately die with equanimity. The condensed history of this patient and the account of his psychedelic session can be found in my book *The Human Encounter with Death* (Ref. 20, p. 80).

This brings us to certain specific aspects of past life experiences that are extremely interesting and deserve serious attention of researchers of consciousness and of the human psyche. The persons who experience karmic phenomena often gain amazing insights into the time and culture involved and, occasionally, even into specific historical events. In some instances, it is absolutely clear that they could not possibly have acquired this information in the conventional way through the ordinary sensory channels. In this sense, past life memories are true transpersonal experiences that share with the other transpersonal phenomena the capacity to provide instant and direct extrasensory access to information about the world.

Another interesting aspect of karmic experiences is that they are clearly connected with various emotional, psychosomatic, and interpersonal problems of the individual. Most frequently, they represent the deepest roots of problems, in addition to specific biographical and perinatal determinants. In some instances, they underlie immediately and directly psychopathological symptoms. In the latter case, deep experiential therapy will activate these symptoms and lead the individual instantly to the karmic theme that explains them and provides the context for their resolution. These experiences thus provide not only understanding of psychopathology, but also one of the most effective therapeutic mechanisms.

Among the characteristic features of past life phenomena that cannot be explained by mechanistic science is their association with astonishing synchronicities in the Jungian sense.[22] I have observed that many individuals experiencing karmic scenes identified the protagonists in these scenes as specific people in their lives—parents, children, spouses, superiors, and other important figures. When they completed the reliving of the karmic pattern and reached a sense of resolution and forgiveness, they often felt that the respective partner was in some sense involved in the process and must have felt something similar.

When I became sufficiently open-minded to make attempts at verification of the relevance of these statements, I discovered to my great
surprise that they were often accurate. I found out that in many instances the persons whom the subject denoted as protagonists in the
karmic sequence experienced at exactly the same time a dramatic shift
of attitude in the direction that was predicated by the resolution of the
past incarnation pattern. This transformation happened in a way that
could not be interpreted by linear causality. The individuals involved
were often hundreds or thousands of miles away, they did not know
anything about the subject's experience, and the changes in them were
produced by an entirely independent sequence of events. They had a
deep transformative experience of their own, received some information that entirely changed their perception of the subject, or were influenced by some other independent development in their environment.
The timing of these synchronistic happenings was often remarkable; in
some instances they were minutes apart. This aspect of past life experiences suggesting non-local connections in the universe seems to bear
some similarity to the phenomena described by Bell's theorem in modern physics.[4]

To clarify my position on past life experiences, I would like to emphasize that I do not consider their characteristics described up to this
point to be necessarily a proof that we have lived before. However, I
feel very strongly that this phenomenon cannot be adequately explained by mechanistic science and represents a serious conceptual
challenge to the existing paradigms in psychiatry and Western science
in general. It is certainly conceivable that some of the essential features of the karmic memories—universality, sense of authenticity, experiential quality of a memory, accurate intuitive insights into the
time and culture involved, therapeutic potential, and synchronistic
events surrounding them—could be explained by a modern paradigm
that would not require the assumption of a separate entity surviving biological death and carrying responsibility for its past deeds. The semantic model based on probability theory developed by the Soviet
mathematician V. V. Nalimov can be mentioned here as an example of
such an effort.[32]

In rare instances, the evidence supporting the reincarnation theory
can be much more specific. A small fraction of past life experiences involves very unambiguous information about the personality and life of
the individual that the subject feels karmically connected with. This
can be names of persons and places, dates, descriptions of objects of unusual shapes, and many others. On occasion, the nature of this material
and the circumstances can be such that they allow for independent test-

ing. In these cases, historical research brings often extraordinary sur-
prises in terms of verification of these experiences down to miniscule
details.

There exists another source of interesting observations related to
the problem of reincarnation. It is the study of children who claim
that they remember various things from their previous lives. This can
include the name of the place where they were born and detailed
knowledge of its topography, names and life histories of their alleged
former relatives, acquaintances and friends, and other details. Ian
Stevenson who has studied many such cases in different parts of the
world has described his extraordinary findings in his famous book
Twenty Cases Suggestive of Reincarnation.[42]

It is interesting to mention in this context the Tibetan tradition to
test the identity of the reincarnated lama by presenting the child, discovered by a special delegation of priests on the basis of various clues
and omens, an extraordinary test. To confirm the authenticity of his incarnation, the boy has to identify from several series of similar objects
those that belonged to the deceased.

The above discussion of the relevant observations related to past
life experiences and to the phenomena surrounding them suggest that
they deserve systematic and careful research. While the observations
cannot be interpreted as an unambiguous evidence for the continuity of
separate individual existence through lifetimes and for the law of karma, it is hardly possible for an unbiased and informed scientist to discard this possibility on the basis of metaphysical adherence to a mechanistic worldview. In the following text, I will illustrate some important aspects of past life experiences by an interesting case history.
The person who is the protagonist in this story started his self-
exploration in a primal group that had separated itself from Janov because of his narrow conceptual framework.

Later, he participated in one of our Esalen month-long seminars,
where we used the technique of holotropic breathing.

During the time when Karl was reliving in primal therapy various
aspects of his birth trauma, he started experiencing fragments of dramatic scenes that seemed to be happening in another century and in a
foreign country. They involved powerful emotions and physical feelings and seemed to have some deep and intimate connection to his life;
yet, none of them made any sense in terms of his present biography.

He had visions of tunnels, underground storage spaces, military
barracks, thick walls, and ramparts that all seemed to be parts of a
fortress situated on a rock overlooking an ocean shore. This was inter-
spersed with images of soldiers in a variety of situations. He felt

puzzled, since the soldiers seemed to be Spanish, but the scenery looked more like Scotland or Ireland.

As the process continued, the scenes were becoming more dramatic and involved, many of them representing fierce combats and bloody slaughter. Although surrounded by soldiers, Karl experienced himself as a priest and at one point had a very moving vision that involved a bible and a cross. At this point, he saw a seal ring on his hand and could clearly recognize the initials that it bore.

Being a talented artist, he decided to document this strange process, although he did not understand it at the time. He produced a series of very powerful and impulsive finger paintings. Some of these depicted different parts of the fortress, others scenes of slaughter, and a few his own experiences, including being gored by a sword, thrown over the ramparts of the fortress, and dying on the shore. Among these pictures was a drawing of the seal ring with the initials.

As he was recovering bits and pieces of this story, Karl was finding more and more meaningful connections with his present life. He was discovering that many emotional and psychosomatic feelings, as well as problems in interpersonal relationships that he had at that time in his everyday life, were clearly related to his inner process, involving the mysterious event in the past.

A turning point came when Karl suddenly decided on an impulse to spend his holiday in Ireland. After his return, he was showing for the first time the slides that he had shot on the western coast of Ireland. He realized that he took eleven consecutive pictures of the same scenery that did not seem particularly interesting. He took the map and reconstructed where he stood at the time and in which direction he was shooting. He realized that the place which attracted his attention was the ruin of an old fortress called Dunanoir, or Forte de Oro (Golden Fortress).

Suspecting a connection with his experiences from primal therapy, Karl decided to study the history of Dunanoir. He discovered to his enormous surprise that at the time of Walter Raleigh, the fortress was taken by the Spaniards and then besieged by the British. Walter Raleigh negotiated with the Spaniards and promised them free egress from the fortress, if they opened the gate and surrendered to the British. The Spaniards agreed on these conditions, but the British did not hold their promise. Once inside the fortress, they slaughtered mercilessly all the Spaniards and threw them over the ramparts to die on the ocean beach.

In spite of this absolutely astonishing confirmation of the story that he laboriously reconstructed in his inner exploration, Karl was not satisfied. He continued his library research until he discovered a special document about the battle of Dunanoir. There he found that a priest accompanied the Spanish soldiers and was killed together with them. The initials of the name of the priest were identical with those that Karl had seen in his vision of the seal ring and had depicted in one of his drawings.

Conclusions

1. Western mechanistic science has been premature in its sweeping dismissal of spirituality in general and of the idea that consciousness can survive death in particular. Such an attitude violates the principles of modern philosophy of science with its understanding of the nature of scientific paradigms and the theory of logical typing. It involves disrespect for observations from a number of disciplines, creation of metaphysical assumptions by illicit extrapolations from the models of natural sciences to psychology, and confusion of maps with the territory.

2. The problems of spirituality and consciousness existing independently from physical body have to be considered in the light of research of non-ordinary states of consciousness, on which beliefs in spiritual realities and eschatological mythologies are based.

3. The survival hypothesis is, in principle, compatible with many observations from experimental psychiatry, particularly psychedelic research, experiential psychotherapies, parapsychology, thanatology, neurophysiology, biology, and the study of multiple personalities. Unbiased analysis of the nature of transpersonal phenomena, particularly of the archetypal dynamics, out-of-body experiences, past life memories, and experiences of communication with discarnate entities is of special interest in this context.

4. While such observations are certainly incompatible with the worldview of mechanistic science, they are reconcilable with the image of the universe and of human nature that is gradually emerging from various disciplines, such as quantum-relativistic physics, astrophysics, information theory, systems theory, cybernetics, thermodynamics, brain research, and biology. These developments have been usually referred to as the new paradigm.

5. The assumption of survival of the individual unit of consciousness after biological death is not the only imaginable interpretation of the observations from modern consciousness research. However, all the alternative conceptual frameworks are in an equally sharp conflict with the Newtonian-Cartesian thinking. Until modern Western science offers a satisfactory alternative that will take into considera-

tion the observations related to transpersonal experiences, the survival hypothesis has to be considered superior to the present attitude of mechanistic science that ignores the facts of observation.

6. A serious reexamination of the existing data is certainly important in the interest of scientific objectivity, honesty, and progress. However, such an endeavor could have important social and political implications. The status of consciousness in the scientific worldview and the question of its survival after physical death are among the most critical influences shaping the human hierarchy of values, ethical standards, moral codes, and behavior. In view of the current global crisis and impending danger of collective suicide, this is a factor that should not be underestimated.

Footnotes

1. F. Alexander, "Buddhist Training As Artificial Catatonia", *Psychoanalyt. Rev.* 18:129, 1931.

2. G. Bateson, *Steps To An Ecology of Mind* (New York: Ballantine Books, 1972).

3. _____, *Mind and Nature* (New York: E. P. Dutton 1979).

4. J. Bell, "On the Einstein-Podalsky-Rosen Paradox", *Physics I*, 195, 1964; "On the Problem of Hidden Variables in Quantum Physics", *Review of Modern Physics* 38:447, 1966.

5. H. Bender, *Umgang mit den Okkulten* (Freiburg im Breisgau: Aurum Verlag, 1984a).

6. _____, *Verborgene Wirklichkeit* (Muenchen & Zuerich: R. Piper und Co., 1985).

7. D. Bohm, *Wholeness and the Implicate Order* (London: Routledge & Kegan Paul, 1980).

8. H. Bonny and L. M. Savary, *Music and Your Mind* (New York: Harper and Row, 1973).

9. F. Capra, *The Tao of Physics* (Berkeley: Shambhala, 1975).

10. *The Turning Point* (New York: Simon & Schuster, 1982).

11. P. Davies, *God and the New Physics* (New York: Simon & Schuster, 1983).

12. S. Freud, *Obsessive Acts and Religious Practices*, Collected Papers, Vol. 6 (London: The Hogarth Press and the Institute of Psychoanalysis, 1952).

13. A. van Gennep, *Rites of Passage*, trans. by M. B. Vizedon and G. L. Caffee (Chicago: University of Chicago Press, 1961).

14. B. Greyson and C. P. Flynn, *The Near-Death Experience* (Chicago: Charles C. Thomas, 1984).

15. S. Grof, *Realms of the Human Unconscious: Observations from LSD Research* (New York: Viking Press, 1975).

16. _____, *LSD Psychotherapy.* (Pomona: Hunter House, 1980).

17. ____, (ed.) *Ancient Wisdom and Modern Science* (New York: SUNY Press, 1984).

18. _____, *Beyond the Brain: Birth, Death, and Transcendence in Psychotherapy* (New York: SUNY Press, 1985).

19. _____ and C. Grof, *Beyond Death: The Gates of Consciousness* (London: Thames & Hudson, 1980).

20. _____ and J. Halifax, *The Human Encounter with Death* (New York: E. P. Dutton, 1977).

21. A. Huxley, *The Perennial Philosophy* (New York: Harper, 1945).

22. C. G. Jung, "Synchronicity: An Acausal Connecting Principle" in *Collected Works*, Vol. 8 (Princeton, NJ: Bollingen Series XX, Princeton University Press, 1960).

23. *Face to Face*, a film based on an interview with the BBC.

24. A. Kardec, *The Mediums' Book* (Sao Paolo: Livraria Allan Kardec Editora Ltda. 1975).

25. _____, *The Spirits' Book.*

26. A. Korzybski, *Science and Sanity: An Introduction to Non-Aristotelian Systems and General Semantics* (Lakeville: The International Non-Aristotelian Library Pub. Co., 1933).

27. E. Kubler-Ross, "Death: The Final Stage of Growth", presentation at the Ninth Annual Conference of the International Transpersonal Association (Kyoto, Japan, April 1985).

28. H. R. Maturana and F. J. Varela, *Autopoiesis and Cognition* (Boston, London: D. Reidel Pub. Co., 1980).

29. R. Monroe, *Journeys Out of the Body* (New York: Doubleday, 1971).

30. R. Moody, *Life After Life* (Atlanta: Mockingbird Books, 1975).

31. ______, *Reflections on Life After Life* (Atlanta: Mockingbird Books, 1977).

32. V. V. Nalimov, *Realms of the Unconscious: The Enchanted Frontier* (Philadelphia: ISI Press, 1982).

33. H. Pietsch, *Shufflebrain* (Boston: Houghton Mifflin Co., 1981).

34. K. Pribram, *Languages of the Brain* (Englewood Cliffs, NJ: Prentice-Hall, 1971).

35. ______, "Holonomy and Structure in the Organization of Perception", in *Images, Perception, and Knowledge*. J. M. Nicholas, ed. (Dordrecht, Holland: Reidel, 1977).

36. I. Prigogine and I. Stengers, *Order Out of Chaos: Man's Dialogue with Nature* (New York: Bantam Books, 1984).

37. R. Rainer, *Ars Moriendi: Von der Kunst des Heilsamen Lebens und Sterbens* (Koeln-Graz: Boehlau Verlag, 1957).

38. K. Ring, *Life at Death* (New York: Coward, McCann & Geoghegan, 1980).

39. _______, *Heading Toward Omega* (New York: William Morrow & Co., 1984).

40. M. Sabom, *Recollections of Death* (New York: Simon & Schuster, 1982).

41. R. Sheldrake, *A New Science of Life* (Los Angeles: J. P. Tarcher, 1981).

42. I. Stevenson, *Twenty Cases Suggestive of Reincarnation* (Charlottesville, Va.: University of Virginia Press, 1966).

43. C. Tart, "Out-of-the-Body Experiences" in *Psychic Explorations*, E. Mitchell & J. White, eds. (New York: Putnam's, 1974).

44. F. J. Varela, *Principles of Biological Autonomy* (North Holland & New York: Elsevier Pub. Co., 1979).

45. A. Young, *The Reflexive Universe: Evolution of Consciousness* (New York: Delacorte Press, 1976).

XI

NEAR-DEATH EXPERIENCES: INTIMATIONS OF IMMORTALITY?

Kenneth Ring

Jump Into Experience

Friend, hope for the Guest while you are alive—
Jump into experience while you are alive—
Think and think, while you are alive!
What you call 'salvation' belongs to the time before death.

If you don't break your ropes while you're alive,
do you think ghosts will do it after?

The idea that the soul will join with the ecstatic just because
the body is rotten—
that is all fantasy.
What is found now is found then.

If you find nothing now, you will simply end up with an apartment
in the City of Death.

If you make love with the divine now, in the next life you will
have the face of satisfied desire.
Plunge into the truth, find out who the Teacher is,
believe in the Great Sound!

Kabir says this: When the guest is being searched for,
it is the intensity of the longing for the
Guest that does all the work.
If you look at me, you'll see a slave of that intensity.

—Kabir
Translation by Robert Bly

It was almost ten years ago that a young medical student published
a slender volume of personal accounts of the experience of dying—and
thereby found, to his astonishment, that he had inadvertently touched
off a massive shift in our understanding of death that was felt
throughout the Western world. That once obscure medical student is
now of course the internationally known psychiatrist, Raymond A.
Moody, Jr., and the book that quickly mounted best seller lists here and
abroad was *Life After Life*.[1] Written in a popular but engaging style by
a man who had been a professor of philosophy before entering medical
school, *Life After Life* was full of anecdotes Moody had collected from
people who told him what it was like to die, and these stories, encased
in Moody's gentle, untendentious commentary, somehow struck a deep
chord of resonance in the collective psyche of the Western world. The
book remained popular for a long time—it still sells briskly, and has
now been translated into nearly thirty languages.
      Now Moody's book is especially relevant to us because it intro-
duced, named and helped to popularize a phenomenon that seems today to have taken a secure place in our thinking about death, namely,
the *near-death experience*, or, as it is often abbreviated, the NDE. To
be sure, others had researched this phenomenon long before Moody, and
another physician, Elisabeth Kubler-Ross, was already a highly visible international figure who spoke compellingly about this same phenomenon. But it was really Moody's book that by labeling the phenomenon rooted it in the soil of contemporary Western culture.
      In the wake of this pioneering work, many books and articles, both
here and abroad, have been published examining NDEs and their implications; numerous professional conferences in the United States, Eu-

rope, and Asia have likewise dealt with this experience; and an international organization, the International Association for Near-Death Studies (IANDS), has emerged as a vehicle for disseminating the findings of NDE research both in this country and around the world. Thus, the attention given to the NDE appears to have triggered a deep absorption with a tiny sliver of life—its apparent last moments—on a very wide scale indeed.

So pervasive is this interest in fact that at least in this country the NDE itself has achieved the status of a *cultural* phenomenon. Not only have hundreds of radio and television talk shows featured discussions, in addition to countless articles in the print media, but these days one can scarcely find anyone who hasn't encountered an NDE in a Hollywood film, television soap, short story, or even a *New Yorker* cartoon. To one sensitized to the existence of NDEs, they seem to be as ubiquitous as convenience stores and just about as well-known. Moreover, literally millions of persons just in the United States are now known to have had NDEs, which means that *many* millions of us are directly acquainted with one or more individuals to whom this kind of experience has happened.

Consequently, the NDE hardly appears to be a passing fad but is instead a salient *fact* of our time and one which continues to exert a very powerful hold on our collective consciousness. Why should this be so?

Among the many reasons that might be offered, I will restrict myself to two. The first has to do with the *nature* of the NDE itself, which I will briefly review in a moment. The second, which deals directly with the theme of this book, is suggested by the *subtitle* of Moody's book (one for which Moody himself disclaims responsibility). That subtitle is "The investigation of a phenomenon—survival of bodily death". Now that subtitle together with the book's affirmative title tends, I submit, to give rise to a *subtext* of sorts within this field of inquiry. In short, what seems to be implied here is that the NDE holds out if not the promise then clearly the very definite hope that there *is* survival of bodily death. This of course is precisely the issue which I will have to confront toward the close of this chapter.

In order to lay the necessary foundation for this consideration, however, I need first to say just a little about the NDE itself. Remember, it is the nature and quality of this experience which tend to be responsible for its strong appeal.

Because of the enormous publicity NDEs have received during the past decade, most of you will already be familiar with their recurrent features; so I will confine myself to a descriptive minimum here.

Although not everyone who comes close to death or enters a temporary state of clinical death reports an NDE, those who do tend to relate a set of experiences which tend to follow a single common pattern. It is in fact the *relative* uniformity of these experiences that has so much impressed researchers and the lay public alike, to say nothing of its effect on NDErs themselves! It is as though each person having an NDE becomes aware of a fragment of the same universal dream. Those who have experienced it emphasize it is in no way like a dream, or hallucinatory, or imagined, but was hyper-real to them, "more real than life itself".

What was the *content* of these experiences? NDErs commonly say that they are aware of a tremendous feeling of peace and well-being; that they feel separate from and *outside* of their body which they often claim somehow to see lying below them; there is a sense of moving through a dark space, sometimes described as "like a tunnel" toward a radiantly beautiful, brilliant white or golden light that seems to exude an overwhelming feeling of pure love. Sometimes NDErs report having a panoramic review of their life; others say that they meet and have a telepathic exchange with deceased relatives or friends that informs them that "they must go back"; still others affirm that they themselves were given a choice and elected to return to their physical bodies. Those of you already familiar with the NDE will be aware that I have omitted a number of elements which serve to define this core pattern, but I think I have mentioned enough of them to provide at least a crude sense of the experience.

Narratives work better than abstractions, so permit me one illustrative case to offer a qualitatively richer *feeling* for the NDE. I have a friend with the improbable (but actual) name of Tom Sawyer. In May, 1978, Tom, then 33 years old, was working underneath his truck when the supports gave way. The truck fell upon Tom, crushing his chest. Before the paramedics arrived, Tom said he could hear his heartbeat slowing up until finally there was no heartbeat at all, but Tom was still conscious—at least for a short time. He then became aware that he was without any pain whatsoever and was moving through a long, dark tunnel at what seemed to him to be a tremendous rate of speed, which he likened to the speed of light. He then became aware that at the end of the tunnel there was a pinpoint of light.

> You then realize that you are coming to the end of this tunnel and that this light is not just a brilliance from whatever is at the end of the tunnel—it's an extremely brilliant light. It's pure white. It's just so brilliant. . . .

And then before you is this most magnificent, just gorgeous, beautiful bright white or blue-white light. The first thing that you realize is the extreme brilliance. It is *so* bright; it is brighter than a light that would immediately blind you, but this *absolutely* does not hurt your eyes at all. . . . The next is this wonderful, wonderful feeling of this light. . . . It's almost like a person. It is not a person, but it is a being of some kind. It is a mass of energy. . . . It doesn't have a character like you would describe another person [but] it is something to communicate to and acknowledge, and in size, it just covers the entire vista before you.

Then . . . the light communicates to you, and for the first time in your life is a feeling of true, pure love. It can't be compared to the love of your wife or the love of your children. Or some people would consider a very intense sexual experience as love and they consider that possibly the most beautiful moment in their life—and it couldn't even begin to compare. All of these wonderful, wonderful feelings combined could not possibly compare to the feeling, the true love. If you can just imagine what pure love would be, this would be the feeling you get from this brilliant white light.[2]

This is just a brief excerpt from Tom's narrative and as such describes only a small portion of his experience. Even so, I think you can perhaps better appreciate why these NDEs seem so compelling, not just to the relative few who undergo them but also to the many of us who hear or read about them. No wonder we long to believe them and to believe in what they seem to signify!

But aside from our understandable and deeply felt wish to accept these accounts at face value, do we really have any justification for doing so? To address this question properly we need to resort to several different perspectives.

First, from the standpoint of mainstream science and philosophy, it is quite clear that NDEs in themselves cannot be taken as proof of survival, much less immortality. This is not to say that NDEs are not relevant to these issues—they are—but only that it is a mistake to think that they *prove* anything. Several principal arguments uphold this view.

To begin with we now know that only a minority of people who undergo and survive a near-death crisis report an NDE afterward. Most people remember nothing. Therefore, even if NDEs are taken to indicate survival, the best one can say on the basis of research data is that it is far from clear that every NDE does. And the very idea that survi-

val may be selective does not seem too plausible to many people anyway, whatever their general leanings may be.

A more forceful and, I think, irrefutable argument may be summarized as follows: Clinical death does not equal biological death. Obviously, the people we interview have not actually died, despite their
often-stated subjective conviction that they have. NDEs are, strictly
speaking, *peri-mortem*, not post-mortem, experiences. As such, they can
only tell us what people are sometimes aware of during the first stages
of a process which, were it to continue, would lead to biological death.
In themselves, they can tell us nothing about what may happen at or
after biological death. Logically, it is quite possible to argue that the
NDE could be nothing more than a final, if glorious, fadeout—
signifying nothing. Accordingly, anyone who contends that NDEs
prove survival is guilty of using a logic of extrapolation. That extrapolation *could* be true, but until some of our nonsurviving patients learn
the knack of returning our questionnaires, our research can never resolve
that point.

In reference to this issue of clinical death, it is sometimes asserted
that a flat EEG reading in conjunction with a reported NDE would be a
strong empirical argument in favor of the survival hypothesis. I suppose it would, but there are still a number of problems with it. For one
thing, though some researchers have claimed such cases, no instances of
this, to my knowledge, have been reported and documented in scientific
literature. For another, even then one would have to show that the
NDE occurred *during* the time the flat EEG reading was recorded—
something that would be almost impossible to demonstrate. Finally,
my understanding is that sometimes even flat EEG readings wouldn't
necessarily rule out some forms of subtle electrical activity in the
brain—so even an apparent clear-cut case of this kind would not be decisive.

A last point is this: It is well-known that there are still a number
of cogent biological and psychological interpretations of the NDE that
do not assume survival. Obviously, unless or until all such interpretations can be ruled out, there is no compulsion whatever to accept an interpretation of the NDE which posits survival.

Thus, anyone looking at the NDE phenomenon from the perspective
of mainstream science or philosophy would be entirely justified in con-
cluding that while the NDE is undoubtedly a subjectively fascinating
experience, it can be subsumed within our current paradigm and therefore in no way constitutes proof of survival. In this conclusion, I believe,
most near-death researchers would concur.

Bear in mind, however, that this way of looking at NDEs is only one of several, so don't necessarily take what I have said as indicative of my own personal assessment. Instead, let us consider an alternate perspective—that of NDErs themselves. What does their collective testimony add to our weighing of this issue?

Perhaps the first thing to note is how strongly NDErs tend to retain their sense of personal identity during their NDEs. Such people will spontaneously exclaim—or will routinely aver when asked—that "it was me" or "I was myself" when they experience what for them is death. Typically this persisting and undeniable impression of one's continuing personal identity at death is accompanied by feelings of surprised delight or even joy. Let me cite here just a few representative examples of this state of affairs from my own archival materials.

A woman who nearly died of cardiac arrest said:

Well, it was like, like I didn't have a body! But it was *me*. Not a body, but *me*. You know what I mean? Like I used to say to my father who didn't know me very well, that he should get to know the *real* me inside, instead of looking out here . . . because that's what's important to me. It was *me*—inside. (The real you.) The real me was up there, not this here. (She points to her physical body.)

A man who was struck by lightning told me:

The most important thing to realize . . . was that I had never, ever, lost me. I lost my body, but I didn't once lose me because as I speak now is exactly the way I was at that moment. I was me! 'Cause I can remember looking around and saying, 'Boy, what have you got yourself into now?' (laughs.) My identity was all around me, so I am 'me' inside me.

Finally, consider this comment from a woman who nearly died while giving birth. You'll see that in her case, her sense of personal identity is clearly associated with a heightened feeling of joy as well as with a definite sense that she had in fact died.

The next thing I knew, I was in—I was standing in a mist and I knew *immediately* that I had died and I was so happy that I had died but I was still alive. And I cannot tell you how I *felt*. It was, "Oh, God, I'm dead, but I'm here. I'm me!" And I started pouring out these enormous feelings of gratitude because I still existed and yet I knew perfectly well that I had died. . . .

Of course, it is this riveting sense of personal identity, coupled with the conviction that one has died, that provides most NDErs with an unshakable assurance that they will—and that all of us will—survive physical death.

There are, to be sure, other elements that serve as potent reinforcers of this understanding. Perhaps one of the most important of these is the so-called out-of-body experience that is a cardinal feature of many NDEs. What is usually reported here is the perception of clearly seeing one's physical body as though above it. This impression seems objective and the body itself is not infrequently described in a rather detached, third-person modality. Here is just one example of this from a woman who was watching a medical team perform a tracheotomy on her:

> I can remember them working on me, but I was completely detached from it. I was very clinical. I mean, it was like, 'They're hurting that girl!' . . . I kinda floated to the ceiling. I can name you what doctor was there. . . . I said (to herself) 'Oh, that girl is going to have a tracheotomy.' It was 'that girl', it was not me. (There was no connection between you and her?) No.

When such experiences occur, NDErs come not just to believe but to *know* that they are not their bodies and since they—the essential part of themselves—seem to exist independently of their physical bodies, the inference again is ineluctable: We survive bodily death.

If time permitted, we could examine many other common features of NDEs and see how they all appear to buttress this conclusion in a subjectively powerful and indisputable fashion. Suffice it to observe, however, what NDErs have to say about their understanding of death afterward, virtually all researchers who have explored this issue with NDErs have noted these twin facts: NDErs almost universally allege to have lost all fear of death *and* to be convinced that the end of life is anything but. Death, they say, as in a single voice, is but a transition into a higher, transcendental realm of being. There is no death.

What has especially impressed me about these statements is not just their near unanimity, but the very obvious and deep quality of conviction that underlies them. Moreover, these effects of NDEs seem in almost all cases to be lasting ones and, as I have tried to show in my own work,[3] exert a profound impact on NDErs' values and conduct. Although I am not arguing here that such testimony must be accepted along with its ontological implications, I do feel from my eight years of research in this field that neither does it deserve to be altogether disregarded. It should and, I believe, must somehow be taken into account in arriving at our own decision on the survival question.

So far, then, we seem to stand suspended between the lack of scientific proof on the one side and the claims of subjective proof by NDErs on the other—and the question naturally arises how to adjudicate between the two. As Willis Harman in his contribution to this volume has already shown, however, this decision is dictated by the particular metaphysic one subscribes to—and obviously people will for the most part continue to go with their pre-existing preferences. A century of psychical research has not settled this question and, as Harman shows, it *cannot* be settled at this level of discourse.

In an attempt to suggest one route out of this impasse which will perhaps have some appeal to persons who now sit on either side of this metaphysical divide, let me conclude this chapter by outlining a *third* perspective on this issue of personal survival and immortality. In fact, I can do no more than sketch in this viewpoint here, but I hope what I do say will at least be sufficient to make a case of sorts for a position that has received less attention than I believe it deserves.

In discussing the problem of survival, we are of course raising the issue of what the tabloids love to call "Life After Death" (usually preceded by the phrase "New Amazing Proof of"). Now if we think about this matter in terms of the issue of "life after death", we immediately run into a problem from the vantage point of the NDE. And that problem is *time*. NDErs are again virtually unanimous in asserting that when they undergo an NDE, they do not experience time as they ordinarily would. One event does not follow another; it is as if everything takes place simultaneously, in an instant *outside of* time. Therefore, from the perspective of an NDEr, "after" is a word without meaning in the context of experience. And thus the phrase "life after death" itself becomes suspect. It may make intellectual sense to us in our ordinary state of consciousness, but likewise it may collapse altogether when we enter into death. How, then, are we to conceive of the problem of personal survival after death—when there appears to be no "after"?

To get us out of this seeming paradox, I would like to resort one last time to quoting a portion of still another NDE—but in this case what is said takes us, I believe, beyond NDEs per se and into the very heart of the matter we have been struggling to penetrate. A friend of mine named Joe Geraci who was clinically dead for two to three minutes as a result of a faulty operative procedure told me this:

> It was then I experienced—experienced what we call a near-death experience. For me there was nothing 'near' about it—it was there.

It was a total immersion in light, brightness, warmth, peace, security. I did not have an out-of-body experience. I did not see my body or anyone about me. I just immediately went into this beautiful bright light. It's something which becomes you and you become it. I could say, 'I was peace, I was love.' I was the brightness, it was part of me. . . . You just know. You're all knowing—and everything is a part of you—it's just so beautiful. It was eternity. *It's like I was always there, and I will always be there, and that my existence on Earth was just a brief instant.* [My italics.]

Those of you already familiar with the extensive literature on mystical experience will now surely recognize something that you may have overlooked before. In their essence, *NDEs have nothing inherently to do with death at all*, much less with life after death. Instead they reflect the shining core of the Self—the hallmark of what many have called "cosmic consciousness". Some of you, for example, might recall this fragment from a famous passage of the book *Cosmic Consciousness*, by Richard Maurice Bucke, who was describing his own mystical experience: "I became conscious in myself of eternal life: It was not a conviction that I would *have* eternal life, but a consciousness that I possessed eternal life *then*."[4]

Well, what, then, does this all point to in the matter of personal survival and immortality? To sum up my own conclusions, I would like briefly to draw on some of the insights of the late English philosopher and student of mysticism, Paul Brunton. Brunton made a distinction between what we may call "egoic survival" and what he labeled "spiritual immortality". The primary distinction between these concepts is that whereas the former perpetuates the personal ego, the latter dissolves it. To appreciate the importance of this distinction, however, it will be necessary to consider Brunton's view of the ego itself.

For Brunton the personal ego was, at bottom, a *thought*, albeit a complex one. In no sense is it, however, anything fixed or definite. Brunton was very clear on the point and uncompromising in his discussion of what it means for the possibility of egoic survival.

Let me illustrate his position by reference to one short quotation from his writings:

The personal 'I' is but a bundle of impermanent hopes and transient fears, a little sheaf of cravings that change with the changing years. Nothing that we know among them is immortal even during this present earth-life; how then can they be immortal through all eternity? To cultivate a belief in a personal ego that will permanently survive in a stage of fixation is to prolong the illusion that even now blinds our eyes to the truth. . . . The mere fact that a person appears abruptly in time makes him inescapably mortal. For whatever has a beginning must have an ending. This is an inexorable law of Nature.[5]

Of course we *can* continue to cling to that bundle of thoughts that constitute the "I" and carry that evanescent identification tag across the threshold of death for whatever fate may await us, but, for Brunton, that is to continue to perpetuate the illusion of the ego and to settle for what he disdained as "mere survival" instead of reaching out for true deathlessness. Thus, "egoic survival" in Brunton's view is actually a failure to achieve the highest prize that death affords, which is spiritual immortality.

What Brunton is challenging us to do is to *transcend* the widespread assumption that a life after death necessarily must mean a personal existence of some kind. If one follows his advice and thought, it is possible to see that in fact eternity—as a state of being—is, just as Joe Geraci understood during his NDE, actually available to us at this moment and has nothing at all to do with death. It is only that the moment of death itself is one of life's supreme opportunities to realize the truth about one's real identity. But that truth is accessible *now*, before physical death, whenever you, along with Kabir,

Jump into experience, while you are alive—
Think and think, while you are alive!
What you call 'salvation' belongs to the time before death.
If you don't break your ropes while you're alive,
do you think ghosts will do it after?
. . . What is found now is found then.
If you find nothing now, you will simply end up with an apartment in the City of Death.

Footnotes

1. Raymond A. Moody, Jr., *Life After Life* (Atlanta: Mockingbird Books, 1975).

2. Kenneth Ring, *Heading Toward Omega* (New York: Morrow, 1984, pp. 57-8).

3. _____, *Life After Death* (New York: Coward, McCann and Geoghegan, 1980).

4. William James, *The Varieties of Religious Experience* (New York: Mentor, 1958, p. 307).

5. Paul Brunton, *The Wisdom of the Overself* (New York: E. P. Dutton, 1943, pp. 190-91).

XII

PANEL DISCUSSION:
SELECTIONS

Saturday

Willis Harman, Moderator: There is widespread consensus regarding the importance of the question under discussion for the past two days. It is a question that has not been fashionable to ask for some decades and Senator Pell is to be commended for the courage in initiating this conference. One of the compelling reasons for the conference and a great many others related to it are questions where our research approaches have not seemed adequate. We have heard that the way you approach the question of survival of consciousness depends on the assumptions that you begin with. Western society has, to a large extent, committed itself to a materialistic, or more precisely, positivistic metaphysic—in other words, what is real equals what is measurable, and what is not measurable we don't talk about, at least not scientifically.

If the question of survival of consciousness is important, it is meaningful to society. What kinds of research should we then be supporting? What promising, fruitful areas that are presently neglected might we think of supporting?

We will begin by asking the members of our panel to respond to the question of research priorities, varieties of research support and which particular areas seem promising. We will also consider questions from the audience.

Jacqueline Damgaard: Charles Tart spoke about the four major types of paranormal phenomena: telepathy, precognition, physical phenomena, and clairvoyance. He said these are established beyond doubt, but there are people who do doubt them. I think that basic research needs to continue to the point at which they are as fully accepted as electricity and magnetism.

I enjoyed Willis Harman's paper discussing the three types of metaphysics. One type of research we should explore is to look at lifestyles of people that operate out of these different metaphysics. If we look at groups of people who believe in these three particular ways and look at variables, such as what kind of health do they have, what kind of emotional states do they have—all kinds of behavioral and lifestyle variables, what are the implications for our quality of present living by these different belief systems?

Sogyal Rinpoche: I think that research must be done on a long-term basis; this is just an opening. I welcome Senator Pell and others who have initiated this idea. Enlightenment is not just an idealistic goal—but there are actual methods; there are ways. From a research point of view, it would be beneficial for humanity to study the different approaches, and I think with Buddhism and Christianity coming together, this is most beneficial. There have been many great teachers, Thomas Merton for one, and we are coming together in understanding.

Paul Davies: The discussion thus far has been between materialism and dualism, the idea that there is some sort of soul-like substance that latches onto the brain, stays with it throughout life; the substance would then survive after death. This is a very old-fashioned concept, particularly in the light of modern computer research and work being done in artificial intelligence, which has a strong bearing upon all the issues we have been raising here. It is possible to have a computer which is in some sense as intelligent as a human being. It would be interesting to have a discussion with that computer as to whether it thought it had a soul, and, if so, what would be meant by that soul. One of the points that I shall bring out is that when we're talking about minds versus brains, we're really speaking about two descriptive levels at the same time. When we're talking about self or consciousness or mind, we have to bear in mind that dualism is old-fashioned these days, particularly among computer scientists and others searching for artificial intelligence. If we are going to approach the issue of survival of consciousness, we ought to be looking at what we mean by our consciousness—by mind versus brain. If we get to the stage of building an intelligent computer, then we are going to come up against this because presumably when we build this computer, we won't be dwelling on any sort of soul or mind "stuff". It would simply be its complexity that gives it the ability to, if I may use the word, "think".

Computer scientists are excited about the prospect that within decades we shall actually have machines capable of reproducing human behavior or with which one can enter into dialogue. At that stage, we're going to have to face squarely the whole idea of whether or not this machine that has been created by scientists can be thought of as having a soul which can then survive the machine's extinction. If such a machine can be made, then we're going to be able to answer some of the questions that have been raised here.

The "ghost in the machine" dualism which goes hand-in-hand with straight-forward materialism tends to view the mind as located inside the brain. This is a view which is not at all traditional, and I think it is one that we really have to challenge if we are to make sense of the nature of the mind or soul survival. I am thinking particularly of belief in the power of prayer, which is practically universally held by a large minority of people in this country. I believe that what happens in our minds when praying can influence people and events in distant places. It's a traditional belief to pray for the souls of people who have died. We may think these beliefs and practices, a living reality for many people, and about which most people are shy to speak, are irrelevant to these topics we are discussing; but I think they are highly relevant to the nature of the Mind. The same idea of an extended mind comes from Jung's theory of the collective unconscious.

Sunday

Willis Harman: We would like to have various persons, convenors and presenters speak—those who would like to insert their own addenda. At the same time, we want all of the panelists and all the audience to be thinking about the question, "Where do we go from here?" We have a momentum here that none of us really expected. We did not expect the numbers of people nor this kind of spirit around the question. And now that we have it, we hate to lose it.

I would like to make several comments about that momentum and what we mean by where do we go from here? Then I will call on two of the convenors who have statements to make. We will then open it up to the panel and then to the audience.

One of the impressive things about this symposium has been that there has clearly evolved two levels of questions being asked. One was the specific question about the survival of consciousness after death, whatever that might mean. The other was the deeper question, "How do we find out more about this issue, since it is clearly important?" Contemporary science, as we have known it, has shed amazingly little light on this area. The world that we perceive is very much a function of the inner beliefs that we bring to that discussion.

In our society we all have a "cultural hypnosis"—the entire culture acts as a hypnotist, giving suggestions about how we should perceive reality. We are at a point in history where basic assumptions are undergoing a shift; we tend to divide into a number of groups. There is an implicit metaphysic that says the material world is here first and evolution takes place and somehow consciousness appears toward the end of that evolutionary path. That picture, or the assumptions underlying it, mean that we then perceive this field of data in a particular way.

There is another set of assumptions that is much newer in our own culture, which is that somehow consciousness is here first and the evolutionary process and the creation of all of this emerges, in a certain sense, from that; not that this is a new viewpoint in history, but it certainly is new in any scientific view of the world.

We seem to be at a point which is analogous to the Copernican revolution. We have a group of people who are frantically trying to add epicycles to the Ptolemaic theory and continue to make it fit as new data comes in. Then we have another group who seem to be saying, But really, we have to have a different set of assumptions, a different picture for this data to fit into; and as a matter of fact, when we reflect on our lives, we find that the positivistic, scientific framework really never fit at all well anyway.

In talking about where we might go from here, we have decided in the Institute of Noetic Sciences that the time has come to open a Washington office. We have a loosely connected network of scientists, some of whom spoke during this symposium, who are moving ahead on a new front, which is really a paradigm change in science. That group may wish to become a more formalized network, and they may be asking the question, "How do we move that network ahead?" In the Institute of Noetic Sciences, we want to encourage that work.

Then there is the question of strategy and policy with regard to national research effort. Our present national research policy is to remain as ignorant as possible about the area we have been discussing. It is virtually impossible to fund any research proposal in this pseudo-scientific area. The question that arises is if we don't know any more than we do about these vitally important questions, what kind of scientific research effort do we need? I call upon Senator Claiborne Pell to offer his comments.

Claiborne Pell: One of the purposes of this conference has been to bring this subject a little more out of the closet because since Victorian times, a few years before then, death and what happens after death has not been discussed. Consider the thirst that people have for these subjects that are outside the physical elements of life; you saw that thirst fulfilled here when this room was filled. My hope is that there will be nationwide conferences similar to ours, that will build support and respectability for the subject, and as a result, we will find a change in the government climate to funding research in this area.

John S. Spong: In 1980 I published a book called *The Easter Moment,* in which I began from my traditional point of view to examine that moment within the Christian story that seems to throw light upon the questions that we are addressing. The fascinating thing about that book to me in my preparation was that using my traditional schools of New Testament scholarship and Christian theology and using the best historical analysis that I could find to explore those texts, I became aware that nowhere in the New Testament is there any serious question about the experience of Easter, but on almost every page there is enormous conflict and contradiction about the detailed content of the experience once it moves from experience into words and concepts.

I am eager to pursue this because I think the Christian church has reached a point in its history where its validity lies more specifically in the questions it addresses than it does in the answers it is attempting to give. I think we must reach the point within organized religious institutions where we see our Scriptures, creeds, traditions, and symbols as simply being that: symbols which point beyond themselves to a truth that cannot be encapsulated in any of those symbols. We need to be in dialogue with biologists like Rupert Sheldrake and physicists like Paul Davies and philosophers like Tony Flew, where we can look with a new set of eyes to transcend those symbols not because the symbols are wrong, but because those symbols were shaped in another age and are inadequate for the way in which we are beginning to perceive the world today.

Needless to say, that will place me in a rather controversial place in my tradition. But I have been in that place for a right long time, and I welcome it because I believe that it is in going through that controversial place that we guarantee a very real future for that institution, and to deny it seems to me to deny a very real future for that institution to which I am committed.

I wanted to share that with you and say I don't know of any two days of my life that I have been as stimulated intellectually and as excited. I have been reading Paul Davies' books for about a year. My daughter is studying for a PhD in physics at Stanford. I discovered that I could no longer speak to my daughter—at least out of my frame of reference. I am enormously grateful to Paul Davies, who gave me concepts, understandings, and words that enable me to talk to a person whom I admire a great deal and to enable her to hear a viewpoint which is not antithetical to the world in which she is living, so that there is a physics-theology dialogue going on in the Spong family that is very rich and very intense and very existential and very real.

My own personal vocation as a Bishop in the Episcopal Church and as a Christian in the whole Christian enterprise is to seek to communicate the Christian Gospel in a way that is big enough to embrace the world that people like my daughter now live in.

Jacqueline Damgaard: In the past 24 hours I have been asked so many times about what the phenomenology of multiple personality is, and what it has to say about our understanding of consciousness. One of the interesting phenomena about experiments that are done looking at different ego states with multiplicity is that they not only differ in terms of inner perceptual experience, but they also differ in terms of objectively observable and measurable variables, such as EEG pattern, visual acuity, taste discrimination, vocabulary, IQ scores, etc.

In one physical body you can have an adult ego state who smokes, wears glasses, is right-handed, good at math, allergic to sulfur, with a normal IQ, that can co-exist alongside a child ego state who has never smoked, has 20/20 vision, is left-handed, paints, has no medication allergies, and scores in the 130s on the same IQ test—of course, this being the same person. To further our amazement, these states may be totally unaware of one another's existence.

What is important about this is that multiple personality, rather than being a demonstration of some form of pathology, is one of the most visible demonstrations of the manifest creativity of consciousness. And the study of multiple personality provides a kaleidoscope of glimpses of the possibility of the human mind as it goes into action to protect itself from becoming psychotic.

If an individual who is amnestically coping with severe psychic trauma, confusion in their affairs, loneliness, and sometimes even fear of the possibility of prosecution for crimes that they don't even remember committing, can at the same time speak several languages that they have never remembered learning, can paint professionally in one ego state and practice medicine in another, what is the human mind and consciousness capable of under the best of conditions?

It is incumbent upon students of the mind, the hopeful for the species, and the respecters of a higher order to seek the inner self-helper within ourselves and to push the edges of our consciousness in search of the fullness of the potential within us now.

Sogyal Rinpoche: Our leader the Dalai Lama is interested in the meeting of not only different religions but different sciences. It is of benefit to all that we synthesize our knowledge not only on a religious level of the different faiths, but also on the level of knowledge. The East could be helped by the Western approach because no longer is East merely East and West merely West. It is very much meeting together.

Question: What are you doing to create harmony among the different levels of understanding to arrive at the essence of this venture?

Stanislav Grof: In Kenneth Ring's final comments, he pointed out that the interest in survival of consciousness after death is actually one aspect of a broader interest which reflects the need for first-hand spiritual experience. There are techniques available in which people could complement what is being discussed intellectually with a profound personal experience.

John S. Spong: I would like to ask Rupert Sheldrake to help me integrate his magnificent lecture with the work of Dr. Wilder Penfield, who argued that the brain was the primary repository of memory. At least, it was by stimulating the brain that he was able to recreate memories, and I am certain that is well enough known so that you must have dealt with it.

Rupert Sheldrake: Dr. Penfield stimulated parts of the brains of epileptic patients. Research suggested that certain parts of the brain, when stimulated, were able to give rise to the subjective experience of memory. This does not prove that memories were located there. Penfield finally abandoned the idea that his experiments showed that memories were located in the part of the brain stimulated. In his last book, published in 1975, *The Mystery of the Mind,* I quote, "In 1951 I had proposed that certain parts of the temporal cortex should be called 'memory cortex', and suggested that the neural record was located there in the cortex near points at which the stimulating electrode may call forth an experiential response. This was a mistake. The record is not in the cortex."

As Jean Houston would say, most of us are cut off before we ever have a chance to reach our human potential, and if we have lessons to learn, we need to stay around long enough to learn them.

Question: Are any of you involved in the life extension research, or do you have interaction with people who are?

Rupert Sheldrake: My own interest in this was stimulated by Michael Murphy, the leading thinker in this field. In San Francisco he has a Human Potentials Archive, which consists of ten filing cabinets in which are descriptions of all sorts of events where human physical potentials have gone beyond the normal limits—extraordinary athletic events, amazing feats of endurance, strange physical phenomena, including the extraordinary series of phenomena collected by Father Thurston, SJ, called "The Physical Phenomena of Mysticism", including stigmata and bodily levitations, obscure effects of so-called physical-mystical experiences.

Question: The question I ask has to do with the premise that we are being communicated with to awaken, to arise to a sense of understanding ourselves, such that we abate calamity on a large scale—a larger scale than we are presently seeing, the phenomena that we seem to be glimpsing through scientific research.

Kenneth Ring: The premise that underlies your question is the conclusion that I come to in a book that dealt with the meaning and implications of near-death experiences—*Heading Toward Omega*. . . . I speculate that what we may be witnessing is an evolutionary thrust toward higher consciousness for which the NDE itself is a catalyst. I basically take the same view that I think you are expressing. Toward that end, a colleague, Elise Agar, and I are going to be creating a new foundation called The Omega Foundation, which will be designed to promote and encourage research in that particular domain—the evolution of consciousness and specifically to the effects of transcendental experiences on human transformation, with special interest in implications for planetary transformation and regeneration.

John S. Spong: I do believe there are periods in history where there has been a "leap of consciousness" that human life has experienced, and I think we may well be in one now, and if we don't get on with it quickly, there may not be a human enterprise.

We must leap beyond "tribal thinking", which sets up one nation-state as the ultimate value and says, "In order to protect this nation-state from extermination, we will exterminate everyone, including this nation-state".

That's a bit of radical irrationality, but it surely permeates the decision-making forces of our world. In Christian theology, the writings of Teilhard de Chardin talk about the evolution of consciousness. Although now deceased, he is a guide into understanding what it is that we're about. I think the next hundred years will be fascinating, and I am glad I am going to be around to see them.

Sogyal Rinpoche: Concerning longevity, in Eastern medical traditions, especially the Chinese, there is a whole field on longevity, a whole science that may be worthwhile looking into. Peace and health are the primary concerns. The best way to prolong a life is not to let the life we have left be prematurely finished. It's really important for us to look into the kind of life we lead. I know that life in the West is difficult. We cannot live without stress, we cannot live without all the things we have to do. But there is a way of easing a little bit, of creating, for example, a little bit more humor, and a little bit more relaxation. I think an especially important thing is space, stay-well spaces in our mind, in our heart.

There is a way of getting an "inexpensive high". As Bishop Spong mentioned, it is a very critical time. There are two things happening according to many of the Eastern prophecies. On one hand there is a crisis, but on the other hand humanity must be evolving somewhere, so there is a rise in the elevation of consciousness. It's a critical time and it's in the hands of the people. As one great master put it, people will complain that times are bad, and the time changes. He says, it's not the time, but it's the people that change. I think it's all tying together, longevity, peace and also the level of consciousness. It's very important to bring awareness and education to understand ourselves and the world because we have two responsibilities—responsibility for the world and responsibility for ourselves.

John S. Spong: There are many levels of truth. If we take the tradition in which you and I both stand and we begin to play with the possibility that whatever Easter *was* happened in 1985 instead of at the dawn of the Christian era, and we had to use words and concepts of 1985 in which to try to encapsulate or incarnate that experience, and we wrote books about it, our words would be very, very different from those used by first-century men and women who had that experience.

The history of the Church is that there is an experience that is valid and real, and then we translate that into words that are quite limited and concepts that are very earthbound, and then almost invariably we literalize those words, making it necessary for people that live in another century or even another culture to have to buy into our limited worldview in order to get to some explanation of that experience by which we live. As a bishop I visit churches of the Anglican tradition every week, and I must confess that the God I meet is, frankly, too trivial to be the God who could be the God of not only the Christian experience but of the human experience.

Question (directed to Antony Flew): Has anything said here led you to change your position in any respect and any more hopeful view for conceiving of life after death in a nontraditional Cartesian way?

Antony Flew: No—no one has addressed the problem I raised. There was nothing incompatible said with anything I believed in advance.

Speaker: I restate what the panelists have said, there is not a division between the physical and spiritual. That is the essence of the conference for me. There is no reason to discount the marvels of the human body in accepting that there are energy states that exist as conscious forms of mind or soul or the inner properties of the spirit. We are not working in the abstract; we are working in a process of experiencing our own unfoldment to the depths of our being. I have traveled and worked with many doctors, psychiatrists and therapists. Many of them have had clairvoyant experiences and are highly intuitive, but are not willing to risk professional status by exposing their own inner experiences.

In response to the question about what we can do to go forward with the energy that has been established here, I simply ask that each of us risk whatever that is that we do risk in sharing our personal and professional lives.

Question: Concerning reincarnation, Dr. Stevenson thinks that some of the cases he has studied rule out the possibility of clairvoyance. Please comment.

Rupert Sheldrake: Stevenson's detailed studies, known as "cases suggestive of reincarnation", show that, in quite a number, people have specific memories which could be verified of particular characters. He did not actually consider this kind of morphic resonance theory of memory in his book because it didn't exist then; I have discussed it with Stevenson, and he thinks this view of accessing memories would account for much of the data.

What inclines him to reincarnationist interpretation in some of them is that the whole personality seems to have a motivational drive or cohesion which he thinks mere access of memories would not give. He is inclined in some cases to think there is a central core of personality which is transferred.

Speaker: Aren't there also body traits that show up that are similar from a previous existence like when a person is killed from a blow to the head and the next incarnation had a birthmark at the injury location?

Rupert Sheldrake: Professor Stevenson spent the last year in Cambridge, England, working on a book with hundreds of examples of people born with birthmarks; some claim that in a previous life they were murdered or stabbed; the birthmarks, which are moles or nevi, correspond to the apparent place of the wound. These are very extraordinary cases and they would suggest that there was some correlation between the memories and the physical structure of the embryo as it developed. They are very mysterious indeed.

Stan Grof: In psychedelic work or in breathing work, when people relive what they feel are past-life memories, they very frequently link it to their present psychosomatic or emotional problems. That seems to be a very meaningful connection between certain aspects of their past life and present complaints. When they complete that experience it has a very therapeutic impact so that could be another piece of evidence that would have to be accounted for if you want to talk about morphic resonance. . . . The way I define transpersonal experiences is that they would fit in two large categories. In the first category basically your identity could expand and encompass anything in space/time, which means anything from the past, present and future of the phenomenal world, you can somehow recognize your essential identity with anything that has existed and will exist within the phenomenal world. There's another category of transpersonal experiences where again you have the feeling of transcending your body-ego, your usual everyday consciousness, and you would move into realms which this culture would not consider to be real. Basically, realms which are archetypal, mythological. You can experience yourself as a great mother goddess, you can experience yourself as being in Shiva's heaven or an Aztec paradise. You can experience some encounters with super-human entities of various kinds. You can experience cosmic consciousness, identify with the universal mind, experience supra-cosmic void and things of that kind. I would call these all transpersonal experiences, but there is definitely a difference, in one of them you stay within space/time, in the other one you transcend, you move into realms which this culture does not consider part of reality at all. The so-called perennial philosophy as Aldous Huxley defined it has a certain classification of it, talking about the subtle realms, and then the causal realms, and then moving into the absolute where you have transcended any forms whatsoever. I think all those experiences are available, are possible, as part of the near-death experience, as part of the psychedelic experience, and, as many people would have it, as part of a spontaneous experience.

Question: Concerning near-death experiences, are there ways that people can experience them and learn from them?

Jacqueline Damgaard: The range of psychospiritual technologies now available is providing people with the opportunity to experience these states and to understand directly something of the transpersonal domain which will eventually impact on the paradigm of science and philosophy.

Question: What is the meaning of "The observer is the observed"? Do I merge with everything that is?

Sogyal Rinpoche: I have just touched the beginning of the process of death. I think in the process of merging, we need to practice meditation. Consider a glass of muddy water; if you keep it still, the dirt settles. Clarity manifests. In the same way our confusion, which is our ego, settles. When it settles, there is a clarity and a oneness. And in that state there is not so much the need to unify, but the unity, the oneness, is there. A Zen master said, "What we call 'I' is but a swinging door that moves when we inhale and exhale". That is compassion. In Tibet reincarnation has been recognized for 16 generations. It is the education that is of most importance. Like a seed which is planted, it is important what kind of environment you have for its growth. Slowly the flower blossoms; the inherent awareness dawns and then the incarnation wakens to past wisdom and knowledge, and through their teaching, we know the level of the incarnation and living a good life. We should appreciate ourselves more. First we must learn to love ourselves well so that we can also love the neighbor. This is very important.

When you are born and when you die—those two times you are alone. And in life, too, you are alone, as you know. It is important to free our fundamental essence, the goodness we call compassion, good nature, or the nature of God—to be responsible in a good life because that is really where you will find insurance for the next life. As the Buddha said, "What you are is what you have been; what you will be is what you do now."

Question: Assuming we find out what's on the other side, how does this affect how we live our lives here?

John S. Spong: I believe in the trickle-down theory of ideas and perhaps even of consciousness. For example, Freud died in 1939—46 years ago. Most people have never read Freud, but they understand what oedipal complexes are and talk about Freudian slips with Freud's consciousness-raising insights. The same thing happens when ideas come of age and are born and trickle down over an increasingly short period of time. I use for example the group of rock stars who gathered to collect money for world hunger. The realization that this is one human family on one tiny planet began to permeate the common ranks. They raised an incredible amount of money, and the consciousness of this generation was touched. . . . I'd like to reiterate some things that Ken Ring said in his poem. If you don't start living now, then it doesn't make much sense to anticipate life beyond this life. When I go to nursing homes and see what some elderly people call "living", I wonder why any of them would want eternal life. Can you imagine an eternity of shuffleboard? To me the issue is that we take the life we have now and we scale its heights, we plumb its depths, we live its treasures, and we invest ourselves in it. Then we can stop being afraid, and drop our masks and live.

Question: How can I help a dying person? If my father, a traditional Christian, were to die and I were there—and I am not a Christian—is there any kind, practical thing that I could do to ease his transition without affronting his beliefs? Also, can we help ourselves make a good death if faced unexpectedly with our imminent death?

Sogyal Rinpoche: I have been working for ten years in the West, helping the dying and teaching from a Buddhist perspective but relating to Western experience. When I was a child I saw my teacher guiding the community—helping them—creating confidence. The main point is to create an atmosphere of love, unconditional love. Give your love fully. Suppose you have not loved the person well in your life. This is the time to do it so that you have no regret later; so you in bereavement afterwards will be better. Let the dying person die in his favorite bed, favorite room, with family and friends surrounding.

It doesn't matter what your belief is, if you believe in God. You visualize in the sky before you with a deep, deep sense of prayer. Invoke the presence of all the Buddhas or the Christ, the God, the embodiment of that in the form of light in the sky before you. And you very deeply pray, meditate that the compassion, the blessing of that help the dying person.

If you find the dying person needs help, then visualize light shooting from the heart of Christ or the heart of the Buddha, going to the dying person and purifying his soul or his consciousness, mind, and then dissolving the person and that his essence is dissolved into his original nature or into God or into Buddha nature. So, to do that and sit with the dying person, to hold hands and give your love—do that practice.

Question: Is there any work being done in developing a language to describe what happens in states of consciousness?

Stan Grof: There are attempts to develop language of unusual experiences. In our culture this is relatively new. In our culture we are anchored in the everyday. We have little sophistication and understanding of unusual states of consciousness. Frequently, we resort to languages of cultures that have a long tradition of the exploration of consciousness.

For example, we use many Sanskrit words, Indian words, and now there is experience in Tibetan tradition. It is going to take time before we develop our own language.

Question (addressed to Candace Pert): Your work points to a physical basis for emotions, consciousness, things we never before thought could be physically based. Do you think there is an outside-the-body location for consciousness or memory, as Sheldrake implies? Also, considering where do we go from here, I think responsibility for answering that question falls most heavily on you, Dr. Pert, representative of our modern scientifically oriented culture.

Candace Pert: This is a time of momentous change in the collective consciousness of the culture. I speak as a scientist, from my experimental persona. Knowing that quantum physics is in a state of flux, knowing the momentous discoveries of the last ten years in our understanding of the brain and body, as a cautious scientist, it is difficult to rule out any of these interesting ideas. It is impossible to rule out that consciousness can be projected in other places, can exist outside the body. We have not formulated how to do these experiments. I am open-minded.

Scott Jones: It is clear we've come to a very natural ending. This symposium is over. Thank you.

The Institute of Noetic Sciences

The Institute of Noetic Sciences was founded in 1973 by Edgar D. Mitchell, Apollo 14 astronaut, to engage in research, dialogue and communication on issues concerning the human mind and consciousness and their role in the continuing evolution of humankind.

Major programs include:

Inner Mechanisms of the Healing Response

Creating a scientific understanding of the mind/body relationship has been a fundamental goal of the Institute. Early work focused on verifying the importance of the link between mind and body through support of practitioners of alternative techniques. Currently, the Institute is operating a research program devoted to studying the mechanisms of the healing response. What are the innate processes within us that stimulate recovery and natural self-repair? Is there an unknown healing system that promotes remission from normally fatal illnesses? The Inner Mechanisms Program supports proposals from selected researchers and supports targeted interdisciplinary working conferences on mechanisms of healing.

Program areas include:

• *Psychoneuroimmunology.* What are the systems of linkage between the mind, the brain, and the immune system? Can these links mediate self-healing in a significant way?

• *Spontaneous remission.* What is the evidence for the existence of spontaneous remission? Which kinds of diseases are more "remission prone"? Which kinds of people experience remission and why? The Institute has created the largest medical database on remission and will soon begin to track the incidence of remission in the United States.

• *Spiritual healing.* How do prayer, meditation and spiritual beliefs affect healing? Does spiritually mediated healing operate by even more powerful pathways than those involved in remission? What is the psychophysiology of "miraculous" healing?

• *Bio-energetic or energy medicine.* Are there measurable magnetic and electrical fields around or inside the body that can aid in our understanding of healing mechanisms? Will further understanding of the body's electrical fields and circuits provide major new understanding of the healing system?

Global Mind Change

Many indicators point to a fundamental change of mind occurring around the world, driven by a complex of interconnected global problems and pulled by an emerging vision of a positive global future. Although the full nature of this transformation is not yet apparent, it clearly involves reassessment of the scientific understanding of the human mind and spirit; of our ecological relationship to the planet; of the assurance of peace and common security; and of the role of business in creating a meaningful and viable future.

The Institute is involved in cooperation with numerous other organizations in various aspects of helping this change be a smooth and nondisruptive transformation. One of the most critical areas is the achievement of global peace. Activities here include participation in an international project on alternate security; promoting a positive view of the achievability of peace; tours to the Soviet Union and other countries with opportunities for cross-cultural dialogues and "citizen diplomacy"; and a booklet by Willis Harman entitled "How to Think About Peace", which is part of a *Peace Packet*. The *Peace Packet* is available from the Institute.

Exceptional Abilities

What are the inner and outer limits of human ability? Is each of us capable of extraordinary achievement, and if so, what are the keys to it? How can exceptional abilities be trained, and what are the implications of new knowledge about them? Answers to these questions—advances in our understanding of "the farther reaches of human nature"—could help define a new, vital vision of human possibilities and renew commitment to positive individual and social goals.

Exceptional abilities range from *ordinary capacities developed to an outstanding degree,* such as lightning calculation or photographic memory, to *anomalous and paranormal capacities* such as remote viewing or absent healing. They also include *exceptional achievement* as manifested in creative genius or in the cultivation of heroic character traits such as *creative altruism,* and *extraordinary systemic transformations* such as spontaneous remission and unusual voluntary control of mind/body functions. These abilities challenge both the adequacy of existing scientific models of human functioning and individual beliefs about the limits of personal excellence and achievement. Research and education to discover more about the nature of exceptional abilities could have far-reaching implications for science, business, education and sports, and individual health and well-being. The Institute is developing a research agenda and supports selected studies of extraordinary human functioning.

The Altruistic Spirit is a major program area within Exceptional Abilities. Through this program the Institute sponsors multidisciplinary research on two questions: What is, and how universal is, our capacity for unselfish love and creatively altruistic behavior?; and, What are the internal and external conditions for fostering the development of intrinsic altruism as a consistent character trait? Moral giftedness is among the topics we are investigating. The annual Temple Award of the Institute of Noetic Sciences will honor one or more exemplars of the altruistic spirit—the irrepressible light of love in the heart of humanity.

•

The Institute's pioneering research, communication and networking activities are financed almost completely by donations from members and other sources of private support. A nonprofit organization, the Institute is open to general membership.

Members are kept abreast of the latest progress in these major new fields of study. Members receive regular publications featuring exciting insights into the work of leading investigators, in-depth articles on critical aspects of consciousness research, announcements of forthcoming conferences, presentations, tours, reviews of new publications, and the opportunity to order books and tapes at a discount directly from the Institute.

Members from the world over join in supporting research that is moving toward understanding and enhancing the quality of life for us all.

For information on becoming a member of the Institute, please send your request to:

The Institute of Noetic Sciences
475 Gate Five Road, Suite 300
P. O. Box 97
Sausalito, CA 94966-0097
(415) 331-5650